SAN CARLOS TO STANLEY

40 COMMANDO IN THE FALKLANDS WAR

Peter Jackson-Lee

Helion & Company Ltd

Helion & Company Limited
Unit 8 Amherst Business Centre
Budbrooke Road
Warwick CV34 5WE
England
Tel. 01926 499 619
Fax 0121 711 4075
Email: info@helion.co.uk
Website: www.helion.co.uk
Twitter: @helionbooks
Visit our blog http://blog.helion.co.uk/

Published by Helion & Company 2022
Designed and typeset by Farr out Publications, Wokingham, Berkshire
Cover designed by Paul Hewitt, Battlefield Design (www.battlefield-design.co.uk)

ISBN 978-1-915070-89-0

British Library Cataloguing-in-Publication Data
A catalogue record for this book is available from the British Library

We always welcome receiving book proposals from prospective authors.

Contents

Glossary

84	See Carl Gustav
66 (Sixty-Six)	Shoulder held light anti-armour throw away rocket
7.62 Link	Linked belt of ammunition for the GPMG
AAC	Army Air Corps
Ac or AC	Aircraft
Acorn	Intelligence Officer
AD	Air Defence
AD Troop	Air Defence Troop
ADS	Advanced Dressing Station
AE	Assault Engineer
AOP	Airborne Observation Post
AP	Anti-Personnel Mine
Asslt	Assault
AT	Anti-Tank, referring to a mine or projectile
ATGW	Anti-Tank Guided Weapon
Bandwagon	See BV 202
BAS	Commando Brigade Air Squadron
BC	Battery Commander
Bde	Brigade
Bergen	Large rucksack
Binos	Binoculars
Blowpipe	British man-portable surface-to-air missile (MANPADS) in use with the British Army and Royal Marines from 1975
Blue on Blue	Accidental engagement between friendly forces
Blues and Royals	See RHG/D
BM	Chief of Staff
BMA	Brigade Maintenance Area
Bty	Royal Artillery battery
BV 202 (BV)	Bandvagn 202 (Bv 202) – a tracked articulated, all-terrain vehicle developed by Bolinder-Munktell, a subsidiary of Volvo, for the Swedish Army and used by Royal Marines in Norway
C/S or c/s	Callsign
Canberra	The English Electric Canberra – a British first-generation jet powered medium bomber developed during the mid-to-late 1940s and later in life proved itself in a photo reconnaissance role. The RAF retired their last Canberra in 2006. The Argentine B Mk.62 B-109, was the last aircraft to complete a mission in the Falklands War and is on display at the Museo Nacional de Aeronáutica de Argentina
Canberra	SS *Canberra*: A cruise ship operated by the P&O Line, deployed as part of the UK Task Force as a troop-carrying ship

CAP	Combat Air Patrol
Carl Gustav	Recoilless 84-mm man-portable reusable anti-tank weapon
CAS	Casualty
CASEVAC	Casualty Evacuation
CBFSU	Commander British Forces Support Unit (Ascension Islands)
Cdo	Commando
CGRM	Commandant General Royal Marines
Chacon	20 x 20-foot container used to store and move equipment
Chinook	Twin rotor heavy lift helicopter
CLIFFI	Commander Land Forces Falkland Islands
CO	Commanding Officer
COMAW	Commodore Amphibious Warfare
Commando	Royal Marine
CORPORATE	Operation to recover Falkland Islands
Coy	Company
CP	Command Post
CTF	Commander (South Atlantic) Task Force.
CTG	Commander Task Group – directly responsible to CTF
CTU	Commander Task Unit – directly responsible to CTG
CVR (T)	Combat Vehicle Reconnaissance Tracked – Scorpion (76mm-armed) or Scimitar (30mm-armed) light reconnaissance vehicle
DF	Defensive Fire
Draft/Drafting	Posting to another unit/ship's detachment or location
DS	Direct Support
EFHE	Harrier/Helicopter landing pads
FAC	Forward Air Controller
FAL/FAL FN/FN	Argentine infantry rifle. Belgian-designed 7.62mm rifle, similar to British SLR but capable of fully automatic fire
FARP	Forward Arming and Refuelling Point
FDC	Fire Direction Control
FDS	Field Dressing Station /Forward Direct Support
FEBA	Forward Edge of Battle Area
Fender	Usually an inflatable buoy to stop two boats banging together
Fighting Order	Main equipment with yoke, (shoulder support) ammunition pouches, belt, and water bottle along with any other items required
First Field Dressing	Sterile dressing with large absorbent pad bandage sealed in a robust flexible waterproof pouch. Can be folded in several different ways to give excellent compression to stop bleeding from wounds
FOB	Forward Observation Base
FOO	Forward Observation Officer
FUP	Forming Up Point/Place
Gazelle	Light helicopter deployed by 3 Brigade Air Squadron
GD	Refers to a General Duties Royal Marine in a fighting company
GMT	Greenwich Mean Time

GPMG	General Purpose Machine Gun
GPO	Gunnery Position Officer
GR3	RAF Harrier used for ground attack
Gz	see Gazelle
HE	High Explosive
HEAT	High Explosive Anti-Tank round for weapon such as the 84 or Milan
Hel	Helicopter
Hexi Cooker	Hexamine metal cooker frame
H-Hour	Time for first assault troops to cross start line
HLS	Helicopter Landing Site
HQ	Headquarters
Intrep	Intelligence report
IR	Infrared – commonly used in this context since infrared emissions from a body are directly related to their temperature
IWS	Individual Weapon Sight – The original first-generation night sight used by the British Army to fit on to the top of the SLR
Jack	Royal Marine name for the Royal Navy (See also Royal for their appreciation of a Royal Marine)
Jock	Scottish person, or regiment if referring to Scots Guards
Junglie	A Royal Marines Sea King transport helicopter of 845 and 846 Naval Air Squadrons (all green in colour not the usual naval grey)
Kip	Waterproof sheet for constructing a slit trench
LCU	Landing Craft Utility – used by amphibious forces to transport equipment and troops to the shore. Capable of transporting tracked or wheeled vehicles and troops from amphibious assault ships to beachheads or piers
LCVP	Landing Craft Vehicle and Personnel – versatile amphibious landing craft designed to transport troops or armoured vehicles from ship to shore during amphibious landing
LFFI	Land Forces Falkland Islands
LPD	Landing Platform Deck (ship) – HMS *Intrepid* and *Fearless*
LS	Landing Site
LSL	Landing Ship Logistics – a term used to describe the Round Table-class of landing ship used in the support of amphibious warfare missions. These ships were operated by the Royal Fleet Auxiliary
Lympstone	Commando Training Centre Royal Marines (CTCRM) – the principal military training centre on the banks of the River Exe for all ranks of Royal Marines
Lynx	A light helicopter
M&AW Cadre	Royal Marines Mountain and Arctic Warfare specialists
Manking	Complaining
MAOT	Mobile Air Operations Team
Matelot	General term describing a member of the Royal Navy

MCM	Mine Counter-Measures
Mexefloat	Low, flat, self-propelled raft in use since the 1960s, capable of carrying 60–180 metric tonnes (130-400,000 lb). Operated by the Royal Corps of Transport and carried on the side of the RFAs
Milan	Infantry-portable wire guided anti-tank missile
ML	Mountain Leader (part of M&AW)
Mne	Royal Marine
MoD	Ministry of Defence
Mor	Mortar
Msls	Missiles for infantry weapon systems
MV	Merchant Vessel
NAAFI	Navy, Army and Air Force Institute
NAS	Naval Air Squadron
NBC	Nuclear Biological and Chemical Defence
NCO	Non-Commissioned Officer (JNCO – corporal, or SNCO – sergeant)
NGS	Naval Gunfire Support
NP 8901	Naval Party 8901 – the original Falklands detachment of Royal Marines at the time of the Argentine invasion
NTM	Notice to move
NTR	Nothing to Report
Nutty	Royal Marines' collective name for Sweets, chocolate, confectionary
O Group	Orders group – a meeting where orders are given
Obs	Observation
OC	Officer Commanding
OCRM	Officer Commanding Royal Marines Detachment, usually onboard a naval ship
OP	Observation Post
Oppo	A close friend – opposite number of a team
Opposed Landing	A landing in which the enemy are either expecting you or are ready for any attack. The result of which would see the landing forces come under sustained fire either as the landing craft approach the landing site or the ramp lowers
Padre	General name given to a person of religion from any denomination with whom you can confide in or speak to freely
Para	Member of the Parachute Regiment
Pinged	Chosen for a task nobody wants to do, possibly by being in the wrong place at the wrong time
Pop up Mine	Anti-personnel mine that when triggered pops up to waist-height then explodes
POW/PW	Prisoner of War
Proffing	Borrowing an item on a permanent basis
Pucara	Argentine ground attack aircraft

Pussers Knife	Naval Pattern 301 Knife issued to naval personnel, with folding blade and a straight tapered marlinspike
PWI	Personal Weapons Instructor
RA	Royal Artillery
RAP	Regimental Aid Post – front line military medical establishment incorporated into an infantry battalion for the immediate treatment and triage of battlefield casualties
Rapier	Ground-to-air defence missile
RE	Royal Engineer
Recce	Reconnaissance
RFA	Royal Fleet Auxiliary
RHG/D	The Royal Horse Guards/Dragoons (Blues and Royals)
Rigid Raiding Craft (RRC)	A fibreglass shallow fast river craft able to carry seven or eight men and a Coxswain
RM	Royal Marine
RN	Royal Navy
Royal	Royal Navy name for a Royal Marine (see also Jack for their appreciation of the Royal Navy)
RSRM	Raiding Squadron Royal Marines
RV	Rendezvous
Saddle	Low point on a ridge between two summits.
Sangar	A field fortification – sangars are normally constructed in terrain where the digging of trenches would not be practicable. During the Falklands peat from the hillsides was used to form a temporary fortified position. Sangars were originally constructed with stones, but can be built of sandbags, gabions or similar materials
SAS	Special Air Service
SBS	Special Boat Service
Sc	Scout light helicopter
Scimitar	Light reconnaissance vehicle with 30mm RARDEN cannon and 7.62mm machine gun
Scorpion	Light reconnaissance vehicle with 76mm gun and 7.62mm machine gun
Scran	Food
Sea Harrier	Naval fighter and strike aircraft capable of vertical landing
Sea Wolf	Naval automatic short-range surface-to-air missile
Seacat	Naval short-range surface-to-air missile
SF	Special Forces (SAS and SBS)
SF	Sustained Fire (GPMG on a Tripod)
Sidewinder	American-made air-to-air missile carried by Sea Harrier
SK	Sea King helicopter
Skyhawk	Argentine A-4 attack aircraft (US-built)
SLR	L1A1 Self Loading Rifle – a semi-automatic version of the Belgian FN FAL used by British forces

SQ	Refers to a Royal Marine with a Specific Qualification such as Driver, Clerk, Chef
Sqn	Squadron
Start Line	A line on the ground (such as a fence or stream) which marks the start line of the attack
Stinger	US man-portable air-defence missile system
Sunray	An appointment/title designated to commander
SUTTON	Operation to land on East Falkland
TAOR	Tactical Area of Responsibility
TEZ	Total Exclusion Zone
Tp/Tps	Troop – a platoon-sized unit
TRALA	Tug Repair and Logistics Area
Unopposed Landing	A Landing in which the enemy are not expecting you and have no forces in place. The result of which would see the landing forces not come under sustained fire either as the landing craft approach the landing site or the ramp lowers
UXB	Unexploded Bomb
Wessex/Wx	Royal Navy medium lift helicopter
White Phos	White Phosphorus grenade – designed to produce smoke but also a useful close quarters weapon that burns skin on contact
Yomp	Royal Marine slang for a long march (from sailors' slang to eat)

Acknowledgements

I would firstly like to thank the many former members of 40 Commando, Royal Marines who have taken the time to assist me by supplying personal stories and images. I will be eternally grateful for their time and assistance. A special thank you must go to the following people: Damian 'D' Irving, who kindly supplied a wealth of information, and images. Alan Stevens, Alex Hamilton, Stephen Lawrence, Ian Headrick, Brien Hobbs who joined 7 Troop Charlie Company from NP 8901 at Ascension, after being rudely evicted from the Falkland Islands by the Argentine invasion force. Roger Stamp, Pete Butcher, Colin Adams, Pincher Martin, Ian Stewart, Alan Holderness, (who turned 18 on the day of the surrender), Terry Barnes, Stu Bratherton, 'Marine A' 40 Commando (who has asked to remain anonymous), Dave Sturgess and Clive Lucking. Nick Kendall-Carpenter, of the Royal Signals Museum, in Blandford Forum for putting me in contact with Bob Hendicott of 59 Independent Commando Squadron, Royal Engineers. Bob was kind enough to fill in a few gaps from his Royal Engineers' records of a unit that is usually forgotten about but proved vital during our time with the Welsh Guards.

I would also like to thank the then Commanding Officer of 40 Commando, Lt Colonel Malcolm Hunt, in assisting me via telephone and email as well as pointing me in the direction of information that would be useful. Malcolm Hunt retired from the Royal Marines having attained the rank of Major-General Malcolm Hunt OBE FRSA.

Lastly, and by no means least, my wife Elaine who has suffered my constant disappearing acts for research and long periods of writing.

Introduction

Within the book, I will occasionally refer to the following senior commanders by name only. This to allow me to make it easier for the reader to see who made what decision and when. Most of the names will be familiar to most readers as they appear and do not require the full name and rank. Under no circumstances should it be taken as showing any disrespect to the person or their rank and experience.

Before 3 Commando Brigade Landing
Admiral Sir John D.E. Fieldhouse: CTF 317 South Atlantic Task Force
Rear Admiral John F. 'Sandy' Woodward: TG 317.8 Carrier/Battle Group
Commodore Michael Clapp RN: CTG 317.0 Amphibious Task Group HMS *Fearless*
Brigadier H.A. 'Julian' Thompson RM: CTG 317.1 Landing Force HMS *Fearless*
Captain B. Young: CTG 317.9 South Georgia Group
Vice Admiral Peter G.M. Herbert: CTG 324.3 Submarine Group

After Landings
Admiral Sir John D.E. Fieldhouse: CTF 317 South Atlantic Task Force
Commodore Michael Clapp RN: CTG 317.0 Amphibious Warfare and Transport Area
Major General John 'Jeremy' Moore RM: Land Forces, Falkland Islands (CLFFI)
Rear Admiral John F. 'Sandy' Woodward: CTG 317.8 Carrier/Battle Group
Vice Admiral Peter G.M. Herbert: CTG 324.3 Submarine Group

Commanders Directly Under Major General John 'Jeremy' Moore RM
Brigadier H.A. 'Julian' Thompson RM: 3 Commando Brigade
Brigadier Mathew J.A. 'Tony' Wilson WG: 5 Infantry Brigade
Lt Colonel Malcolm P.J. Hunt RM: Commanding Officer 40 Commando RM
Lt Colonel John F. Ricketts WG: Commanding Officer 1 Battalion Welsh Guards

Company Commanders of fighting units within or attached to 40 Commando RM
Major Shane Cusack: Alpha Company Commander
Captain Simon J.D. Bush: Bravo Company Commander
Captain Andrew R. Pillar: Charlie Company Commander
Captain Roger J. Williams: Support Company Commander
(Captain Robin Gilding was to replace Captain Williams who was to take up his position at the Staff College during the Falklands)
Lt Bob Hendicott: 1 Troop, 59 Independent Commando Squadron Royal Engineers

The Falklands War or Falklands Campaign?
A campaign is a phase of a war involving a series of operations related in time and space and aimed towards a single, specific, strategic objective or result in the war. A campaign may include a single battle, but more often it comprises several battles over a protracted period

or a considerable distance, but within a single theatre of operations or delimited area. A campaign may last only a few weeks, but usually lasts several months or even a year.

There is limited information in the official documents on 40 Commando and their attached units, such as 59 Independent Commando, Royal Engineers, who were to remain in San Carlos during the fighting in the Falklands. The work undertaken by the men of these units has and shall always be vastly underappreciated due to the lack of historic documents. Without the likes of 40 Commando and 59 Independent Commando, there would have been no advance or backup troops available for the forward units.

The records of A and C Company who moved forward with the Welsh Guards are to be found in the Welsh Guards' documents, but again this is very limited in its detail. The documents fail to point out the issues that were seen in the lack of readiness and fitness of the Welsh Guards upon arrival.

The title of this book may seem a little strange to some as 40 Commando, as a unit, did not actually enter Stanley at the end of the Falklands. Given that it is 40 years since the Falklands War I felt it was now time to put right a historical aspect of the Falklands that has long been ignored. Using information from official files and the recollections of those who were there I hope we can now recognise 40 Commando's role in the Falklands. 40 Commando has had an almost complete lack of acknowledgement from historical professionals and military personnel from various fields who have concentrated on the various battles and nothing else. Notwithstanding the actual landings, 40 Commando, and many other elements of the Task Force have effectively been erased from the history books as far as the Falklands War is concerned.

My aim with *San Carlos to Stanley*, which was to originally be titled *Falklands' Forgotten Commando,* was to recognise the professionalism and skill of the men from 40 Commando and attached units such as 59 Independent Commando Royal Engineers. This recognition is only briefly noted in a few of the books on the Falklands War, which only ever mention the landing and two companies, usually not which companies, who were sent forward with the Welsh Guards following the tragic events at Bluff Cove. From then on, 40 Commando seem to completely disappear unless you include the numerous mentions of Welsh Guards and 5 Infantry Brigade. It is generally assumed that 40 Commando languished at the beachhead and after the initial air raids, they were not involved in the conflict at all.

San Carlos to Stanley has been set out in a diary format to show the daily progression of events and to explain how 40 Commando was an important part of this brilliant military achievement which was at the time thought to be an impossible task and totally against all the odds. This brilliant achievement was brought about through the professionalism and skill of those units taking part and their hard-fought battles for the various mountains which formed the ring of steel around Stanley. 40 Commando were constantly moving location over East and West Falkland, patrolling, and setting up OPs in the San Carlos and Port San Carlos areas, all to protect the beachhead and thus the advance.

Other factors that are commonly missed are the high-level bombings by Argentine Canberras, and air raids which included the direct bombing and strafing attack on ground forces on 27 May, at San Carlos and Ajax Bay. These raids resulted in fatalities and numerous injuries in both San Carlos and Ajax Bay. Following this air raid on 27 May, 40 Commando's Milan troop were attached to 45 Commando for the epic yomp after 45 Commando's Milan were destroyed during the attacks on Ajax Bay.

Following the *Sir Galahad* tragedy, the defence of the beachhead would be by a combination of HQ, B and Support Company of 40 Commando with the surviving Welsh Guards. A and C Companies, 40 Commando, would move forward with the Welsh Guards as reserve for the final push on the mountains, followed by the final fight in the Falklands, on Sapper Hill by 9 Troop, C Company.

9 Troop, C Company had just secured Sapper Hill following the only helicopter assault of the Falklands War, with both aircraft being hit by small arms fire. This assault was in plain view and within a few hundred metres of at least two companies of Argentine marines and infantry who were dug in on Sapper Hill. Once they had disembarked from the helicopters, 9 Troop took whatever cover they could and engaged the enemy using all available firepower. 9 Troop were closely followed by C Company HQ. This spirited attack convinced Brigadier General Joffre, the commander of the Argentine 10th Infantry Brigade (responsible for Sapper Hill) that further resistance was pointless. He spoke to General Menendez and shortly after reports started trickling through of the appearance of white flags flying over Stanley and an Argentine surrender.

A Company, the remainder of C Company, the Welsh Guards, and 1 Troop, 59 Independent Commando, followed shortly after and were the closest British troops to Stanley when the white flags were flown. Due to the uncertainty of the surrender holding, and the distinct possibility of some elements of the Argentine forces refusing to surrender, 40 Commando, the Welsh Guards and 1 Troop, 59 Independent Commando, were told to hold on Sapper Hill and not to enter Stanley. They were soon to be joined by 45 Commando, who had 40 Commando's Anti-Tank Troop with them for the famous yomp. If it were not for the order to hold position, 40 Commando, Welsh Guards and 1 Troop, 59 Independent Commando, would quite possibly have entered Stanley as per the order shown later in the book.

Through the passage of time, it has emerged that Jeremy Moore had wanted one of 5 Brigade's battalions to take over 40 Commando's garrison duties, but Michael Clapp was worried about protecting his anchorage in San Carlos Water. He was relieved when Jeremy Moore decided that the protection of the anchorage in San Carlos should be undertaken by the Royal Marines who were experts in helicopter and landing craft drills, as well as amphibious warfare. Julian Thompson asked for 40 Commando to return to his command on at least three occasions but to no avail. Jeremy Moore and Michael Clapp were both worried what might be happening in West Falkland as the Argentines were known to be building up their forces there. If Jeremy Moore needed to carry out a coup de main or pre-empt any enemy action, 40 Commando would be needed. Jeremy Moore had been warned by intelligence from Northwood that the Argentines were planning an airborne assault, artillery barrages and even a full-on counterattack on the beachhead. If San Carlos fell, the advance would have been finished and this would have been a very humiliating defeat for the British. It was imperative that they had an experienced fighting unit there not only to protect the beachhead but the whole operation to retake the Falkland Islands.

Michael Clapp did not think that Malcolm Hunt, 40 Commando's Commanding Officer, would ever forgive him if he knew that he supported Jeremy Moore's decision. Michael Clapp later stated in his book *Amphibious Assault Falklands: The Battle for San Carlos Water*, that he had little doubt that it was the correct decision and not an easy one for Major General Jeremy Moore to take. There was also the consideration of the radio nets having to move if the Welsh Guards moved to San Carlos and 40 Commando took over the Welsh Guards' positions. This is not withstanding the helicopter assets that would be required but were unavailable as they were busy moving men and equipment forward in the main advance.

Throughout the Falklands War, 40 Commando and attached elements such as 59 Independent Commando Squadron defended the beachhead from possible artillery barrages, counterattacks and air raids as well as supporting the advance by supplying stores and equipment. Their contribution to the Falklands War should never be forgotten, as without the constant supply of stores and ammunition, there would not have been an advance, especially if the beachhead was lost in a counterattack by the Argentinian forces on West Falkland.

The various timings used in the Falklands War stem from headquarters at Northwood insisting at Admiral Woodward's requests that the campaign be fought in Zulu Time (suffix Z) which equates to GMT. This meant that there was no need to do any mental arithmetic to reconcile orders, reports and actions. The time in London was BST which had started on 28 March 1982 and was an hour ahead of GMT, with the Falkland Islands four hours behind. Taking account of the diplomacy it becomes apparent that the many principal participants were spread across six time zones of France and West Germany, where important discussions and meetings were held at GMT +2 hours: a further hour ahead of London. To complicate matters further Argentine time was only three hours behind Zulu and during the occupation this was imposed on the Falklands, although this was ignored by the residents as in normal times the Falklands were four hours behind.

By and large for the time periods within *San Carlos to Stanley*, I have used Zulu Time, as this is how timings appeared in many of the documents I have consulted. The Task Force therefore began the day three hours before their Argentine counterparts. Readers can make the necessary calculations to note that at 0630 local time in the Falklands it was already 1130 in London. Table 1, taken from the *Official History of the Falklands Campaign*, shows the relationship between the main areas involved.

Table 1: Time Zones during the Falklands War		
		Local Time at Noon GMT
Lima	GMT -5 Hrs	0700
Santiago, New York, Washington, Falklands	GMT -4 Hrs	0800
Buenos Aires, South Georgia, Falklands Under Occupation*	GMT -3 Hrs	0900
	GMT – (Z)	1200
London	GMT +1 Hrs	1300
*During the occupation Argentina introduces Buenos Aires Time		
		Official History of the Falklands Campaign

Throughout *San Carlos to Stanley*, the reader will see reference to Callsigns (c/s) which relate to the military radio reference for the individual sections or troops within 40 Commando. Some of the main designations used are as described it Table 2:

Table 2: 40 Commando Callsigns				
Company	**Troops**	**Callsigns**		
A Company	1-3 Troop	11 (1 Troop)	12 (2 Troop)	13 (3 Troop)
B Company	4-6 Troop	21 (4 Troop)	22 (5 Troop)	23 (6 Troop)
C Company	7-9 Troop	31 (7 Troop)	32 (8 Troop)	33 (9 Troop)
Each troop was further split into sections so B Company 6 Troop 2 Section would be 23B. Other elements within that Commando unit or those attached to it, such as the Support Company Mortar Section would have other callsigns such as Callsign 53.				

All personal accounts are as given to me by the respective person, or within the written memoires that have been provided. In a few places I have shortened a few of the accounts to allow the story to be told in a brief and precise manner.

1

Pre-Deployment

During 1980/81, the Royal Marines were suffering a manpower shortage and so those passing out of training would generally divert to the Arctic units of 42 and 45 Commando to bring the units up to complement strength. Both units would undertake a deployment to Northern Norway every year as part of the NATO Northern Flank commitment. With an influx of new recruits, it was now 40 Commando who were to be brought up to full complement strength. 40 Commando's programme for the next 12 months was not overexciting, with exercises on Salisbury Plain and at Thetford followed by a brief amphibious exercise with both HMS *Invincible* and HMS *Hermes*. This was to be followed by a planned deployment to South Armagh, known as Bandit Country, in Northern Ireland, in January 1983.

During the Falklands War, A Company, 40 Commando left the UK onboard HMS *Hermes* as a possible advanced force to retake the islands. When HMS *Hermes* arrived at Ascension Island, Shane Cusack and the SBS commander onboard discussed the possibility of using A Company as a backup force for the SBS who were already ashore on the initial phase of retaking the islands. During the Falklands War, the SAS called upon 40 Commando to stand by to assist in the extraction of a four-man OP at Port Howard, West Falkland. The OP had been compromised, and Captain Hamilton of the SAS had fought hard to extract the OP team, but he was, unfortunately, killed and one man was captured. The SAS also requested company-strength support for a raid on Pebble Island, but unfortunately, none of the tasks took place.

The Royal Marines operate around the world in many forms of warfare, including conventional, jungle, arctic and amphibious operations, and this was one of the reasons why Michael Clapp was keen to see a Royal Marines unit ensure the safety of his anchorage in San Carlos Water, much to the dismay of the Commanding Officer, Malcolm Hunt, and the rest of 40 Commando. However, two companies were later to take part in the fighting alongside the Welsh Guards. Today, as was the case in 1982, the Royal Marines form a high proportion of the Special Forces intake, which can be seen in the extract below:

The contribution that the Royal Marines make to UK Special Forces (UKSF) has been a common theme in the evidence we have received. In the past the Special Boat Service recruited exclusively from the Corps, and the link with the SBS remains strong. The Special Reconnaissance Squadron and Special Forces Support Group also receive substantial support from the Royal Marines personnel. The evidence indicates that somewhere between 40 and 50% of the UKSF personnel have a Royal Marines background – yet another indication of the disproportionality high contribution that the Royal Marines make to Defence given their size in relation to the rest of the Armed Forces.

Special Forces are of great utility in amphibious operations. The Falklands Campaign demonstrated the value of covertly inserting small SF teams ahead of the main landing force to gather intelligence and guide forces to the landing zone, disable nearby enemy installations, provide fire control for air strikes and naval gunfire, and if necessary, to engage the enemy units that might be in a position to interfere with the landing.

The contribution made to UK Special Forces by the Royal Marines is disproportionate to the size of the Corps and is indicative of the quality of the people who pass through the ranks. The growth in the use of Special Forces in recent years makes the continuing 'pipeline' of trained and resilient personnel vital. Reducing the strength of the Royal Marines will substantially reduce the recruitment pool available and reduce the Special Forces' amphibious warfare expertise.

House of Commons Defence Committee Report HC622, *Sunset for the Royal Marines? The Royal Marines and UK Amphibious Capacity.*, para 39-4, *Third Report of Season 2017-2019* (4 February 2018)

25 March

Malcolm Hunt, the Commanding Officer of 40 Commando, had been warned that his Commando might have to travel to the Falkland Islands to pre-empt an invasion of the islands. Soon the requirement for a full Commando unit was reduced to a single company (A Company). He was not allowed to make any preparations, including bringing his men to short notice, nor was it revealed how the men and equipment would travel the 8,000 miles to the Falklands. In a ship travelling at 30 knots, it would take 14 to 16 days and the only way to Stanley by air was via the normal civilian route through Argentina. Given the lack of airport security at the time it was thought a small team, possibly air defence, could travel as civilian musicians and disguise their weapons systems as musical instruments.

The Air Defence Troop were stood down on 31 March following a meeting in Downing Street. The airfield at Stanley was too short to take a long-range transport and while Hercules aircraft were capable of landing at Stanley Airport, they were too heavy for a long stay on the runway apron. Added to this, they were not fitted with any air-to-air refuelling systems; a Hercules would need to refuel not only at Ascension Island but also carry out mid-air refuelling to reach the islands. This was dramatically shown when Vulcan XM 607 required eleven Victor tankers to provide air-to-air refuelling to enable it to bomb Stanley Airport in an outstanding achievement in planning and execution of the raid.

On arrival, the Hercules would have to land whatever the weather, and the Royal Marines of 40 Commando would exit the aircraft – which would now have to be abandoned – then secure and hold the airfield to deny its use to the Argentines and wait for reinforcements. The plan was abandoned, and 40 Commando were stood down. With tensions clearly rising the Commando was brought to 72 hours' notice to move. A similar operation – Operation Mikado – using C-130 Hercules and 55 men from the SAS was planned, and abandoned at the last minute, in May of 1982. Their plan was to fly to the Argentine mainland to destroy the remaining Exocet missiles, then escape through Chile.

26 March
The invasion of the Falkland Islands, codenamed Operation Rosario, started with the Argentine Navy leaving from mainland Argentina. The operation had originally been called Azul (Blue) during the planning stage.

31 March
Intelligence reports reach Whitehall that the Falklands would be invaded on 2 April, when according to Prime Minister Margaret Thatcher:

> I shall not forget the evening of Wednesday 31 March 1982. I was working in my room at the House of Commons when I was told that John Knott wanted an immediate meeting to discuss the Falklands. I called people together. John was alarmed. He had just received intelligence that the Argentine Fleet, already at sea, looked as if they were going to invade the islands on Friday 02 April. There was no ground to question the intelligence. John gave the MoD's view that the Falklands could not be retaken once they have been seized. This was terrible, and totally unacceptable. I could not believe it: these were our people, our islands, I said instantly: If they are invaded, we have got to get them back.
>
> Prime Minister Margaret Thatcher, *Memories of the Falklands* (2002) p.2

01 April
- The War Cabinet meets to discuss the possible invasion of the Falkland Islands
- HMS *Hermes* and HMS *Invincible* told to prepare to sail

40 Commando were at Altcar Ranges, near Liverpool, carrying out weapons training when rumours started to circulate about the Falklands being invaded. Initially everyone thought it was an April Fools joke. As history would tell, this was no prank.

> I can recall getting the news that we were to travel back down to Plymouth from Altcar on or about the 01 of April. It got us out of the monotony of one of the most boring jobs, range butt duties. Endlessly lifting and pulling down Figure 12 targets, pointing to where shots had hit then gluing paper squares over the holes. I can remember Cpl Porthouse commenting that this is as close as ever we will ever be too been [sic] shot at.
>
> Travelling back to Plymouth there were lots of rumours especially the one about it being an April Fools' joke. All I was aware of was that we were not going to get any Easter leave and my two weeks of drinking back home in Ipswich, had been put on hold.
>
> Marine Terry Barnes, 9 Troop, C Company

02 April
- Falkland Islands invaded
- HMS *Hermes* is put on 4 hours' notice, all leave stopped, and general recall started at 0615
- 800 Squadron Captain recalled from Gibraltar
- A flash Signal was sent to Commanding Officer of 40 Commando notifying him that 3 Commando Brigade Royal Marines had been chosen

In the months leading up to the Falklands War, 40 Commando had carried out amphibious exercises with both HMS *Invincible* and HMS *Hermes* which were to prove invaluable during the months ahead. 40 Commando undertook the amphibious trials with the new HMS *Invincible* in the latter stages of 1981. This gave many of the younger Royal Marines, me included, their first taste of sea time with the Royal Navy and stood them in good stead for the months ahead. On return from this exercise the Commando embarked on an adventure training programme in the UK and Europe. I opted to go skiing in Avoiraz, France.

HMS *Hermes* had been a Harrier strike carrier during the previous 12 months and her amphibious expertise was somewhat rusty. In February 1982, 40 Commando Group embarked by air and LCVP in Plymouth Sound and carried out two landing exercises on the south coast of England over the next fortnight. Accommodating over 2,000 men for a short stay along with their vehicles and stores on the flight deck provided many problems. We were to see these problems all over again in the not-too-distant future, albeit with smaller numbers and less equipment.

In the Defence Review of 1981, it was envisaged that the Royal Navy, and consequently the Royal Dockyards, would play a small role in any future conflicts due to everyone concentrating on NATO and the European scenario. The review called for a drastic reduction in the number of workers in the dockyard, and the first round of redundancy notices were issued in early 1982, just prior to Argentina invading the Falklands. As part of this, the Royal Navy wanted to dispose of the amphibious ships, thereby killing two birds with one stone. Getting rid of ships would save money, and without the ships and landing craft the Royal Marines would then have no means of conducting amphibious operations, and thus they would be without a role. They could be legitimately offloaded onto the Army, if the Army wanted them.

There were no contingency plans in existence for the Falkland Islands, or indeed anywhere else outside NATO, to support any deployment much larger than a brigade, and there was neither the time nor the hard information to form detailed plans now. The nearest thing to the current situation was for deployments to Northern Norway. Helicopters would be at a premium, both for moving men and equipment from ships standing offshore and then taking them forward on land, but the ships would have to be protected.

The Ministry of Defence's thoughts on retaking the Falklands were put in a box years ago and marked '*Mission Impossible*.' Pandora's Box had been opened and we were now charged with carrying out that impossible mission. Within 48 hours of receiving the call, 40 Commando was concentrated at Seaton Barracks, Plymouth preparing for whatever might be ahead. A Company were to leave on HMS *Hermes* and the remainder of 40 Commando would follow on *Canberra* with the main Task Force.

For most of the first week of April supplies were being moved by road using the Royal Corps of Transport and Territorial Army vehicles (now known as Reserve Forces) and drivers in 100 chartered 44-foot flatbed lorries. Around 39,108 tons of freight was moved by road, and by the second week 44 special trains had been hired with key items having to be found around the country, arriving piecemeal fashion at their destination. This included 100 vehicles, 2,000 tons of ammunition and hundreds of tons of stores. All the stores would eventually be unloaded and stored in the San Carlos Bay area, either at the beachhead with 40 Commando or in Ajax Bay across San Carlos Water.

The danger of a direct transit was that it would see the men arrive with reduced fitness. Furthermore, the stores would be unable to be offloaded in an organised fashion into the shore stores areas and thus enable the LSLs and merchant vessels to leave the danger area. This would also be the problem for an airhead to allow the establishment of a base close to the area of active operations where supplies and troops could be received and evacuated by air. The answer to this problem was Ascension Island, situated 3,700 nautical miles from the UK, which had a former Second World War airfield with a 10,000-foot runway. In 1962 a lease agreement was signed which allowed the Americans to use the island. However, a caveat was placed in the contract that allowed for the British to have military use of the island at any time that it was required. This foresight into the potential possible emergency use of Ascension Island was a solution to the Falklands' logistics problem.

And so, our epic journey to a task that everyone said was impossible began.

2

HMS *Hermes* to Landings

03 April
- A Company 40 Commando arrive at Portsmouth to board HMS *Hermes*

04 April
- Commanding Officers from 40 Commando and 42 Commando attended a briefing at 1100 in Devonport with the commander of 3 Commando Brigade, to begin organising the logistics of fighting a campaign in the South Atlantic
- HMS *Conqueror* leaves Faslane Naval Base on the west coast of Scotland

Initially it was planned that all personnel under 18 years of age were to be left behind but Shane Cusack, the Company Commander of A Company, waived this matter aside for now. This was a good decision as the order was later rescinded. The suspicion was that the Royal Navy would have a serious logistical and manpower problem removing all personnel under 18 years of age from the Task Force.

As the coaches approached HMS *Hermes* at 0557, the usual Commando mess decks were already allocated, and A Company were to be farmed out into pockets to any available mess deck that contained a spare bunk. Shane Cusack made vehement protests to the captain of HMS *Hermes*, Captain Linley E. Middleton, but suggestions that sailors vacate the allotted embarked forces' accommodation promptly fell on deaf ears. Captain Middleton's response to Shane Cusack's plea that the fighting effectiveness and morale of his men would suffer was, I imagine, taken with a quiet sharp intake of breath by Shane Cusack: "You must feel free to use the ship's Tannoy system to get messages to them, just as I do when speaking to the ship's company".

During the time it took HMS *Hermes* to sail to Ascension, the numbers of Argentine troops on the islands increased dramatically. Not only had the plan to fly A Company to Ascension gone out of the window but the intelligence reports were now suggesting 10,000 Argentines were on the islands, which ensured this was not a viable option anymore.

> We were told about the Falklands invasion and the only thing I knew about the Falklands was that it was a rubbish draft for 18 months, bloody miles from anywhere. Diego Garcia in the Indian Ocean was better. I can recall feeling so pleased with myself on two accounts; one that I had managed to crush everything in and two that I had already painted my name, service number and 6 (representing 40 Commando Royal Marines) on the base of my kitbag.
>
> Marine Terry Barnes, 9 Troop, C Company

05 April (Monday)
- HMS *Hermes* plus A Company, 40 Commando, and HMS *Invincible* sail from Portsmouth

- The remainder of 40 Commando Royal Marines are put on 12 hours' notice to move
- Embarked were: 800 Naval Air Squadron (12 BAE Sea Harriers, including seven absorbed from 899 Training Squadron and trials); part 809 Naval Air Squadron (four BAE Sea Harriers absorbed into 800 Squadron); part No. 1 Squadron, RAF (eight Hawker Siddeley Harrier GR.3s); 825 Naval Air Squadron (four Sea King HAS.2s; formed from 706 Training Squadron); 826 Naval Air Squadron (12 Sea King HAS.5s); 846 Naval Air Squadron (six Sea King HC.4s). The flight deck and hanger areas were quite full so our flight deck training would be limited, especially when we were at flying stations.

06 April
- First Amphibious ships sail
- Naval Party 1222 arrived at Ascension (effective from May 1982 and disbanded 31 Dec 1986). The main task for this temporary detachment was to receive men, stores, equipment, and helicopters flown out from Britain and then ship them south to the Falklands

07 April
- HMS *Hermes* starts Zulu time
- Work starts on *Canberra*'s modifications

08 April
- 40 Commando travel from Seaton Barracks, Plymouth to Southampton to board *Canberra*

Around midday the first of the 2,500 troops started to embark onboard *Canberra*. It went on all afternoon with hundreds of men loaded with bergens and personal weapons in a never-ending stream moving into new accommodation more used to pleasure-bound passengers. Overhead cranes swung heavily chacons/containers onto the games deck. It was now that the troops heard from Captain Scott Masson over the Tannoy for the first time:

> This is an unusual role for this ship, and we hope you will be as happy as the passengers that we normally carry but of course with the added advantage that you are not paying for it. P&O has a long history of association with Her Majesty's Services, and we are delighted to welcome on board 3 Battalion Parachute Regiment, 40 & 42 Commando Royal Marines and all the embarked services personnel. We believe this voyage to the sunshine cruising area for which we are well adapted will provide a unique experience for those on board. Nobody knows exactly what the future holds for us, but I have no doubt that working together we shall accomplish everything that is asked of us and, believe me, you have the full support of all the ship's company which I command. It has been most encouraging to receive an enormous number of good wishes for the unusual deployments that we are about to embark on.
>
> Captain Dennis Scott Masson, SS *Canberra*
> *A Very Strange Way to go to War – The Canberra in the Falklands* (2012) p.62

Within minutes we were called to be working party to load stores onto *Canberra*. I thought here we go again; we'll be here for hours. As we were loading some "nutty" boxes in a chain gang formation from the gang plank to ship, I remember one of the lads grabbing a box and running back down to his cabin before the civilian staff noticed he was missing. True Royal Marine style, "proffing" anything that's available.

Marine Terry Barnes, 9 Troop, C Company

09 April

- *Canberra* sails for the South Atlantic

At 2000, after a day of frantic activity with all men and stores on board, *Canberra* slipped her moorings, and by 2013 lines were clear and she eased out into the channel with the band playing 'We Are Sailing.'

Half a mile down Southampton Water the ship passed close to the shore and banners could be seen with *'BACK SAFE AND SOON'* and *'GIVE THE ARGIES SOME BARGIE'*, others simply *'GOOD LUCK'*. The captain sounded the ship's horn to blast out a resounding farewell to the ship's homeport. As the sights and sounds faded away, everyone on board gathered their thoughts, with the Task Force having an average age of 20.

I was promoted to Substantive Sergeant on, of all days 01 April 1982 at Altcar Ranges and just a matter of days later 40 began the journey to Southampton to load on the *Canberra*. As the most junior of the Senior NCOs, I was appointed Duty Senior for the next 24 hours.

I think I could write a book on that first day, organising as many as 1,000 ranks on working parties, pissed up Paras, stow-a-ways, abandoned vehicles on the jetty, even a possible proxy bomb, due to an army officer leaving his case next to a wall. After we slipped moorings, it didn't stop there.

Finding Marine drivers' and getting them back to their previous sections/ companies, finding accommodation for others, Paras robbing the wardroom flats of coffee, tea & biscuits, Casualties from overcrowded escalators that crashed under their weight, setting up a guard room, it was early hours of the morning before it began to calm down. My report to the RSM, Gus Pearson, the next day, went like war & peace. Well done, Pincher, you will not get another duty. In my head I heard somebody saying … Yeah!! you could be dead before it comes round again.

Sergeant S. 'Pincher' Martin, Support Company

The first few days were to see a not so intelligent act when the British Forces Post Office announced the designated postal address for *Canberra* was BFPO 666. Despite the hilarity at Satan's postmark, on board nobody at P&O appeared to get it as they informed relatives of the crew how to write to their loved ones. It was three weeks before somebody provided a new postal address with the firm instruction that the previous number 666 should not be used.

40 Commando Royal Marines were given the William Fawcett Room to relax in, have lectures, briefings, and entertainment. At first, we ran in just sports kit and training

shoes, then fighting orders, carried weapons and boots. I managed to get some large blood blisters on one foot.

Behind a curtain in sick bay, we could hear cries of pain as the treatment was being administered. We could not stop laughing at the shrills from the discomfort being carried out to our colleagues. When my turn arrived, I was told to lay face down and to bend my leg at the knee and place my foot up in the air. It felt like someone had whacked the sole of my foot with a cricket bat. I turned around to see the medic with a needle in his hand and a sadistic smile on his face.

Marine Terry Barnes, 9 Troop, C Company

For the men of A Company, 40 Commando, onboard HMS *Hermes* the daily training and daily exercise on the flight deck had the added problem of working around the various aircraft taking off and landing. There would normally be a specific hour allocated for everyone onboard to use the available space of the flight deck to train and keep in shape. As we were now operational, aircraft operations took preference over training.

All manner of other training activities filled the remainder of each day, including weapon handling, radio procedure, survival techniques, aircraft recognition, advanced first aid, the list was endless. On *Canberra*, the comprehensive first-aid instruction, especially on the later leg from Ascension Island, was given particular attention by all, and included how to suppress bleeding, insert drips, and administer painkilling drugs, amongst other procedures.

On the way to Ascension Island, on HMS *Hermes*, we had a full training schedule. We carried out PT on the flight deck every day. We frequently found ourselves on the flight deck without hearing protection as the Harriers were landing and taking off and all we could do was cover our ears.

Rifles were integrated into the PT sessions. We practised with our weapons, SLR, GPMG, 84mm Carl Gustav, 66mm LAW, completing both drills, and live firing from the flight deck. We were even allowed to carry out training on the quarterdeck at times. At the time, as a young Marine, I did not understand what an "honour" that was. We also practised helicopter drills and reviewed various fieldcraft skills.

During this time, I tried wearing the new Cairngorm boots that I was issued and immediately felt them rubbing on my heels. I decided that there was not enough time to break them in and wore my German Para boots instead for the whole conflict.

Marine 'A', Alpha Company, 40 Commando

A consignment of instruction films for the treatment of gunshot and blast injuries from Korea and Vietnam was brought onboard *Canberra* at Ascension. These formed an illustrated lecture by Surgeon Commander Rick Jolly that became known as 'Doc Jolly's Horror Show'. Also undertaking this training were journalists, which for them included the use of first field dressings and basic battlefield first-aid, vials of morphine, treating sucking chest wounds, burns and applying tourniquets without strangling anybody, amongst other useful information.

Running parallel with the medical lectures were military briefings on weapons, mines and survival. Every public room was in use as men were going through the information. Any available space became an impromptu lecture theatre where brown paper bags that were normally used for rubbish were slit open, folded out and taped up to form makeshift backboards. Diagrams of Argentine regiments' insignia and rank structure, and identification charts began to appear around the ship.

10 April
- Michael Clapp is appointed Commander Amphibious Task Force
- Sandy Woodward is appointed Commander Carrier Task Group
- Julian Thompson is appointed Commander Landing Force

11 April
- A sports day onboard *Canberra* for the crew and embarked forces

9 Troop, Charlie Company's representative in the race was a young Marine by the name of Ricky Miller. Ricky was focused, not only on finishing and winning but he had to ignore the pain he was suffering after borrowing a pair of training shoes from another marine, possibly Andy Gaunt, that were too big, and well-worn in.

Marine Terry Barnes, 9 Troop, C Company

12 April
- Maritime Exclusion Zone established

14 April
- Initial planning for the landings was now taking place

Admiral Fieldhouse argued that sea control and a reasonable degree of air superiority over the Falkland Islands could be established and the area close to Stanley was the most suitable landing spot. In terms of decisive military result and with tactical surprise this might just be achieved.

The three principal options for landing were:
- West Falkland

This option promised minimal opposition, and ground cover for deployed troops, distance from any mobile Argentine forces, and minimal risk of casualties. Against this was vulnerability to mainland base attacks and lack of direct pressure on the main Argentine force. Another move to East Falkland would expose the men to hazardous, and possibly unsuitable, beaches.
- The South of East Falkland

The advantage of the south was that there would be light opposition and minimal risk of civilian casualties, but problems of inadequate cover and a difficult approach to Stanley.
- The North of East Falkland

Offered proximity to Stanley and immediate pressure on the Argentine force but a greater risk of opposed landing, a loss of tactical surprise and an early confrontation with Argentine quick reaction forces.

It is assumed that the north of East Falkland Option formed part of Op Order 1/82 (see appendices). This option would see the following tasks undertaken by 40 Commando which were to be carried out in Berkeley Sound just north of Stanley:

Phase 1: land one Commando by LCU, secure COW BAY and VOLUNTEER BEACH and established a beach head. The Landing Force moves ashore by LCU and helicopter into beach head.

Phase 2: launch successive Commando/Battalion assaults from the beach head to secure JOHNSON HARBOUR SETTLEMENT, PORT LOUIS SETTLEMENT, URANIE BAY BEACH and LONG ISLAND – MOUNT LOW ridge line.

40 Commando would be involved as follows:

Phase 1: Land by LCU and secure COW BAY and VOLUNTEER BEACH. Establish a beach head and prepare defensive positions.

Clear MOUNT BRISBANE and secure fire base for 79 Battery in area grid 3695.

15 April
- The Chief of Staff issued a directive to *'land with a view to repossession.'*
- 2 Para (900 men) transferred from 5 Brigade to 3 Commando Brigade
- The Prime Minister agrees additional ships to be sent
- HMS *Intrepid* ready by 28 April and MV *Norland*, which would carry 2 Para, added to list of ships arriving around 18 May in time for the Landings on 21 May

16 April
- Sandy Woodward discusses campaign strategy with Michael Clapp and Julian Thompson onboard HMS *Fearless*
- Sandy Woodward moved his flag to HMS *Hermes* which now became the Task Force Flag Ship

HMS *Hermes* arrived at Clarence Bay, Ascension Island at 1239. The various other ships of the Task Force were a sight to behold. There were ships in every direction as far as the eye could see. I could see one ship later identified as the *Atlantic Conveyor*, had a Harrier seemingly landing behind containers. We now know these were to protect the aircraft and helicopters on deck.

As we arrived at Ascension, Captain Middleton's orders to Shane Cusack were brief, *'We are putting you ashore before we sail'*. Shane Cusack then asked as to where and what provisions existed for his men, the reply was, *'I don't know'*. Shane Cusack wondered about the tons of ammunition we had brought onboard in Portsmouth. This would be no use in the South Atlantic onboard HMS *Hermes* rather than being used for training in Ascension Island, and if A Company were to be put ashore then the ammunition and stores would have to come as well.

Shane Cusack noted that he would have to solve this problem himself and asked a signaller to contact the RFA that had been sighted at anchor in the bay. This RFA turned out to be *Sir Tristram*. After making his request, the Captain of *Sir Tristram* said that he would be more than happy to offer A Company a new home and he would also take the considerable amount of ammunition currently onboard HMS *Hermes*.

The commander of the SBS onboard HMS *Hermes* stated that he would prefer it if A Company were to remain onboard as a company-strength backup force for the SBS who were already ashore. This request was refused by Captain Middleton and A Company were transferred to *Sir Tristram*. The proposed SBS backup role would have been right up our street and relished, especially given the earlier plans to send A Company from RAF St Mawgan to Ascension, and then by RFA to the Falklands.

Sir Tristram was to make A Company welcome as their embarked force of Royal Marines. The following day we were joined by Z Company, 45 Commando, who had flown to Ascension from the UK. Wednesday 20 April, *Canberra* arrived, and we sadly bid farewell to *Sir Tristram*. We were most grateful for her last-minute hospitality. Sadly, when we next had sight of her it would be in far less happy circumstances.

17 April
- Sir John Fieldhouse and Jeremy Moore fly to Ascension to meet Sandy Woodward, Julian Thompson, and Michael Clapp onboard HMS *Hermes*

18 April
- Carrier Battle Group leaves Ascension: HMS *Hermes, Invincible, Glamorgan, Broadsword, Yarmouth, Alacrity* along with RFA *Olmeda* and *Resource*

19 April
The time at Ascension enabled the various commanders to assess the readiness of the Task Force and get in some very valuable training. A Company's cross-decking exercise from HMS *Hermes* to *Sir Tristram* highlighted the routine that would be required for a successful transfer later in the programme. At the Wideawake Range area, all personal weapons were checked, and zeroed, including the 84s firing HEAT rounds at old oil tanker trailers to simulate vehicles known to be on the islands.

In a statement by 40 Commandos' Commanding Officer Malcolm Hunt, he notes that the PWI training HQ Defence Troop, who were all qualified Royal Marines but had specific day jobs, would, as this situation showed, automatically revert to being a Royal Marine if required. During the time in the Falklands, parts of HQ Company were heavily committed in manning OPs and conducting patrols, clearly demonstrating that clerks, chefs, and storemen retained their basic military skills; after all, they had all completed the 32-week basic training at Lympstone and earned the right to wear the Green Beret with Globe and Laurel Cap Badge. They may have been given a different career path to the GD Marine to help increase the manpower levels in certain jobs within the various units, but they still had to complete the annual fitness and weapons tests.

'Always the bridesmaid and never the bride' sums up my experience of 1982. My war started somewhat earlier than most as I was on the outgoing NP 8901 due to leave the Falklands on April 2nd, 1982. When we were deported back to the UK after the invasion, we were given the contact number of a captain to call if we were being hassled by the press, Captain Graham if memory serves; I rang him and told him that the press wasn't bothering me, but my conscience was, and could I please go back with the Task Force? He was clearly pleased to hear this (the old detachment was never asked to return, unlike our replacements). "Good Show!!" he said, "I'll send you a ticket to

Plymouth, report to Stonehouse and take it from there!". When I got to Stonehouse, there were a few other guys as well, so I was not the only one. About ten returned on this basis and saw it through to the end, which happened to be a drafty [sic] Sapper Hill. Almost everyone went to 40 Commando, in my case for old time's sake; I went to 7 Troop Charlie Coy as I had spent three years in Forty in the mid-seventies, also in 7 Troop at the time were Michael Wilkins (Ugly Mick) and the formidable Julian Thompson, under whom we were the first unit, army or otherwise, to serve a tour in South Armagh without any fatalities (1976). A couple of the South Georgia chaps from our detachment went to Juliet Company in 42, I say this as a point of accuracy, it might seem to be pedantic, but these volunteers should be recognised for their willingness to 'get back on the horse' after a nice spot of terror; anyway, at least this time we had some prospect of being on the winning side.

After collecting a complete Arctic issue of kit and weapons, we were on our way to Lynham to be taken to Ascension by C-130, via Gibraltar and Dubai; the latter was a dump by all appearances, nothing like now. After 24hrs on the Hercules, we landed at Ascension, the first thing we were greeted with was "Why have you brought so much kit?" Because nobody told us otherwise of course! Our detachment commander Major Noote was there and asked us which unit we wanted to go to; Forty was favourite as several of the others had served there when I did, besides that, Seaton Barracks was in prime position for the delights of Plymouth. We heard that some of the old detachment were returning to the UK via Ascension where we met them; four of the group immediately turned round, Brasso Hare and Steve Porter went to Charlie Coy, Steve Chubb and Derek Hunter to Juliet Coy. Eventually we made our way to the *Canberra*, me less one fighting order which someone decided they needed more than I did when I went for a run. I was interviewed by O/C Charlie Coy Captain Andy Pillar and WO 2 Bill Howie; they let me in! I went to 7 Troop run by Taff Lloyd and 2nd Lt Paul Allen. It didn't take long to settle in and obtain some webbing, in very short supply to my surprise, which is also why I ended up with one of those tortoise shell shaped steel helmets a la Rhine Crossing!

I was pleasantly surprised by the leeway given for having a few drinks if desired under the auspice of work hard, play hard; we were generally left alone when work finished, quite a change from *Bulwark* and *Hermes* on which I had previously been deployed. I don't recall this being abused, especially when we heard about the Sheffield; it became clear that we would have to fight, and this was very real.

Marine Brien Hobbs, Charlie Company, 40 Commando

20 April
- *Canberra* arrives at Ascension Island

27 April
- Plans for landings presented to war cabinet
- Cabinet in London gives approval for the landing, to be known as Operation Sutton

The Task Force were practising helicopter assault stations daily with the aim to get troops ashore first in one coordinated wave of seven or eight helicopters, followed by individual aircraft as quickly as they could be loaded and dispatched. If we had to do this for real, we would have to be within a mile or so of the Falklands. It was this preparation that would have been vital for an initial proposal of a helicopter assault in Berkeley Sound, just north of Stanley, before San Carlos was agreed upon.

The 1:50,000 maps issued to the Task Force were originally drawn up from aerial photographs taken in 1956 and printed in 1961. They did not have the much-needed grid lines marking the latitude and longitude lines, which would be used extensively in referencing locations and targets. Ordnance Survey worked frantically to produce new 1:25,000 maps and rush them out to the Task Force. These even showed the Royal Marines' Moody Brook barracks as derelict thanks to the Argentine Forces thinking the barracks were occupied, but NP8901 were ahead of the game.

> Not until the very end of the campaign were there any air photographs showing enemy dispositions, defensive positions, strong positions, compositions and so forth. Even they arrived so late, so poor they had no influence in planning. So, for the first time probably since Gallipoli in 1915 an amphibious operation had to be mounted with no air photography of the enemy. Detailed intelligence would therefore have been gleaned by the mark one eyeball which referred to both SAS and SBS patrols on the ground behind enemy lines.
>
> Brigadier Julian Thompson RM
> *Signals of War: The Falklands Conflict of 1982* (1990), p.333

29 April
- San Carlos with its sheltered waters emerged as the favourite both on HMS *Fearless* and at Northwood

06 May
- *Canberra* sails from Ascension with HMS *Ardent* and *Elk*

07 May
On board *Canberra*, the doctors called for volunteer blood donors to build up a blood bank. This was taken up by everyone and it also allowed for 10 days to recuperate before blood could be given again. With typical military humour the military medical staff regularly had comments such as '*I want mine back when we get there*' or '*look after that doc it is only on loan.*'

10 May
- Michael Clapp and Julian Thompson took the final decision that San Carlos would be the landing point
- Sir John Fieldhouse was pushing to send a firm instruction to 3 Commando Brigade to prepare to do more than sit tight once landed

12 May
- 3 Commando Brigade HQ issues Operational Order for the landings in San Carlos Water
- Amphibious Task Group ordered to repossess the Falklands as quickly as possible

Op Order 2/82 issued 12 May 1982 from HQ 3 Commando Brigade RM HMS *Fearless* (See appendices)

Op Order 1/82 issued in May of 1982 should not be confused with LFFI Op Order 1/82 issued by hand in San Carlos on 01 June 1982. (See appendices)

13 May
- Julian Thompson gives 3 Commando Brigade orders for San Carlos landing onboard HMS *Fearless*

14 May
- The following were promoted to Local Corporal for the duration of *Op Corporate*:
  - L/Cpl K. Hargreaves
  - L/Cpl K. Brennan
  - L/Cpl A. Parker
- The following rank has been promoted to Lance Corporal:
  - Mne G P Edwards

15 May
- Michael Clapp holds his pre-landing conference
- The following rank was promoted from Local Sergeant to Sergeant:
  - Sgt N Holloway

The wording on the Chief of Staff directive was to '*land with a view to repossession*' was thought to be restrictive and too ambiguous. It suggested that the next step would be to argue for holding back on extra ground forces or establishing a presence with a view to further negotiations or preparing a beachhead from which future operations might be developed. This task would eventually fall to 40 Commando as it was felt that an experienced Commando unit would be better prepared to fight off any counterattack on the beachhead. Early intelligence reports suggested a counterattack would be expected alongside the numerous air and ground attacks that were seen following the landings.

18 May
- War Cabinet was presented with and approved the San Carlos option
- Michael Clapp and Julian Thompson order the redistribution of troops prior to landing subject to final confirmation on 20 May
- The following ranks were promoted to Local Sergeant for the duration of Op Corporate:
  - Cpl J K Mullans
  - Cpl N M Clarke
  - Cpl R P Brown
- The following ranks were promoted to Local Corporal for the duration of Op Corporate:
  - L/Cpl S Bambury
  - L/Cpl D F Irving
  - L/Cpl A J Allen
  - L/Cpl I D Smith

Carrier Battle Group (TG 317.8) and the Amphibious Group (TG 317.0) finally came together. The Amphibious Group had arrived overnight at a holding area on the eastern edge of the TEZ. To the irritation of the commanders and the Task Force as a whole, news that the two groups had joined up were leaked out via the BBC. This would not be the last time the BBC would endanger lives of the task or landing forces.

As the landings took place, Special Forces would seek to destroy key enemy positions and equipment, Pucara ground attack aircraft, helicopters air defence systems, fuel and ammunition; harass the enemy, and reduce morale; as well as deceive the enemy as to the location of the main landing. At San Carlos, the Amphibious Group would enter the North Sound after last light with the key ships of the assault wave consisting of HMS *Fearless*, HMS *Intrepid*, SS *Canberra, Norland, Stromness* and five LSLs along with *Europic Ferry*.

The SBS patrols and SAS patrols which were deployed with the Task Force had been committed to covert reconnaissance and intelligence-gathering tasks. The teams had been operating since early May and crucially, all undetected. Argentine patrols had been avoided through regular changes in position and good camouflage. This allowed for a more accurate intelligence picture of the enemy's dispositions. These operations would continue until the surrender.

The ships would move right into San Carlos Bay and the initial landings would be carried out by landing craft. It was planned that the distance of the run from ship to shore would not exceed 10 miles and with eight hours of darkness the Royal Marines and Paras would be ashore by first light.

19 May
- Cabinet gives approval for amphibious landings
- 40 Commando, less HQ Main and B Echelon cross-deck to HMS *Fearless*

At this point, the planners realised that they had all their eggs in one large, big white target, SS *Canberra*. Sandy Woodward was also of the same opinion but wondered how he was to achieve the cross-decking of 1,500 men and limited assets in the time available and in the middle of the South Atlantic.

Helicopters would be fine for small numbers, but the sheer scale of the operation would make a very long-drawn-out affair with additional hours and stress put onto the aircrafts' engines, pilots, and mechanics, when these would be very much needed after the landing to ferry supplies and men from the ships and around the islands as the need required, and for how long?

Cross-decking via the old naval method of a jackstay, which was a tried and tested naval process, required rigging steel hawsers between the ships and winching each man across, along with his kit and weapons, using a harness. This was not without its obvious hazards and anyway for an operation as prolonged as this it would be desperately slow compared to a helicopter.

The landing craft from HMS *Fearless* and *Intrepid* could come alongside *Canberra* to load the men and their full kit on board and ferry them away to what would be a temporary home. However, in a sizeable sea the landing craft would rise and fall around 15 feet against the hull with every wave, and the soldiers with all their kit would have to try to jump onboard, and then clamber out at the other end of the trip, quite likely very cold and wet.

Lady luck was on our side and the following day the sea was unnaturally calm enough to consider the option of using the landing craft. The larger LCUs were chosen for the job and throughout the day they transferred 40 Commando (minus HQ Main and B Echelon) to HMS *Fearless* and 3 Para to HMS *Intrepid*. The landing craft were making their way across 1,000 yards of open ocean with the weather worsening by the minute and wind gusting at 25 knots. As the landing craft bounced through the South Atlantic, sea spray soaked the men huddled in the hold. The reality that we were going to land and do this for real started to hit home when we were told to write our wills and final letters.

Prior to boarding the landing craft, 40 Commando were in the Meridian Room listening intently to Malcolm Hunt who spoke about what was to come in the next few days and weeks. We then moved, in single file, snaking down the staircase and along the passageways for three decks, shuffling forward a few steps at a time, with our bergens and equipment. From the promenade deck, down through D and E deck stairs and passageways, and through to the port doors. The crew, cheerful as ever, wished us luck and hoped they would see us again soon. Those at the front started to feel the chill of the breeze as they stood by the open door looking down at the LCU bobbing up and down in the mid-South Atlantic.

At 0930 the men of 40 Commando commenced their cross-decking to HMS *Fearless* via the Port E deck door. From there they would be on forced rest until the actual landings. The jump into a waiting LUC had to be timed perfectly, as it was not only rising and falling up the side of *Canberra* by some considerable distance, but the swell also caused the landing craft to move away from the ship and then slam back into the side with some force. This was despite the landing craft being secured to the promenade deck above. The impact of the LCU against the side of *Canberra* could be felt throughout the whole ship.

One by one the marines handed their bergens to the waiting crew of the LCU, and gauged the rise and fall of the landing craft, registering the faces looking up and shouting encouragement, before stepping out and hopefully landed on the deck of the landing craft. Any miscalculation, allowing for the swell, or the loss of footing, could be fatal.

It was very nearly fatal for one man when, just after 1000, there was a roar of '*Swim you Bugger!*' Dave Sturgess of C Company lost his footing trying to board the LCU and had fallen into the cold waters of the South Atlantic between LCU (F4) and *Canberra*. There were only moments to spare before the LCU would crash back against *Canberra* and Dave's head would then act as an ineffective fender and be crushed between the LCU and *Canberra*. Stunned by the bitter cold of the South Atlantic, Dave was jerked back to reality by the LCU's crew telling him to swim. He made it to the stern of the LCU just before the next collision, with the marines in the LCU using their rifles to stop it crashing against the *Canberra*. The wake had sucked him in then pushed him out just before the stern came back in again. The crew managed to act quickly to stop the stern coming back in and then hauled him around the side. Being soaked in cold water in this weather was no joke and the danger of hypothermia quickly setting in was very much a reality.

The crew ripped off Dave's fighting order and put him in the engine room, which was the only warm place available, as they could not stop the cross-decking. It was not known how long the South Atlantic would hold with this good weather and there were a lot of men to transfer. Hopefully, hypothermia would not set in before Dave could be given appropriate treatment and dry clothing on HMS *Fearless*. By 1100 the job was complete, and 40 Commando were housed in a now very cramped HMS *Fearless*.

We transferred through the big loading doors in the side of *Canberra*; into the landing craft which was moving up and down in the swell. We were fully loaded, with extra ammunition, and one man in C Company missed and fell into the sea between the landing craft and *Canberra*. He was in serious danger of sinking or been [sic] crushed between the two vessels. All the men in the landing craft held the two ships apart with their rifles and the man was able to keep afloat and swung around and he was pulled out. It brought home to us that this was how it was going to be; we were on active service and there will be none of the safety facilities normally presented. We are very cramped in *Fearless* and the whole of my company was in the wardroom. We spent much of the next day and half asleep.

Marine Michael Spence, B Company, 40 Commando

Marine Dave Sturgess, C Company, 40 Commando told his story of the transfer and falling between *Canberra* and the landing craft:

I can't remember much, and a few things are sketchy.

I got to door and there was a rope with a knot in the end. The landing craft crew got the weapon and as there was a swell, I think we were told to jump on the third swell as this brought the landing craft closer to the door. I leaned out to jump but this third swell did not come up enough and there was something like an eight-foot drop. I went to step back onto the doorway and not sure what happened, but I went off and remember my toes catching the edge of the landing craft as it moved out and away from *Canberra*. I could hear the engines of both the landing craft and *Canberra* and eventually came up to the surface, but not quite breaking the surface and could see the sun through the surface of the water as I was letting the last of my breath out.

I eventually broke the surface with water coming out of my nose, much like a fizzy drink, and I shot out the back of the landing craft. There was a rope put in front of me to grab but my hands were too cold to grab it and I tried the ladder on the side of the landing craft, and the three crew pulled me onboard after hooking me with a boat hook. I was an extra weight as I had a trip flare, 66mm and 1,000 rounds of link ammunition as I was the No. 2 for the GPMG with Clive Lucking as my No. 1 and he was next to transfer into the landing craft.

Got onboard *Fearless* I went to sick bay to get a hot shower and some gear from the stoker's mess. Sgt Peter or Steve Kay (ML) who was possibly part of the landing craft crew onboard *Fearless*, gave me his woolly pully. I do remember unlinking all the ammunition and cleaning the rounds and clips so they could be used on the landing the next day.

Marine Dave Sturgess, C Company

My memory of Dave Stug's swim was we stood next to the open bulkhead; Dave was next to go. The army SNCO at the doorway seemed to place a hand on Dave's shoulder as he prepared to jump but the vessels parted as Dave jumped and I watched Dave drop like a stone in between the two vessels.

I was the next man to make the jump and the SNCO went to place a hand on me to tell me when to jump so I politely informed him to not touch me, and I would jump when I was ready. Training took over that day as I made that jump. I next saw Dave on one of the mess decks of HMS *Fearless* in borrowed clothes as his where being dried.

Lady luck looked down on Dave that day for sure. The one thing it proves is that the battle swimming test works. The sad thing being the crew that saved my best friend and number 2 of our gun team where all lost later in the conflict.

Marine Clive Lucking, C Company

20 May

- Michael Clapp received orders to land from London
- Jeremy Moore had become the Task Group Commander (CTG 317.1) with both 3 Commando Brigade, and 5 Brigade under his command

At 1522Z Jeremy Moore sent the following signal to all ranks of 3 Commando Brigade:

As you prepare to land in the Falkland Islands, I wish you all well good to have the red beret alongside the green again. We did so well together at Suez and we will do so again tomorrow I know. Best Luck.

Onboard HMS *Fearless*, the Royal Marines of 40 Commando prepared for the landings but intelligence reports could not indicate either an opposed or unopposed landing. In true Royal Marines tradition, they prepared for an opposed landing, and were ready to take on any situation they come across. One thing was certain, the men of 40 Commando Royal Marines would secure the objective come what may.

When we got too [sic] *Fearless*, 2 Troop, A Company were in the galley/dining room area. The room was empty, and we left our kit in the room and humped some stores around the helicopter landing deck for a while. The next day, we received the O Group for the landing. The last words of the troop commander in the O Group were "if the landing is opposed, we will just have to keep going forward and secure the objective".

We were told to wear steel helmets during the beach landing, and this was later changed to wear your berets in true Commando tradition but secure your steel helmet to your webbing and take it with you when you land.

Marine 'A', Alpha Company, 40 Commando

3

Landings and Initial Days

21 May

- 3 Commando Brigade lands on Falkland Islands and establishes beachhead at San Carlos
- HMS *Ardent* sunk
- 40 Commando Landed Blue Beach 1
- A Company cleared White Rincon and moved to defensive positions on the reverse slope of Verde Mountain
- B Company cleared Little Rincon and moved to defensive positions on reverse slope of Verde Mountain
- C Company cleared San Carlos Settlement and moved to defensive positions south of the settlement
- Recce Troop moved to their OP positions

At 0145 HMS *Fearless* and HMS *Intrepid* steamed into Falkland Sound with HMS *Fearless* one mile ahead of HMS *Intrepid*. Both vessels came to their prescribed anchorage areas at 0345 and 0347 , respectively. Ships then followed, anchoring inshore of the LPDs on the route that the landing craft would need to take to get the troops ashore. They stopped just a few minutes later than planned and the anchor ran out 15 fathoms (90 feet or 27.4 metres) of water, the deafening sound of each link in the chain clanging unavoidably noisily against the hull and splashing into the water. The long repetitive sound of the clanging would have been heard for miles in the still night air. So far, so good, and with the main task immediately ahead, thoughts turned to the landings and any last-minute changes to the plan due to enemy action.

HMS *Plymouth* swung into her allotted place with her guns facing southeast ready to fire over Port San Carlos to the east or down the more southerly bearing of the wider San Carlos Water directly in front of her, so she was now ready for an incoming attack from either direction. HMS *Brilliant* brought up the rear of Group 2 and cleared the narrows just before 0300 (midnight local). She took up position to the shore of West Falkland with her Sea Wolf missiles ready to deal with an air attack from any direction.

The Argentines above them on Fanning Head never even noticed as the 12,120-tonne HMS *Fearless* with 40 Commando on board slid past Jersey Point almost 800 feet below. The stern gates of the flooded dock opened, and the landing craft pushed out into the sea beneath a star-filled sky. As the weather cleared, the moon acted as a floodlight. The second wave of ships was through the Sound, entering in single file and protected by the guns of HMS *Plymouth*. *Canberra* steamed through the narrows, ghostly white beneath the southern stars and took up her position with *Stromness* and *Norland* in the gateway of the inlet.

HMS *Fearless* initially had a problem in that her ballast pump refused to work, and she was unable to sink low enough to float out the LCUs with the vital first wave of 40

Commando for San Carlos – Blue Beach. It was a frustrating wait sitting on the enemy's doorstep waiting to knock. The landing craft of HMS *Fearless* eventually floated out an impressive 11 minutes after dropping her anchor. The flotilla of eight landing craft were now in the water. There was a delay with 2 Para's disembarkation from *Norland* for Port San Carlos – Green Beach. The final LCU to load from *Norland* had difficulties as a member of the Parachute Regiment had fallen between the craft and the ferry, crushing his pelvis. Over a short radio call the planners discussed if they should send the fully embarked 40 Commando on ahead to retrieve something from the H-hour timings or should wait even longer until the Paras were ready.

Julian Thompson wanted the landing craft containing 85 percent of the first wave of troops to set off immediately and allow the last landing craft to finish loading correctly.

So started the operation to retake the Falkland Islands from a foreign invader.

The attached grouping for 40 Commando for the initial landing was as follows as outlined in the Operational Order:

> 8 Battery – indirect support including BC and all FOO parties
> 3 Troop, B Squadron, Blues and Royals – in direct support
> 2 Scouts (anti-tank guided weapon/reconnaissance helicopters) – in support and
> under command for movement
> One Royal Engineer Reconnaissance Section
> One Combat Engineer Tractor
> Number 1 Air Defence Section (Blowpipe) – in support and under command
> for movement
> Naval Gunfire Observer (NGFO) party – in support and under command
> for movement
> Two frigates (naval gunfire support) – in support

It was still all quiet in the Sound and HMS *Antrim* waited silently to the east near Cat Island. In her Ops Room radio signals from the SBS, six miles north on the freezing height of Fanning Head, were being logged and recorded to allow the 4.5-inch guns to make any final adjustments. At 0350 they were ready, and the guns opened fire onto the granite headland far above them. The barrage finally awakened the Argentines as they crouched in the freezing wind on top of the cliff. HMS *Antrim* filled the area with more than 250 rounds in less than 30 minutes, sufficient probably to flatten something the size of Windsor Castle. The Argentine 25 Infantry Regiment's Combat Team Güemes had not posted lookouts and thus had not noticed the large black silhouettes of warships, the ghostly white figure of *Canberra*, or heard the ships anchoring.

The men of 40 Commando had travelled down the narrow passage onboard HMS *Fearless* to the tank deck and into the landing craft. The men in the after two craft had to climb up the dolphins that divided the dock, onto the narrow catwalks until they arrived at the aft craft then down into their LCU. As they filed onto the ramp leading into the LCU, the Company Sergeant Major issued grenades, 84mm and 66mm rounds, and to some men two 81mm mortar rounds. The mortar rounds would be dumped on the beach for use by 40 Commando's Mortar Troop until resupply could be arranged.

Julian Thompson stood on HMS *Fearless*'s tank deck and when the line occasionally paused, he would take the opportunity to speak to the nearest man. Darkness gave them a measure of anonymity, but given the situation, it was not a case of officer and men, but Royal Marine to Royal Marine and so anything could have been said or asked. One marine was asked how he felt, and his reply was that he felt a bit of apprehension. Julian Thompson assured him that everybody felt the same way and he was not alone in this, and once he got going, he would be fine.

Parts of 40 Commando, including myself, would land in landing craft carried on the davits on the side of HMS *Fearless*, and which would be lowered into San Carlos Water once full. To reach these landing craft involved a journey similar to that taken by the men going to the dock. A long heavily laden snake of men scrambled down ladders and narrow passageways, tripping over obstructions, or bumping into each other in total darkness other than dim red light. This dim red light was used to protect the night vision as it allowed eyes to quickly adjust to a night sky when going from internal compartments to the ship's deck areas. As the landing craft left HMS *Fearless,* the flashes of 4.5-inch shells and the lines of tracer on Fanning Head could be seen.

Two of the eight landing craft had either a Scorpion or Scimitar to protect the troops on the run in to the beach. The vehicles were ready to fire at any enemy on the beach over the lowered bow ramp at the start of the run in.

H-hour was set at 0630 , and this gave the troops time to reach defensive positions before dawn and the expected ground and air counterattacks. 40 Commando's landing craft would be left circling while 2 Para were landed at Bonners Bay. 40 Commando would then land across Pony's Valley Bay to the north and secure San Carlos Settlement where they would find 31 civilians, including 14 children.

Both 40 Commando and 2 Para thankfully landed unopposed.

A Company cleared White Rincon (north of the target beach) before moving up to defensive positions on the reverse slope of the Verde Mountain, area grid 604855. B Company cleared Little Rincon before also moving into defensive position on the reverse slope of Verde Mountain, grid 609844. C Company cleared San Carlos Settlement itself by 0950 , where they hoisted the Union Flag, before taking defensive positions south of the settlement by 1044 . All defensive positions were on the reverse slope of hills with observation posts being placed on the crest. In this way any attacking force would be silhouetted as they came over the hill.

The whole Commando (less HQ Main and B Echelon) were now in position and had started work on defensive positions which were secure by last light. Recce Troop began moving to their OP positions, but their progress was slow due to difficult terrain.

0950 hrs a signal was sent 'HELL CAT' – San Carlos Secure going to plan pop 31 Inc 14 children increased by 2 families from Stanley. Evacuation details by first light. Enemy in company strength have visited for 3 days last week. For your Acorn to pass to CALLSIGN 60 – Local civilians suggest that description may also include house at grid 597814.

Landing site "Crow" made secure.

Civilians state all roads between San Carlos and Stanley have been mined. All subunits in position by 1350 main HQ ashore 1800 .

Signal notifying San Carlos was now occupied by Royal Marines of 40 Commando.

Simon Buzza had tried to dissuade me from being in one of the first landing craft (F5 with 3 Troop). He was concerned that I should be so far forward and might be in an unacceptably dangerous position. I explained to him I needed to see at first-hand what was happening, and I was acutely aware just how young and inexperienced my three troop commanders were; I wanted to be close at hand if anything went wrong. Simon too was not exactly safe himself as he and the remainder of Coy HQ were only 100 metres behind travelling in F8.

As ordered, I sighted the Company on the high ground to the East of the Settlement, in four close groups facing the Verde Mountains. Left forward was Tim Webster and 1 Troop; to his right about 100 metres away was Richard Walker and 2 Troop; tucked in 100 metres behind Tim were 3 Troop and Andy Salmon; to complete the boxed square (a defensive layout that I favoured) and behind 2 Troop was the right rear subunit of Company Headquarters.

Labours were frustrated though within minutes when a very high water table filled our initial holes with water, making them useless. With a switch of tactics, I ordered the men to create sangars. Cut blocks of peat made an admirable substitute for stone and considerable progress had been made by the time the first air attacks took place.

Wet boots though were of major concern as it proved impossible to dry them out. To try and overcome this, many marines turned to wearing their NBC over boots as additional boot protection. Constantly wearing wet boots, was to have serious consequences on us before we left San Carlos.

Major Shane Cusack, OC A Company, 40 Commando, *The Summer of 82*

Everyone was applying cam cream, checking their fighting orders and weapons, and getting ready to move. There was one bergen filled with 1,000 rounds of 7.62mm link for the GPMG SF and one of the youngest, if not the youngest Marine in the troop volunteered to carry it ashore, in addition to his own kit. As soon as the Troop Sgt asked for a volunteer, he said, "I'll take it". I was highly impressed, and the bergen must have weighed over 100lbs, so with that, plus his own kit he must have been carrying well over 150lbs when we landed. He was 17 years of age.

We made our way through the ship to the landing craft dock, and pretty much every sailor was patting us on the back saying, "good luck lads". We all picked a container holding two 81mm mortar rounds to be dropped in a pile ashore.

Marine 'A', Alpha Company, 40 Commando

We were briefed as to our job on landing, the task for Charlie Coy was to move through San Carlos Settlement driving out any enemy encountered and dig in the far side. I don't remember much about the briefing itself; the drama was (and still is) somewhat overshadowed by Major Norman's final brief before the Argentine landing. We longed to get off *Fearless* and get ashore. I think everyone must have thought as I did; "Get us off this ship and ashore and we will never be defeated; get our feet on the ground and we can do anything, just get us off the ship … ..!

Marine Brien Hobbs, 7 Troop, Charlie Company

Prior to landing, I started asking the section one by one if they were for "crucifixion" as we had watched "The Life of Brian." Answer yes and you'd get 2 grenades, 2 x 81mm,

1x 66mm, 1 x smoke. One guy did say no, so I said he could go home he was free. Company Sergeant Major did not find it funny.

Upon landing we shuffled off the LCU by the weight of our equipment and 81mm mortars we carried. 9 Troop cleared the righthand side of the settlement with the reporter Max Hasting in tow. We went to the first farm building whilst Captain Pillar knocked on the door and told a swearing Falklands farmer, because he had been woken up by all the noise, that we were back! He didn't give a "nats nadger" about that. I remember us all running for cover as he opened the door and a large shaft of light illuminated us all. We cleared the settlement and moved out 1 km and dug in.

Local Corporal Damian Irving, 9 Troop, C Company

Our chaps surrounded the manager's house when Andy Pillar knocked on the door to ask if there were Argies about. There was some delay before Mr Short appeared and said something like "Oh you've come then" a common reaction throughout the settlement. There were no garlands of flowers [or] kisses on both cheeks. If we had been grassed skirted Chinamen with daggers in our teeth the reception would have been the same.

Captain Roger Williams, Support Company, 40 Commando

The Islander's inner gratitude to the British servicemen who came to liberate the island was deep and genuine this is Pat Short's memory of the event.

About 1:30 am my son Derek heard shelling – we later found out it was on Fanning Head. Then we heard engine noises out in the bay. I went outside [and] couldn't see anything. There was a pup in the porch and woke up, wagged its tail and hit a tin. It made me jump and I went back in again. I went back to bed, waiting and wondering what was happening. Then, at 4–4:30 am there was a hefty knocking. I tried to unlock the door but dropped the key and kept them waiting while I scrambled about on the floor to find it. When I opened it there were all these blokes with paint on the faces and camouflaged. I asked them if they were British, and one said hello Pat do you remember me? I couldn't pick anyone out that I could recognise, and he told me it was John Thurman. I had met him when he had been out here a year or so ago and he visited us at the settlement. I shook his hand a few times I think, and they told us to go back to bed and forget all about it until the morning.

Mr Pat Short, Settlement Manager, *The Falklands War* (2014), p.211

The landing day began early at 2.15 am when we were called to breakfast. By 03.00 the ship's broadcast was calling us to Assault Stations. A Company, landing from the four smaller LCVP landing craft, mustered in the main dining hall whilst the remainder of the Commando gathered further aft nearer to the stern ramp. The dining hall was very cramped with over 150 marines all carrying weapons, spare ammunition and large bergens.

Adrenaline was beginning to run and then much to the relief of all it was time to be led outside and loaded into the landing craft. These were still high on the davits and yet to be lowered into the water. As soon as we were onboard the winches started and down, we went. After circling for 5 or 10 minutes the small craft lined up astern of each other and we set off for the two-hour run in to the beach. The passage was a smooth one and mercifully the sea was calm and the weather kind. Landing craft were cramped at the best of times, but that night they were overladen with bodies and, with insufficient space inboard, we over-spilled onto the main deck in front of the conning position.

With 10 minutes to go before landing we slipped out of our assault life jackets and prepared ourselves for whatever was coming next.

The landing craft made a hash of the next 10 minutes. 100 metres short of the beach, our craft suddenly went astern. Either we were about to go aground, or we were heading for the wrong landing point then we lined up again and went ahead. We were worried that the extra noise would have been heard and just wanted to get out of the boat as quickly as we could. The wait was driving us mad.

The coxswain gave the order "down ramp and out troops" – however the ramp did not fall! The retaining clips then needed several thumps with a sledgehammer to release them; obviously, they had not been greased and checked beforehand.

Any expectation of a semi-dry landing was extinguished immediately. We plunged into icy cold water up to our waists. The next problem was not to fall over as we were not very stable on our feet. Heavy bergens and full fighting order, as well as being loaded down with ammunition, made movement very difficult in such deep water. Surging forward – instinct took over – we reached the beach in about 20 to 30 paces.

From our beach where we stumbled ashore, the beach exits were non-existent. Instead, resembling something out of a Keystones Cops or Charlie Chaplin movie, we all crashed into the person immediately in front of us. Our beach assault came to an abrupt halt. Within 15 paces we reached the edge of any so-called beach [and] what lay ahead was a vertical 6' high peat wall. Two marines turned and faced each other with either end of a rifle in their hands. As we stepped forward onto the weapon we were elevated onto the higher ground.

We swiftly deployed and cleared the nearby area known as White Rincon (our first task). Then at a fast pace we climbed up onto the high ground where we were to occupy a defensive position.

As soon as we could do so we furiously began digging even though it was not yet light. Eagerly we sought to get the first stages of some protection around us before the expected Argentine aircraft arrived.

Major Shane Cusack, OC A Company, 40 Commando, *The Summer of 82*

The troops took two days' rations ashore with them, so the major task on D-Day was landing ammunition, with some being delivered to the unit sites, but a vast majority was delivered to Ajax Bay. The Commando Brigade were able to move about reasonably freely, which allowed the landing of stores and equipment to be carried out as quickly as possible to establish the beachhead. The position was reasonably secure, and everyone was in the knowledge that they were not being observed and could not be engaged by direct fire from heavy artillery or heavy machine guns.

The construction of sangars rather than traditional trenches was due to the ground water table in the British positions on the hills above San Carlos. This entailed taking sods of grass from the hillside to form the sangar walls, but this left large scars on the hill and showed the position to any enemy forces, which was not ideal. Patrols were sent out to check and ensure there were no Argentine movements in the area. The positions also enabled the setting up of mortar, artillery, and naval gunfire on reference points against possible enemy movements or counter attacks on the beachhead. Regular patrolling by day and night on both the forward and reverse slopes of the ridge ensured that any enemy OP positions would not last long.

A working party was called for and like all good Royal Marines I ducked for cover. It was not until Marine Spooner (Hall) returned to the troop's positions that we found out that he had gone back down into San Carlos Settlement to raise the Union Flag and have some photographs taken. Little did I know that this picture was to be published all over the world in the next few days with the heading "we're back" on the front page of many UK tabloid papers.

Marine Terry Barnes, 9 Troop, C Company

To avoid any unnecessary confusion and possible blue on blue incidents, such as a Harrier in hot pursuit of a Mirage being shot down by one of our own frigates or ground forces, it was agreed that a ceiling of 10,000 feet above the landing area was to be part on an invisible box roughly 10 miles across. This box was to be declared a Harrier No Go Zone. Inside the box the helicopters could ferry anything to and from the beaches and ships and they would go to ground whenever enemy aircraft came in. This would give the troops and ships complete freedom to fire at any fixed wing aircraft that was inside the box as those aircraft would only be Argentine. Meanwhile the Harriers would be waiting outside the box knowing that if anything came out of the box it would be Argentine.

The helicopters with their underslung loads continued to fly to the beachhead, and the Mexefloats and their Royal Corps of Transport crews continued to carry stores ashore during air raids. In the nine hours of daylight on the first day, the helicopters picked up 288 loads and put ashore 520 men, with another 220 tons of stores from 11 different ships, taking the loads to 21 different sites. They had landed the rest of the guns, and the four light batteries and a good deal of ammunition, although not enough should the beachhead at San Carlos and Ajax Bay be seriously attacked as the brigade had expected them to be.

Until there were at least 30 days' stores ashore, which would be several thousand tonnes, the brigade could not fight far from the beachhead without undue risk to the operation. Indeed, every battle would need the support of at least one Light Gun battery, requiring 11 lifts by eight Sea Kings to take the guns forward with 500 rounds for each of the guns.

At Goose Green the SAS observers noticed six Pucara aircraft preparing to take off. They called in NGS from HMS *Ardent* and only one aircraft, flown by Captain Jorge Benitez, got airborne. He was later shot down by a Stinger missile but only after he had reported on the activity in San Carlos Water. The landing was now known and even with this intelligence there was still uncertainty as to this being the real site of the British landings to retake the islands. This was the moment which the Argentine Air Force had been waiting for and they were soon unleashed. The first Daggers left Río Grande at 1225 heading for San Carlos.

The first day proved to be a long one, not only for the initial landing and digging in, but the Argentines had taken umbrage at the British wanting their land back and making good on their promise to take it back by force if necessary.

The first wave consisted of nine Daggers from the 6th Fighter Group at San Julián and six Skyhawks of the 5th Fighter Group from Río Grande. They were detected entering the Sound near Swan Island at 1325. They went for HMS *Antrim* and HMS *Broadsword*. HMS *Antrim* was damaged and temporarily out of action with wounded men and an unexploded

1,000lb bomb. HMS *Broadsword* received cannon fire which wounded eight men and damaged its two Lynx helicopters. Another raid came in with aircraft going straight for HMS *Antrim* which had little to fire back with in return as the Seacat system was out of action, while another went for RFA *Fort Austin*, which was only defended by GPMGs. One of the aircraft was to be caught by a Sea Wolf from HMS *Broadsword* before more damage was done. There was then a lull for more reconnaissance by Pucaras from Goose Green which led to one being shot down.

Another lull ensued befor the next serious set of air attacks which began at 1730 . The first raid was assessed as a possible Super Etendard. Sea Harriers went to intercept the aircraft but found four Daggers, one of which was shot down and the other three pressed on. Four A-4 Skyhawks arrived undetected by flying in low over West Falkland and attacked HMS *Argonaut*. The two bombs that hit her failed to explode, which spared the ship, but she was nonetheless immobilised with two men killed. HMS *Argonaut* dropped anchor just in time to avoid going into the rocks by Fanning Head. A dozen more Argentine aircraft flew up the inlet attacking whatever was in their path or they could see through the smoke.

Eventually an Argentine attack succeeded and the final burst of action for the first day was the most effective of the day. Seventeen aircraft burst through to the landing area and in the savage action both sides took severe losses; eleven Daggers and six Navy Skyhawks had taken off and all but one reached the landing area, flying in small tactical groups of two or three aircraft. One aircraft was shot down by a Sea Harrier and another flew into a hill. It may have been this aircraft I noticed as an instant cloud in the distance. At 1755 three Navy A-4 Skyhawks sighted and attacked HMS *Ardent*. At 1830 HMS *Yarmouth* came alongside HMS *Ardent* and took off the ship's company who would later transfer to *Canberra*. Overnight HMS *Ardent* burnt alone and sank after 12 hours.

In the beachhead, the headquarters was set up and camouflaged near the settlement manager's house which, as it happens, was close to the large white flagpole upon which the Union Flag had been hoisted 24 hours earlier. It was thought that this would make an excellent aiming mark or reference point, for incoming aircraft and any Argentine observation posts watching the San Carlos area, especially the beachhead, so the flagpole was taken down. This was even more important as seven Bv202 bandwagons were formed into a command post configuration. The whole complex was covered by camouflage nets and difficult to see from the air or the ground at a distance.

Callsign 1 reported the sighting of a six-man patrol moving south and using torches at grid 615895 (2130). Artillery fire was requested but was refused with instructions to continue observation. An IR source was seen later at grid 625892 (2230) and this time permission to engage was given but it was decided not to.

Nightfall brought relief from the relentless action and the work to unload the ships so they could be sent out of the Sound to relative safety at the TRALA. Northwood were anxious that *Canberra* was an obvious target, and they were trying to work out ways in which the *Canberra* could be used despite its huge target potential within San Carlos Water. One of her main options was as a barracks once a beachhead had been established. To emphasise the point that this was a bad idea a picture was drawn to show the inherent dangers of amphibious landings and operations with this big white target, sitting on the bottom of San Carlos Water fully loaded with troops and supplies.

Argentine commanders at Stanley had discussed the possibility that the British might land well away from Stanley and had recognised that a direct attack against such a British move would be difficult to accomplish. Brigadier General Menéndez's first action was to request air attacks from the mainland, which had clearly been granted. The Argentine attacks made no difference to the actual landing and the vital process of getting equipment installed ashore.

It was a surprise that the Argentines had got their response so wrong. Not only had they failed to provide fighter escort to take on the Harriers, but they had also gone for the frigates and destroyers rather than the amphibious ships and troop carriers which were there for the taking, with one being so very prominent, large and white, that she may as well have had a target painted on her side. By contrast the Royal Navy had planned and carried out one of the most successful amphibious landings in military history, and 8,000 miles from home. They had put forces ashore with most of their equipment on the first day of the operation, which was always the most dangerous.

So ended 21 May. The number of aircraft dispatched from mainland Argentina was 45 (26 Skyhawks and 19 Daggers) and 36 of these aircraft reached the Falklands. The British had destroyed 14 of their aircraft (seven Mirages, five Skyhawks and two Pucara) and three helicopters on Mount Kent seen by an SAS OP. HMS *Ardent* got one of the Pucaras on the ground with NGS, and small arms fire accounted for a Skyhawk. HMS *Plymouth* and *Broadsword* got one each with missiles. HMS *Ardent* was sinking and HMS *Antrim* and *Argonaut* were temporarily out of action with unexploded bombs onboard. HMS *Brilliant* and *Broadsword* were damaged by cannon fire. Thirty-two British sailors were dead, and more than 20 others were injured.

By the end of day one the 40 Commando's Official Diary records the locations as:

Grid 598842
First Callsign 1 – grid 604855
Second Callsign 2 – grid 609844
Third Callsign 3 – grid 602838
Fourth Callsign 50 – grid 602848
Fifth Callsign G21 – grid 610844
Sixth Callsign G22 – grid 608868

22 May
- 3 Commando Brigade Ashore
- Brigade Maintenance Area established at Ajax Bay
- Preparation of defensive positions continued throughout the day
- The CP was almost complete and finally occupied at last light

At 0200, movement was seen on the shoreline in the vicinity of Fern Valley Creek by B Company through IWS. Two men were waist deep in the water and a third man was ashore. A subsequent investigation by daylight revealed nothing.

40 Commando were ordered to be responsible for the defence of a Rapier Detachment at Lookout Hill, grid 595882 with effect from first light. Callsign 31 was tasked.

Before first light, Malcolm Hunt ordered all rifle companies to make maximum use of their GPMG against Pucara aircraft since the companies themselves were well protected from the air.

All companies received instructions that the enemy helicopters are not to be engaged unless positively identified as the enemy has three light attack helicopters of Augusta Bell type, which are similar in appearance to Royal Navy Lynx helicopters.

Just after 2000 two Daggers followed by three A-4B Skyhawks attack San Carlos Water after approaching from the south. One aircraft ditched its bomb at the entrance and the second did not press home its attack. The aircraft had slipped through the British ship and Rapier defences and were only seen at the last minute. The first Rapier systems brought ashore to the bridgehead had not performed well, with only one missile being fired and that had malfunctioned. The concern about Rapier was reflected in a request back to London for every available spare part, especially those known to suffer higher failure rates, to be sent to the Falklands as soon as possible, even if this meant cannibalisation of UK-based Rapiers.

The next day was surprisingly quiet as unknown to us thick cloud had prevented the Argentine aircraft from taking off from their bases on the mainland.

Top of our objectives was to locate an Argentine observation position known to be broadcasting information to the enemy planes. Intelligence believed it to be close by but that could mean anywhere on a long range of hills perhaps 5–8 kilometres in length. It was like looking for a needle in a haystack, if indeed it was even on our side of the Bay.

Major Shane Cusack, OC A Company, 40 Commando, *The Summer of 82*

Patrolling programme as noted in Log Sheet for the day:

1. A Coy – One OP at LOOKOUT HILL in sec str. Local patrols from that CALLSIGN. One OP (G22 and 56A) at CHAPEL ROCKS Sec str clearing patrols to grid 615855 to view possible OP position and give local clearance from 2200 to 0100.
2. B Coy – 6 man standing patrol to grid 623809. Out at 2400 in at 0500 to remain in position for 2 hrs.
3. Support Coy – CALLSIGN 73 and 60A from LOOKOUT HILL to grid 5890. Return dropping off CALLSIGN 60A to grid 586893 as OP for 72 hrs duration.

SITREP as at 222400Z

1. Area busy but incident free day.
2. General – Day began with move ashore of Brigade HQ and continue to offload stores onto beachhead.
3. Narrative –
   a. Brigade consolidated def positions ashore and BMA being established.
   b. OPs established.
   c. Vigorous patrol prog.
   d. Airfield denial OPs WEST FALKLANDS. Suspect enemy at CHARTES. Intend recce DUNNOSE HEAD, CHARTES and FOX BAY with follow up raid by coy if req.
   e. Airfield recce completed at PORT SAN CARLOS grid 6192.

4. Warning Order – patrol vigorously. Insert OP grid UC 1338. Start planning for bn raid DARWIN / GOOSE GREEN.

23 May

- BBC Announce during a broadcast on the World Service that the bombs are not exploding once dropped
- Four frigates; HMS *Broadsword, Plymouth, Yarmouth* and *Antelope,* take up position at the entrance to San Carlos Water and Port San Carlos
- Damaged *Argonaut* anchored in San Carlos Water
- During the day intelligence reported that the area west of Fox Bay on West Falkland was thought to be of vital interest to Argentina
- HMS *Antelope* sinks

Intelligence reports that area west of Fox Bay is of interest to the Argentinians. A photo recce of Port Howard shows a large convoy possibly moving reserve forces to Fox Bay. Anti-tank and anti-personnel mines have been laid in a standard grid of 1.5 metres for anti-tank and 0.5 metres for anti-personnel.

Callsign 60A and 73 left San Carlos together by air and arrived at grid 598900 where 60A was left as planned to observe a 360-degree arc. Callsign 73 returned via Lookout Hill and A Company's position early afternoon. Callsign 60A returned from the OP position with nothing to report.

At 1635 the first attack from four A-4B Skyhawks took place; these were spotted by 2 Para as they crossed into Grantham Sound. The aircraft split into two pairs and were now faced with a barrage of Rapier, Blowpipe and small arms. The attacking aircraft concentrated on HMS *Antelope*. The attack came just 12 after the frigate had joined the Task Force. One A-4 was caught by a Sea Wolf from HMS *Broadsword* (although this was also claimed by a Rapier team it has since been officially attributed to HMS *Broadsword*) and small arms from HMS *Antelope*. The A-4 managed to release its bomb but then collided with *Antelope's* mainmast and crashed. Another A-4 was damaged, and the frigate received two hits from 1,000lb bombs but neither exploded. One man was killed, and another seriously injured. After half an hour another three naval A-4Q Skyhawks came, again without warning. One aircraft was unable to release its bombs and crashed when it attempted to land at Río Grande; the pilot was killed when he ejected.

Another raid at 1805 , was ineffectual and led to one aircraft being shot down over Pebble Island by a Sea Harrier's sidewinder. HMS *Antelope* was able to restore power and move slowly down San Carlos Water. The first bomb to be tackled by the bomb disposal team on HMS *Antelope* unfortunately exploded, killing Royal Engineer bomb disposal officer Sgt Jim Prescott with the second member of the team, WO Phillips, losing an arm.

Jim was standing right next to me. We had a momentary glance at each other as if to say "oops", then I was flying through the air. The build-up of pressure had been so great that it ripped the hinges on the doors off and blew them towards us. The nearest one hit Jim square in the chest and killed him outright, and at the same time took my left arm.

WO II J. Phillips Royal Engineers (Bomb Disposal)

That evening Brigade Headquarters was moving its bandwagons and command post into a purpose-built recess in the ground, which had been dug by the Combat Engineer Tractor. There was an explosion which lit up the night. The crew of HMS *Antelope* began to gather on the upper deck wearing the standard issue orange once-only emergency suits. Everyone was completely unprepared for the huge explosion that erupted soon after sunset. A large lump of superstructure flew through the air as the explosion ripped through the ship just forward of the Seacat missile system. Several helicopters immediately took off from HMS *Fearless* and *Intrepid* and began to illuminate HMS *Antelope* and the surrounding water to search for survivors and assist the landing craft, who had all diverted from their tasks to head over to HMS *Antelope* to recover survivors. I had just gone on watch; all you could do from A Company's position on the hills above San Carlos was watch this terrible heart rendering sight and hope everyone got off.

The immense bravery of both the helicopter and landing craft crews frantically searching for survivors, or taking off those men on the upper decks of HMS *Antelope*, was outstanding. The helicopters were using searchlights and without a word, co-ordinating the search for men in the water with the landing craft, such is the trust and understanding between the Royal Navy pilots and Royal Marine landing craft crews. Several secondary explosions took place, but the helicopters continued to fly above HMS *Antelope*, illuminating her in the hope they were able to save members of the crew. Suddenly a dozen men appeared on the port waste. One landing craft coxswain seeing this returned to HMS *Antelope*'s side to take them off via a ladder. It was a most impressive rescue, and no one even got their feet wet.

The second explosion comparable to the first went up half an hour after the rescue. HMS *Antelope* finally sank during the night, and the following morning she could be seen with her bow and stern poking out of the water in an act of defiance, and what could be described as the tips of 'V' for victory. Everybody felt a great loss, she was more than just a ship; she was also a guardian and protector.

LCU Foxtrot 4 and her crew – who had earlier saved Dave Sturgess from the cold South Atlantic on the night before the landings – were now rescuing the men of HMS *Antelope*. Foxtrot 4 was the home to Recce Troop during our short stay on HMS *Fearless* before the landings. Sadly, Foxtrot 4 was attacked by Skyhawks in Choiseul Sound two weeks later, which resulted in the crew being killed. See appendices for the crew list in the Roll of Honour.

Corporal Alan White received a commendation from the Task Force Commander, Admiral Sir John Fieldhouse, for his part in rescuing 41 crew from HMS *Antelope* using a Mark 2 LCVP, one of four carried by HMS *Fearless*. The landing craft, Foxtrot 7, was in the Royal Marines Museum in Portsmouth prior to its closing down in April 2017. It was hoped that the museum was to be moved to Portsmouth Historic Dockyard in 2020.

After the landings, several reports of bombs failing to explode were circulating, and an MoD briefing to an American correspondent included the possible reasons for the failure, which may have been fusing, age or mode of delivery. The morning press briefing again referred to the unexploded bombs and included the additional information that they were being rendered safe onboard the ships. The BBC had, not for the first time nor the last, thought fit to announce this to the world. Yes, you could say it was the MoD stupidly mentioning this in the briefings, but a modicum of common sense would tell you this is not the sort of information you want out there at this time. The BBC, who decided to announce to the world that the Task Force was now in the Total Exclusion Zone, had now decided it was in the interest of the public, but not the thousands of service personnel and civilians in the naval or merchant ships in and around the Falklands, to announce the possible reasons why the bombs were not exploding. Later they would announce the Paras' attack on Goose Green the day before it was due to take place.

There was outrage and anger at this and the inescapable coincidence that all three bombs that hit HMS *Coventry* had exploded. Comments (many of which are unprintable) such as the BBC employing half-educated morons, with no common sense, who were either completely thoughtless as to the consequences of their actions or looking to further their careers in this exclusive scoop, ignoring the cost in lives and ships, and quite possibly even a smattering of both. Needless to say, some reporters on the ground and in ships were not popular after this.

The initial shock and violence of those first raids subsided [and] we adapted into life without air superiority and unloading stores. The air raids were not too bad (well as good as it gets having 500lb bombs dropped on you and random strafing by 30mm cannons). For all the bravery and accuracy of the Argentine pilots they were not having that much visible success. Step up the BBC World Service, announced to the world that the Argentine bombs were incorrectly fused and therefore not exploding on contact. Well done that reporter.

Another vivid [and] not very pleasant memory of this consequence was seeing battleships light up the night sky as they exploded, backs broken, sinking the next day, a sad, sad sight bringing home the gravity of our situation. I would not have been a Matelot for all the tea in China.

The free for all of the first few days was reigned in. During one raid Scotty was sat with me and Taff Davis's trench. As the raid progressed his trench took a hit, we looked on even more bemused as Kenny Hargreaves, who was having a wash, sprinted half naked with fighting order and first field dressing through the carnage leaping into an empty trench.

During another raid Eric was selected by a random Skyhawk as a target. Legging it like Usain Bolt from open ground towards his trench he dived in headfirst.

Colin Adams, Milan Troop, 40 Commando

Just after midday 40 Commando were detailed as the alternative Brigade HQ.

Two possible enemy helicopter sightings were made at 1455 by Callsign 62 due east of their position, then at 1505 an Argentine Iroquois helicopter was sighted at grid 6675 heading south.

At 1530 Callsign 62 sighted four men moving northeast at grid 680748. At 1625 these men took cover when overflown by aircraft at grid 6657652. 2 Para later stated that the patrol may have been theirs. It was pointed out that they had been asked at the time and had denied having a patrol out. This was a classic possible blue on blue situation which was luckily avoided.

Callsigns 1 and 2 were informed that a farmer would be moving his cattle around their locations after first light on the 24th. Life must go on I suppose.

End of day two, HQ was located at grid 598842, // A Coy 604855, // B Coy 609844, and // C Coy 602838.

24 May

- Confirmation that the river on our near boundary is exclusive to 40 Commando RM TAOR
- Brigade notified 40 Commando that the enemy is liable to use one of their Commando companies to harass their positions

The Argentine strategy for the day involved concentrating their attack into a half hour period between 1345 and 1415. Instead of approaching largely from the north and west, as before, this time they would come from the southeast. Five Skyhawks flew in low over San Carlos Water and they managed to survive the Rapier, Blowpipe and Seacat systems as well as small arms fire, before hitting *Sir Galahad* and *Sir Lancelot*, but the bombs either failed to explode or passed through the ships.

The second raid by four Daggers at 1405 strafed HMS *Fearless* and *Sir Galahad* with cannon, whilst *Sir Lancelot* was again hit by a bomb striking the ship's side and causing some internal damage. The third group, also four Daggers, coming in at the same time along the north coast of West Falkland were seen near Pebble Island by a Sea Harrier and shot down by the Harrier's sidewinder. Ten minutes later another three A-4C Skyhawks came in to attack but thankfully hit nothing.

Whilst all this was happening, the unloading continued, and vital airfield construction and fuel handling equipment was getting ashore. During the air raids, the helicopters landed with their rotors still running or tried to hide in any way they could as the attacking aircraft came in. As soon as the air raid was over, they immediately finished the task that had been rudely interrupted, before going onto the next task. Emptied of stores, RFAs *Stromness*, *Sir Percival* and MV *Norland* left San Carlos. The rush to get materials ashore meant that storage on land was less than ideal and new headaches were being created for the logistics teams. *Sir Lancelot* had almost finished when she was hit, and *Sir Galahad* was still full of ammunition. It took *Sir Galahad* until 28 May before it became fully operational again, while *Sir Lancelot* was not ready until 7 June but could still be used for accommodation and helicopter refuelling.

During one air raid at 1430, B Company's Callsign 21 reported an unexploded missile at grid 61208402, approximately 30 metres from their position, along with one casualty. Asked for a description, the following was passed, dark green, five feet long, nose disintegrated, four fins on body and tail, NATO No 410 99 964. Reply – appears to be Rapier missile and holdfast minor were on their way to deal with the missile but may take some time to reach the requested location.

B Company claimed one of their GPMGs hit an A-4 Skyhawk, and tracer was seen striking a wing and cockpit. This was also reported by two subunit commanders. The aircraft crashed after the engagement. It was also reported by Callsign 60 that the enemy aircraft were using Mount Usborne and Rabbit Mountain in their approach run. One company was strafed with cannon fire from an A-4 Skyhawk.

Following a discussion between the Commanding Officer of 40 Commando, Commanding Officer of 2 Para, and the BM it was agreed that earlier instructions from Brigade not to use GPMG against enemy aircraft should be amended to:

> In view of 40 Commando's success earlier, aircraft should be engaged only if friendly positions are being directly attacked.

Finally, and rather nicely, a note of encouragement and good luck was received from former 40 Commando members, unfortunately there was no address to which a reply could be sent. (See appendices)

A planned night fighting patrol to Verde House grid 677855 was carried out but nothing was found at that location.

All units were made aware of Argentine Huey activity at grid 5898.

It was now assumed that Argentina was likely to put in OPs to observe the beachhead. 40 Commando were to ensure that they had OPs covering the likely Argentine OP areas by observation at least. Night vision devices were to be used to cover the enemy likely approaches and possible OP positions. It was thought likely that the OPs would already be in place around Mt Usborne and Table Rock (7868).

25 May

- HMS *Coventry* sunk
- *Atlantic Conveyor* hit 90 miles northeast of Stanley by an Exocet
- *OP SUTTON* short orders received from 3 Commando Brigade RM
- General Daher, General Menéndez chief of staff arrived in Buenos Aires to explain the situation on the islands and the San Carlos counterattack

In the early hours of the morning several explosions were heard, and it was thought to be artillery fire 10–15 kilometres away to the south-east.

The air attacks continued and at 1530 Skyhawks from the 4th Fighter Group made an indirect approach overland to attack the San Carlos anchorage. One of the Skyhawks was quickly brought down by a combination of Rapier, HMS *Yarmouth*'s Seacat and 20mm rounds. A Skyhawk coming in very low over the water and in full view of those on the hill was struck, flipped over onto its back and crashed into the water. Ironically, it ended up very close to the spot where HMS *Antelope* had sunk.

From the Verde Mountain we watched the pilot being rescued by a rigid raiding craft and he was then transferred into a landing craft. The raiding craft coxswain, in his enthusiasm to get the pilot out of the water as soon as possible, ran over him, which resulted in him bursting his ear drum and adding this to the dislocated knee he had suffered after ejecting from his aircraft. The pilot, First Lieutenant Ricardo Lucero, aged 26, who was based at Santa Cruz became something of a personality in the hospital at Ajax Bay, and pictures of both him and his injuries being treated with respect on board HMS *Fearless* were shown in Argentina during a television news program that night.

Captain Robin Gilding RM arrived as OC Support Coy designate to relieve Captain Roger Williams RM who was flown home as part of his planned draft to take up his position at the Staff College.

OPs were out in the following locations to protect the beachhead and surrounding areas: 599899, // 594881, // 609867, // 609848, // 612844, // 616833, // 625835, // 624812, // 684792, // 721811, // 616834, // 619843.

B Company, on Verde Mountain, reported white lights coming from the beachhead and this was thought to be an Argentine listening patrol. One flare was fired along with five rounds. A clearance team was sent to check out the area but found nothing.

26 May

- News about the loss of HMS *Coventry* and *Atlantic Conveyor* with four Wessex Helicopters used for night missions, and one for Rapier support, in addition to a number of Chinooks. Julian Thompson now had only six Sea Kings plus five Wessex and one Chinook to move his troops towards Stanley
- An Argentine radio interception suggests that the command in Port Howard on West Falkland had been tasked with an artillery barrage at 0700 on the 26 May 82 until 0730 . It is assumed that this barrage may be starting at 0630 , but nothing happened
- Intelligence officers assessing the enemy artillery position at grid 778898
- Just after midday Harriers destroyed the HQ and gun positions at Port Howard

The remaining Recce Troop OPs were to be relived using a rolling replacement programme.
OP locations as at 250715 May 82:
599899, // 594881, // 609867, // 609848, // 612844, // 616833, // 625835, // 624812, // 684792, // 721811, // 616834, // 619843.
Amended list of OPs sent in reply to Brigade's initial list for clarification:
Callsign 13B595881, // Callsign 56B 618830, // Callsign 32C 2625813, // Callsign G22 609866, // Callsign G21 611844, // Callsign 61 728792, // Callsign 61A 772811, // Callsign 62 687793, // Callsign 62A 730853
A summary of future intentions was received from HQ Commando Brigade which indicated C Company 40 Commando would move at first light 27 May to Ajax Bay to relieve 45 Commando which will now move to Douglas on 28 May. C Company was also detailed as a guard for the Rapier Detachment at grid 567808 as well as those on the ridge at Ajax Bay accompanied by a Mortar Section (Callsign 53). Instructions were received from Brigade HQ that they should be ready to move tomorrow, with kit, from Blue Beach by 1030 .
Operations mounted in the next two days would see 40 Command hold all three major positions to allow the advance to Stanley to proceed.
2 Para was to move south to Darwin and Goose Green and their location was to be taken up by one subunit of 42 Commando.
45 Commando were to be taken by landing craft to 42 Commandos location to set out on foot to Douglas Settlement at first light on the 28 May.
C Company 40 Commando were to go to 45 Commandos location to relieve the whole unit.
3 Para were to move on foot from Douglas Settlement to Teal Inlet settlement.
When 2 Para's tasks were complete the subunit of 42 Commando is to revert back to 42 Commando.

27 May

- San Carlos Settlement bombed with Marine McAndrews, 40 Commando, and Sapper Gandhi, 59 Independent Commando, Royal Engineers killed
- Six men from 45 Commando and the Commando Logistics Regt were killed and others were wounded at Ajax Bay
- The field dressing station at Ajax Bay had an unexploded bomb in the roof

- 45 Commando's Milan systems were destroyed in the bombing at Ajax Bay and 40 Commando Milan Troop were to be tasked to join 45 Commando for the mega yomp to Stanley
- 11 Field Sqn RE came under command of 40 Commando as a defence company
- Lights seen at Third Corral Shanty grid 777898

With Ajax Bay now full, as far as storage capacity was concerned, San Carlos was now being established as an overflow Brigade Maintenance Area. C Company's move to Ajax Bay went smoothly with 40 Commando being ordered to assume responsibility for the facility. They were not to know that in the early evening Ajax Bay and San Carlos would be part of the change in the Argentine planning from attacking shipping to attacking land-based elements by bombing and strafing, with tragic results. Immediately after the air raid on Ajax Bay, 16 men from C Company were unaccounted for and it was thought they were casualties, but by 2230 everyone was accounted for.

San Carlos Water was almost empty of transport ships and realising they had failed to prevent the beachhead being established, the Argentines turned their attention to its disruption. The first raid came from Canberra bombers at 1715 when two aircraft dropped their bombs without much effect near 2 Para's positions on the Sussex Mountains.

Just after 1930 four A-4B Skyhawks of Grupo 5 came in low over Grantham Sound into San Carlos Water, in two pairs separated by a few minutes, and proceeded to bomb and strafe the troop and supply positions. At 1735 B Company announced that they had captured an Argentine who was later to identified as a Lieutenant Commander in the Argentine Marines, Captain De Corveta Camiletti. The prisoner, having earlier being escorted into San Carlos with his head covered to prevent him seeing anything, was now being taken along the jetty to his transport to Ajax Bay and interrogation. Unfortunately for Captain De Corveta Camiletti, he was on the jetty as the attack, possibly coordinated by him, came in and he was able to experience this first-hand.

This would be the first time that a deliberate attack was made on the actual beachhead. A young unknown Royal Marine described the attack:

> I was watching some local men excavating trenches for us with a tractor. My mate was telling the first one he didn't expect to see bombing as the Argentine Air Force had almost had it when two planes came along our side of the bay hugging the hillside we were on. There hadn't been any alert at San Carlos, though there might [have] been somewhere else. There was tracer going out after them but the planes were just too fast and after they had disappeared over the hill a missile fired by one of the ships came over and nearly blew up 40 Commando as it landed in their lines.
>
> I watched them release; it was getting commonplace by now and you don't flap anymore. They looked as though they were going miles over when the parachute opened. That surprised us we had never seen that before. The first one landed on the beach near the jetty and the others worked their way up. They didn't explode, some of them did, five, I think. The planes made a lot of noise, then the bombs exploded – that really was a terrific amount of noise. It was the same with every attack, the noise. Then we saw the smoke and a lot of guys rushing about. I was surprised later that only two guys were killed.
>
> Young marine of 40 Commando *The Falklands War* (2014) p.235

The second pair of aircraft seemed to head for the area around the jetty and the armourer's shop which had been set up in one of the huts. A trench collapsed due to the proximity of a bomb explosion and the area behind the large sheep sheds was hit with cannon fire. Men were seen to head to the trench as everyone in it was now buried, so they used anything to hand to dig them out. Marine S. G. McAndrews of 40 Commando and Sapper P. K. Gandhi of 59 Independent Commando Squadron, Royal Engineers, were killed. One of the Skyhawks was hit by a 40mm Bofors fired from either HMS *Fearless* or HMS *Intrepid* and crashed over West Falkland near Port Howard. Casualties would have been worse if the attacks had come half an hour earlier when the area had been full of men, and if more of the bombs that were dropped had exploded.

An account detailing the bombing of San Carlos can be found in the appendices.

This bombing and subsequent strafing runs had been remarkably accurate and well directed onto the important shore-based positions. It is possible this could be linked to the capture earlier that day of the Argentine officer who had been found by a patrol from B Company hiding in the hills overlooking San Carlos. It seems the Argentine Marine officer had positioned himself on the high ground overlooking San Carlos and was presumably reporting British movements back to Stanley. He refused to give any information on what he was doing there or how long he had been there. It was assumed with a high probability that he had been observing the landing and quite likely with a small team who were never found or confirmed. No radio was found but it would not have been difficult for him to hide this. (A document relating to the capture and questioning of Lieutenant Commander Dante Camilette and the contact with his team can be found in the appendices.)

> That night with one of their number captured, it is thought that the remnants of the Argentine observation group decided to withdraw back towards Stanley. Moving up a gulley very close to our position they were spotted and challenged by Corporal Jones on sentry duty. Armed with a single shot 303 sniper rifle, he had got off several well-aimed shots before they disappeared into the darkness.
>
> Corporal Jones was adamant that he had hit at least two of them. When we returned to San Carlos at the end of the war shallow graves containing two dead Argentines were found on the high ground about two kilometres away. He had, as he said, shot and killed two of them.
>
> Major Shane Cusack, OC A Company, 40 Commando, *The Summer of 82*

The first week was now over and everyone was a little battered, but the beachhead was intact and more than 10,000 tonnes of supplies landed from the various ships. There had been some setbacks from air attacks and bombings which was an experience no one would forget.

The Argentine commanders in the Falklands realised that as the days passed it became more obvious that the landing at San Carlos was more than a diversion. The 12th Regiment at Goose Green, 17 miles away, could have mounted a counterattack. The 5th and 8th Regiment at Port Howard and Fox Bay could have mounted a limited counterattack on San Carlos. The British tried to discourage these possibilities by bombarding those locations with naval gunfire at night. It was even suggested that the Argentine IV Air Mobile Brigade be flown to the Goose Green airfield and attack the beachhead from there. Nothing was done for two reasons. Firstly, Stanley was regarded as the key to the Falklands and if the

British landed elsewhere then they would be forced to come to Stanley and fight in front of the defences already set out in that area. Secondly, any move from Stanley to counterattack the British, especially a Parachute Regiment from the mainland, would face enormous transportation difficulties and the British air superiority.

My section, plus 2 surveillance guys, were flown to Wreck Point to guard an isolated Rapier site, occupied by members of 45 Commando. As it was isolated the Rapier site was under constant threat of attack from Argentinian SF. The Rapier was replaced by a "Blind Fire" RAF Rapier that was positioned outside our defensive perimeter. All the guys were told to move position and rebuild a protective perimeter for the RAF as we couldn't protect them. We laid grenade booby traps on likely approach route for the Argie SF, tin cans with grenades in them with the pins out attached to some trip wires and barbed wire strung out all over the place at knee height. I made Chris Pretty put the pins back in when we left.

Local Corporal Damian Irving, 9 Troop, C Company

I was sat in my shelter looking over at San Carlos when suddenly this almighty roar came just over my head out of nowhere. One after the other, two Skyhawks crossed our ridge at very low-level heading for the San Carlos settlement which they proceeded to bomb and shoot up with their cannon. Very shortly after another pair of Skyhawks came along the ridge only a couple of hundred feet up if that, I was looking down on them; they dropped a series of bombs across Ajax Bay. I had the unpleasant experience of seeing people running about before vanishing with the explosions.

Before we moved out, Brasso and I went to have a look at the area struck by the bombs including the one in the rafters. We had only been given 180 rounds before the landing, so we picked up a few boxes of 7.62 for our rifles and a cylindrical container of grenades before departing. On our way back we saw the unit Padre, he was sat on his own on some crates looking very downhearted. We stopped to say hello, but he was clearly distracted so we soon left.

Marine Brien Hobbs, 7 Troop, C Company

The day we were hit I was in the middle of giving a set of orders for our next task, I had my boys sat on my trench, when it started, and Mac Andrews let off a 66mm.

That day, I went in front of the FEBA, going through the Rapier Section on top of the Far Hill. The Task was to drop Sgt Fred Poyser and 3 Reece Troop guys as a forward Op warning of incoming Aircraft. Speaking to the Army Rapier Section Senior, we were either returning late at night or early morning as I did not want a blue on blue. It turned out to be early morning. Using a professional approach, I sent Cpl Kev Brennan and one marine in first, to warn them of our approach. Kev returned to me stating,

"You're not going to believe this. No sentry all in their slugs"

"You better wake them up God help us"

On returning back to San Carlos we found the Officers had put a Sign on the farmer's out building "Officers Only" they had blocked the toilet, due to being too lazy to flush with a bucket of sea water, we were stripped bullocky buff getting washed down when someone said "Can't you read" … .to get a universal reply … Fuck Off.

Sergeant S. 'Pincher' Martin, Support Company

A few more nights in that frozen muddy hole in the ground and it was time to return, as we squared ourselves away Sully and his patrol returning in the open when a Skyhawk popped up over the horizon heading straight for him. He swears the pilot gave him a wave followed by a strafing of 30mm cannon, like a slow-motion film as the ground around tore up with the rate of fire, hilarious to see but I suppose you had to be there.

Marine Colin Adams, Milan Troop, 40 Commando

Trench foot is an insidious problem and one which was starting to become a problem with both the Royal Marine and Para units. The official medical description for this condition was 'non-freezing cold injury.' This was a simple description to describe the myriad of changes to the feet of the men who, night after night were suffering in the open, gaining what little, if any shelter was about, in sub-zero temperatures, with boots that never dried out properly. The men, who in most cases had got their feet wet on the initial landing were suffering even more. The residual salt crystals in the leather of their boots had acted rather like hygroscopic magnets and attracted further moisture. Furthermore, the cheaply manufactured DMS boots, so adaptable and smart in normal daily use back in UK were now falling apart under operational conditions that were considerably tougher.

Jeremy Moore was to describe the DMS infantryman's boots during the Falklands with the memorable and excellent term 'leather personnel carriers.' It was a scandal that the standard issue boot had been designed to an inadequate specification, then built to a low price by contractors, who cared not a dot as to how these items subsequently performed under arduous conditions.

Rick Jolly notes:

One of the doctors in the hospital ship Uganda (a chap who had better remain nameless) was to suggest to me that trench foot was just the latest way for marines and Paras to get out of the war! He might have said this because of the speed with which their signs and symptoms improved under the ideal conditions aboard Uganda, but my reaction to this slur on the integrity of the Parachute Regiment and Royal Marine Commandos, as well as the slight on John Williams' clinical judgement, was rather vehement. This individual's later apology was much more graceful when he had been given an opportunity to understand the background to the story.

Senior Medical Officer of 3 Commando Brigade Royal Marines Richard (Rick) Jolly
(Doctor for Friend and Foe, Kindle Edition)

28 May

- B Company 40 Commando to Sussex Mountains to relieve L Company, 42 Commando

40 Commando were given communication instructions that all bridgehead locations were to come onto the Commando UCN and 40 Commando would then assume responsibility for monitoring the Local Anti-Air Warfare Commander/Co-Ordinating Net (LAAWC) and pass air raid warnings on to the appropriate units.

Extensive searches were made around Third Corral Shanty at grid 777898 for signs of the possible enemy lights that were seen last night. In two follow up patrols along the fence line and returning via Lookout Hill, neither patrol had anything to report but observed that many tracks were seen and could possibly be from old enemy OP locations.

29 May

- Jeremy Moore, Sandy Woodward and Michael Clapp meet on board HMS *Hermes*
- Michael Clapp becomes Commodore Falkland Islands
- A Company sent to clear Camilla Creek House (grid 6465) to escort POWs from Goose Green to Blue Beach 2
- Upon return to San Carlos, A Company were to occupy their old positions and become Brigade Reserve at 1 hour's notice, but C Company were nominated for this by CO
- Callsign 61A were replaced by Callsign 62 who reported helicopters at grid 7477 and asked if friendly forces were in the area
- The UXB close to the jetty on Blue Beach 2 from the air raid on 27 May was blown up at 1200

A Company were tasked to go to Camilla Creek House and escort the prisoners from Goose Green back to San Carlos. Throughout the yomp to Camilla Creek House, the prisoner numbers were constantly increasing and eventually the number reached 1,400. At 1445 , A Company were ordered to return to San Carlos along with the accompanying Scimitars. *The Official History of the Falklands Campaign* conservatively reports 961 Argentinian prisoners taken, although as its author Lawrence Freedman notes *'the counting process was possibly less precise than the number suggests'*, and other accounts of the battle have reported a larger prisoner count.

We were tasked to make a day-long march over Sussex Mountains to escort the Prisoners of War back to San Carlos the next day. By now the giving of orders to my officers was a brief event. All that they and the men wanted to know was –

Where [sic] the enemy there?

What were we being asked to do?

When would we leave?

What was the order of march?

Only if low on rations or food would the other question be; when would Colour Sergeant Stollery arrive with our re-supply?

Colour Sgt Stollery was a stalwart throughout the campaign, and no matter where we went (and I never had time to tell him where we were going even if I knew myself), he always turned up, sometimes on a tractor, sometime in a lone helicopter. He took a weight off my shoulders making sure we never ran out of food or water.

We trekked about 11 kilometres towards Goose Green before it was calculated that some 1200 enemy had surrendered. Someone re-thought the enormity of the task given to us and ordered that we return from whence we had come. We turned round and arrived back at San Carlos but too late to re-occupy the hill.

Grabbing a few hours of rest in the sheep shed within the settlement, we moved before first light towards the hill and our old positions. I was always uneasy staying down in the settlement any longer than necessary.

Major Shane Cusack, OC A Company, 40 Commando, *The Summer of 82*

30 May

- SAS Patrol returns to San Carlos following successful ambush of two Argentine SF teams on Mount Kent
- Warning Order received for 40 Commando to be relieved by 5 Brigade on the night of 31 May/01 June with C Company as Brigade Reserve in Ajax Bay
- San Carlos is subject to a high-level bombing raid by a Canberra of the Argentine Air Force which caused no casualties but startled the ground crews and pilots of 846 NAS when 1,000lb bombs landed without warning 100m away
- Bombings had become a feature of nightlife in the beachhead
- The QM and 2I/C moved to Port San Carlos for a recce
- Callsign 21A reports sighting of medium-sized helicopter 10km southwest of grid 55686[?] (last number missing from report documents)
- POWs were dropped at Blue Beach at 2025 to await transportation to Ajax Bay POW camp facility
- Brigade notified 40 Commando of an aircraft sighting of five-man patrol at 0229 in grid 8076, 8077 moving north

The Commanding Officer's diary notes that 40 Commando was informed it was to be relieved by 5 Brigade on the night of 31 May/1 June. A Company on Verde Mountain and B Company on Sussex Mountain to be relieved, C Company was to leave Ajax Bay but to remain as Brigade Reserve. 40 Commando was to establish a defensive position around Port San Carlos to be sufficient for local defence with the intention being that 40 Commando would march to Teal Inlet. The Commando echelon and non-essential Commando HQ elements were to move to Port San Carlos in preparation for the arrival of 5 Brigade on 31 May.

The big air raids had reduced somewhat but about this time, the Argentines reminded us they were still around, I was coming off watch after stand-to when there were four flashes with attendant thuds over towards San Carlos apparently dropped seemingly at random by a Canberra bomber.

Marine Brien Hobbs, 7 Troop, C Company

31 May

- The day began with another night bombing with four 1,000lb bombs in the area 610863 between A Company and the FOB. It had been thought that the Argentines had no night capability
- There was a short notice requirement for one JNCO and three marines to act as protection party for a research team going to the Argentine ship *Bahia Paraiso*. This was later cancelled
- It was agreed that the original company position could be occupied by 5 Brigade elements during the day on 1 June rather than overnight

- Lights seen at John's Rincon at grid 7291 and investigated. A very busy and eventful day of maximum flexibility
- Enemy sighted below Lookout Hill/Old House Creek at grids 5788, 5888, with five men seen running from a cave. A Company (Callsign 11) were tasked to send a patrol to investigate but found no evidence of enemy occupation
- It was decided to move the Commando Brigade Headquarters forward to Teal Inlet settlement where they set up in the manager's house

Julian Thompson made his intentions clear in a daily situation report to Divisional HQ, extracts of which are noted below:

40 COMMANDO RM. WARNING ORDER ISSUED FOR RELIEF OF UNIT POSITION AM 1 JUNE BY BATTALION FROM 5 BRIGADE. 40 COMMANDO TO MOVE TO PORT SAN CARLOS IN RESERVE. [That is in reserve for 3 Commando Brigade, not anyone else. And to move forward – see next part of signal]

FUTURE INTENTIONS

31 MAY / 1 JUNE. 40 COMMANDO TO BE RELIEVED [i.e. by a unit of 5 Brigade]

3 JUNE. LSL TO TEAL. 40 COMMANDO TO DOUGLAS OR TEAL

01 June
- Marine M. Gibson promoted to Lance Corporal
- 5 Brigade begin disembarking in San Carlos Water and landed with no firm orders. They were to move into defensive positions with MV *Norland* disembarking 1/7 Gurkhas
- 3 Commando Brigade forward base established at Teal Inlet in preparation for major engagements
- J Company 42 Commando was to come under the Command of 40 Commando on completion of tasks at Darwin and Goose Green
- B Company arrived back in San Carlos late evening having handed their positions on Sussex Mountain to 1/7 Gurkhas

Throughout the day lights could be seen at various locations, each of three-second duration at grid 753763. Flashes of light were also seen at grid 7977, along with intermittent flashing lights in low ground to the north, 5–7 km away. Vehicles were seen moving east–west along the track to the north of Cerro Montevideo, grid 665928.

Baltic Ferry arrived with new Scout helicopters, and *Atlantic Causeway* had eight Sea King HAS.2As of 825 NAS and 20 Wessex HU.5s of 847 NAS which were to be based ashore at Port San Carlos as well as San Carlos Settlement. Julian Thompson never felt they had enough lift capacity, especially as the need to resupply grew disproportionately as the units moved further away from San Carlos. The sheer weight of the loading tasks in San Carlos to which was added support for forward units at Teal and Fitzroy and other tasks such as minesweeping and Special Forces operations, all added to the shortage. The eight LCUs, eight LCVPs and four Mexefloats were at full stretch, but needed to give a little more.

1/7 Gurkha came ashore looking like heatseeking missiles, thoroughly thankful to be ashore in an environment they were happy with. They were flown to Goose Green by Chinook which then released J Company to re-join 42 Commando.

Tony Wilson informed his staff that unless the Argentines gave in so that 5 Brigade could garrison the islands, the options open were either to reinforce through the existing bridgehead or to mount a separate attack in a different area, possibly from the south. It was clear that his preference was for the latter option. One difficulty was that 5 Brigade were carrying insufficient logistic support with them and they had brought almost no additional means of moving men, materials, and equipment. Tony Wilson proposed a more equal allocation of the existing helicopter support assets between the two brigades as a means of allowing 5 Brigade to advance separately and so support a southern strategy.

Michael Clapp described Tony Wilson as clutching at a promise of parity with 3 Commando Brigade over the availability of assets. Tony Wilson's demands for helicopters yielded little and he was of the mindset that the Royal Marines seemed to be getting preferential treatment. 3 Commando Brigade were in the middle of a series of critical tactical moves that required the very limited elements of air transport that were available. There was nothing to be gained by the sudden reallocation.

5 Infantry Brigade started its push forward when elements of B Company, 2 Para, flew to Swan Inlet House in Scout helicopters where Major Crosland made his famous phone call to find that Fitzroy Settlement was clear of Argentines. With the agreement of Tony Wilson, 2 Para commandeered a Chinook and flew the 50km forward to Fitzroy. They had no means to back this move up and had not consulted those upon whom they would have to depend for the backup. This bold but unilateral initiative placed Jeremy Moore in a very difficult position. He either had to tell 5 Brigade to undo the move or immediately back them up. A withdrawal would have been humiliating for Tony Wilson and the Paras, and would have been difficult to explain to Northwood, who were constantly looking for good news to give to the politicians and thus the press. To back up 5 Brigade would put even more strain on a fragile logistics chain at Ajax Bay and San Carlos which was already struggling to sustain 3 Commando Brigade in the north. Jeremy Moore chose to back up the advance along the southern route.

> We were to remain on the Hill for nearly a further week before our next move. Conditions were as bad as they had been previously.
>
> Drinking water was a precious commodity on the hill and not to be wasted. There was insufficient to do anything but use what was supplied, for cooking and drinking. To save water we only shaved about every three days. Those in the settlement were more fortunate and seemed to have plenty, so much so that someone even sent us dehydrated rations not realising that we did not have the water to rehydrate them.
>
> Major Shane Cusack, OC A Company, 40 Commando, *The Summer of 82*

At 0415 01 June Jeremy Moore issued Operational Order LFFI OpO 1/82 and subsequently followed by OpO2/82 on 9 June with the mission '*To secure Port Stanley*'. (See appendices)

Op Order 1/82 was delivered by hand and informed 40 Commando that it was to come under the command of HQ LFFI as Force Reserve with the task of defending the forward maintenance area.

Julian Thompson's intention had been to move the battalion to Douglas or Teal Inlet, and he had sent orders to this effect on 30 May. It was expected that units from 5 Brigade would relieve 40 Commando as soon as they landed at San Carlos. However, this move was cancelled late on 1 June when 40 Commando received an order from Jeremy Moore's HQ to stay back to defend the beachhead. Jeremy Moore and Michael Clapp were both worried that if they needed to carry out a *coup de main* or a sudden surprise attack to pre-empt any enemy action against San Carlos or Ajax Bay, let alone the ships in San Carlos Water, the specialist Royal Marines of 40 Commando would be needed but this was never relayed to Malcolm Hunt. The decision to leave 40 Commando at San Carlos infuriated Malcolm Hunt who went to see Jeremy Moore to try and get him to reconsider his decision.

Following the surrender, Malcolm Hunt wrote a letter to Jeremy Moore to bring to his attention the feelings he still had over the decision to leave 40 Commando at San Carlos. Following discussions with Julian Thompson it was agreed that Malcolm Hunt's feelings should be recorded in the Commander's Diary:

> It is not my opinion that the units of Five Infantry Brigade would be so well prepared for the task (later proved to be so in my view) and anyway I did not consider that this comparatively static task was making the best of Commando troops. Having listened patiently to me, not surprisingly, General Moore did not change his plans. There was considerable resentment in the Commando of this decision, and it was to be reinforced later after 1 WG suffered appalling sad casualties at Bluff Cove when rather than being relieved by 40 Commando the unit, in fact, reinforced the Battalion with two rifle companies.
>
> Lieutenant Colonel Malcolm Hunt, Commanding Officer 40 Commando
> *The Official History of the Falklands Campaign, Pt 2* (2005) p.589

Michael Clapp was relieved by Jeremy Moore's decision as he trusted 40 Commando to defend his anchorage and to use his assets with intelligence. However, he did not think that Malcolm Hunt would ever quite forgive him if he knew that he supported Jeremy Moore's decision.

It was with sadness that we were to move forward following the tragic events at Fitzroy, with the Welsh Guards, and that is a whole new chapter to follow.

02 June

- *Canberra* disembarks Scots and Welsh Guards at San Carlos
- Completion of the FOB at San Carlos allowed helicopters to refuel but they could not be re-armed. The FOB was immediately used by two GR3s and next day two Sea Harriers. The Sea Harriers found it more useful as it gave them extra time over the Falklands after refuelling before returning to the carriers

Divisional HQ decided that B Company would move to Port San Carlos along with 11 Field Squadron, Royal Engineers, and elements of Commando Logistics Regiment would come under the command of the 2I/C of 40 Commando Major A. C. Gowen. They were to be tasked with coordination of OPs and local defence.

40 Commando informed Divisional HQ of its intention to withdraw two Recce Troop OPs, leaving only one at grid 718795. The two teams are to be redeployed as mutual support in the area of Swan Pond working back by radio to Port San Carlos.

Malcolm Hunt put A Company on two hours' notice with effect from 2215 but told Major Cusack not to draw any conclusions. The remainder of the Commando was moved from 24 to 12 hours' notice with effect from 0030.

Canberra anchored south of Fanning Head at 0617 with the first LCU secured alongside at 0630 to begin the transfer along with her two 825 NAS Sea Kings. So anxious was the ship to disembark her – what have been described as not so popular – passengers and be on her way that four of *Canberra's* boats were willingly pressed into service to help with the disembarkation. At one stage *Canberra's* crew formed the chain gang to move the Guard's stores.

The Scots Guards took over positions around San Carlos until their move to Bluff Cove on 5 June. As 3 Commando Brigade had discovered, digging trenches was a nightmare as water filled the trenches almost immediately, so peat sangars became the order of the day for the new arrivals.

The Welsh Guards seemed somewhat of the mindset of being on an exercise on Salisbury Plain as it was quickly noted that equipment was being left. This was apparently due to their not having time to store it before deploying. They did have an exercise on the Brecon Beacons prior to deployment to enable them to be prepared for the Falklands, so they could have left this equipment either at home or on the QE2, but they chose to bring it to a war zone. It was rumoured that 5 Brigade was to be the Falkland Islands' garrison following the retaking of the islands. This would go some way to explain the low level of fitness and the extra kit they had brought with them, including a disco.

The Welsh Guards' battalion diary states that the men were bewildered after 22 days at sea and staggering ashore from LCUs weighed down by their bergens, webbing and ammunition. The initial orders were to establish 5 Brigade in San Carlos Settlement and the Sussex Mountains area. Once disembarked, the Welsh Guards remained in concentrated areas in San Carlos around the old horse paddock, three miles south of San Carlos, while the Gurkhas relieved 2 Para at Darwin/Goose Green as well as B Company 40 Commando on Sussex Mountains.

In his book *Walking Tall: An Autobiography*, Simon Weston makes a statement about the Welsh Guards coming ashore in San Carlos and their initial position:

When we went ashore, the marines made fun of the fact that some Welsh Guardsmen had worn plastic bags over their boots – only a few, but enough to warrant slagging. The marines said it was to keep them nice and shiny. In fact, it was to keep our feet dry. To them and all other detractors I'd just say this: any Bootneck can get his feet wet; it takes the ingenuity of a Guardsman to keep them dry.

The day after the surrender at Goose Green. There was lots of activity on the jetty. We staggered up towards a building at the end of the jetty, past hundreds and hundreds of dismantled tents. That was an encouraging site. Perhaps we wouldn't have to bivvy in trenches at all. There seem to be plenty of helicopters, too, but they were shifting containers not troops. That wasn't so good. We went on past soldiers who were resting and patrols who were coming back in. We eventually reached a little gully in the foothills some distance away and [were] ordered to dig in. That night you could see little campfires twinkling all over the hillside. It wasn't lax security; in thick, low cloud, visibility was down to just a few metres.

Simon Weston, *Walking Tall: An Autobiography* (1989) p.92

Within the Welsh Guards' diary, it notes that the Welsh Guards' first landing craft arrived at Blue Beach at 1300 and by 1430 the remainder of the battalion was ashore except for B Echelon which was to stay on board *Canberra* to oversee the landing of the battalion's kit. The battalion's four Land Rovers landed from the *Baltic* on 1 June were to be used to ferry kit and bergens. The battalion reached its positions and settled in for the night, with the mortar platoon taking over 700 mortar rounds, which it is believed had been left behind by 2 Para during their move forward. The second in command persuaded or bribed the help of two civilian tractors and drivers to assist in moving the battalion's kit to its current location.

The resentment within 40 Commando worsened when they noticed one of 5 Brigade's battalions, being fresh and all their kit dry, failing to march a relatively short distance. A Company, 40 Commando, who had undertaken the initial wet landings on 21 May, and who had been ashore for 11 days, living on Verde Mountain above San Carlos, had earlier yomped to the Sussex Mountains and back the same day tasked with returning with the POWs from Goose Green.

Following a seven day stay at San Carlos and five days on Sussex Mountains, 40 Commando's B Company returned to San Carlos and occupied the old positions of C Company, with a move to Port San Carlos the following day.

Callsign 31 was in the area of San Carlos River to follow up on a Recce Troop report of lights at John's Rincon grid 7091 // 7092 // 7191 and 7192. They split into two groups, north and south upon their arrival at 1615 and noticed two sets of footprints in the spongy ground, although no definitive boot marks were found. The patrol continued north to a small re-entrant at grid 715918 and found a 3.5-inch RCL round and a further search found the weapon in two parts approximately 20 feet away. Two more rounds were found within 30 feet of the weapon body along with another two single rounds. All the equipment was within a 35-foot circle in the stream bed itself. Approximately 60 feet further north the patrol found 7.62mm rounds and sweet wrappers. It was believed that the equipment was discarded by the Argentines following the landings at San Carlos. At grid 710921, and running in an eastward direction, the patrol found vehicle tracks which did not have any distinctive track marking.

On the night of 2 June, a friendly fire incident took place between the SAS and the SBS. An SBS patrol were mistaken for Argentine forces and in the brief firefight one of the SBS patrol, Sergeant Ian 'Kiwi' Hunt, was sadly killed. He was the only member of the SBS to be killed during the Falklands War.

The comments below describe the disbelief of the units located in San Carlos as to their initial impressions of the Welsh Guards upon landing and in the days up to the surrender. These were the same people A and C Companies, 40 Commando, would join for the remainder of the Falklands War following the tragic events with *Sir Tristram* and *Sir Galahad* a few days later.

On the day they arrived, they were off loaded in San Carlos and the Royal Marines were tasked to unload their equipment. Forming a human chain along the rickety jetty they began passing boxes of equipment, until it became obvious, these were boxes of metal polish. Then boxes of disco lights, speaker boxes etc. Summed it up really, after all the excuses, they came ill prepared or under some illusion that they had Saturday night off.

We had an equally surreal afternoon in a working party during preceding air raids unloading disco equipment belonging to the Welsh Guards but that is another story.

We watched them discarding their personal kit in the short 3,000 metre yomp like Fred Kernow army, first to go were the 2 x 81 mm mortar bombs, followed by steel helmets, respirators to reduce the weight. Then hearing the excuse that they had come direct from London Duties. They had how long sailing down to get fit after the London Duties?

Surely these 'professional soldiers' would have made an effort to get fit on the way down or bin the disco equipment/leave it on the *QE2/Canberra* and not bring this ashore, or would they?

Did the professionals not have an exercise in Wales before deploying, which I believe did not go well anyway.

Following the Welsh Guards (Prince of Wales Company, I think), I saw one guy carrying two boxes of ammunition, I said to him "You won't get far like that mate, why don't you strip them down?", he ignored me and pressed on. Sure, still in sight he put them down and shook his hands, picking them up again when the column moved on.

The racket they were making in their plastic waterproofs that most of them were wearing did not make a good impression on me.

We had to give the Guards a hand with their heavy kit, including Browning 50 cals that they had brought with them. Regrettably, some of this kit got dumped by the wayside later, which pissed everyone off because of the effort we made to help them.

Comments from various members on the beach head

03 June

40 Commando was tasked to provide 80 guards for 800 prisoners of war beginning at dawn. Malcolm Hunt objected to the task and negotiated that only 1 Troop of C Company would be made available due to other manpower commitments, and 20 ranks of HQ Company would be ready to move at 15 minutes notice. It transpired that they were not required. The troop task at John's Rincon had to be postponed due to manpower considerations.

B Company moved to Port San Carlos by landing craft as part of the Divisional Reserve Troops and ensure the security of that location. Upon arrival, they seemed to be the only effective fighting unit in the settlement and perimeter security was their responsibility along with all OP tasks and patrolling. This patrol tasking was normally carried out at troop-strength and the first patrol was to check the area of Fanning Head for an enemy force capable of launching a land-based Exocet missile at the ships in San Carlos Water. The patrol found nothing except for a few pieces of equipment left there by the Argentines before the attack by the SBS on the day of the landings.

Most of the 1/7 Gurkhas flew in the lone Chinook to Goose Green to relieve 2 Para, and this left a gap in the defence of that area would have to be closed by C Company, 40 Commando, who deployed a rifle troop for the task.

The Malcolm Hunt discussed with CO CLIFFI the problems of light discipline at night among units of 5 Brigade.

Divisional HQ warned 40 Commando of an intelligence assessment of a possible helicopter assault from West Falkland on to East Falkland, with the Port San Carlos area being the most likely target of a landing at last light. This was tied in with helicopter activity to the north and enemy OPs. COMAW considered putting helicopters on ships overnight to ensure their safety from this possible assault.

04 June

- A troop task at John's Rincon was cancelled due to the availability of helicopters and flying weather
- A further order warned that 40 Commando was to provide one 84mm team with two 66mm on the night after next to go with the SBS for an anti-submarine patrol. A Company were nominated for this by Malcolm Hunt

C Company was issued with a warning order stating that three patrols were required to move out today to cover Fanning Head, Race Point and Cape Dolphin. Unfortunately, the patrols did not take place. It was planned that Fanning Head would be patrolled the following day, beginning at 1300 , when a search for possible enemy land-based Exocet was to be conducted.

Routine patrolling on Verde Mountain by Callsign 89 continued from San Carlos Paddock grid 6184 to Rocky Mountain east grid 6281, Callsign 1 patrolled the ridge to the north, Callsign 2 patrolled grid 623920 // 607927 // 597946 // 627934 // 642919 and 621925. This patrol found one US-made compass at grid 636924 and one UK-type pilot's knife 200 metres north of the wreckage of the Gazelle at grid 638923.

05 June

- A signal was received ordering 40 Commando to coordinate the defence of the forward maintenance area
- At 0440 lights were reported by 21C approximately 1.5–2 km to his front
- Order from HQ LFFI requested that when Harriers and helicopters land at Port San Carlos at night all air defence weapons are to be tight. Through the day when aircraft are positively identified weapons are free
- B Company completed the clearance of Fanning Head and they intended to move to Cape Dolphin tomorrow
- C Company were told to prepare to move a troop to Head of the Bay House. Callsign 61A visited Cape House and established that there had previously been Argentine helicopter activity at grid 694106 and they were possibly FAC troops. It was decided that Callsign 61 would join 61A and they would observe the landing site

Malcolm Hunt spoke to HQ LFFI about activities in San Carlos and relations with the local people. He was concerned about the discourtesy shown by members of 5 Brigade and the fact that they had left large amounts of kit in their trenches when leaving San Carlos. They had also unlawfully commandeered civilian tractors. He suggested that a senior officer should visit to talk to the residents.

06 June

- B Company's clearance of Cape Dolphin was postponed due to lack of helicopter assets
- Patrols in Swan Pond grid 6805 and Rodeo Mountain grid 7297 to be withdrawn tomorrow

Julian Thompson asked for another battalion to be switched to him to provide a reserve, with a preference for 40 Commando, who were languishing back at San Carlos and becoming increasingly bitter at being left behind. The request was again refused, and Division gave him no assurance that fresh troops of 5 Brigade would be ready, nor a forecast of when they would.

A conversation between Malcolm Hunt and Lieutenant Colonel Stevenson (HQ LFFI) discussed the possibility of using 40 Commando for company tasks on West Falkland including a company raid on Pebble Island, a raid on Sea Lion Island, and either Mount Rosalie or Edgeworth.

Just after midnight Callsign 1 cleared an area of San Carlos Paddock. They also found an empty meat tin at grid 604854 which was only just starting to rust but still had grease in it so it must have been used recently. This was a possible OP position for five men to lie up. Several footprints were also seen in the area.

07 June

The Welsh Guards had to return to San Carlos on HMS *Fearless* and, unknown at the time, 40 Commando were to see the level of fitness – or lack of fitness – of the Welsh Guards in the coming days due to tragic events with *Sir Tristram* and *Sir Galahad*.

Hugh McManners, a member of 148 (Meiktila) Commando Forward Observation Battery, who was awarded a Mention in Despatches, worked closely with the SBS and SAS during the Falklands and made the following observations on the Welsh Guards:

> The Navy are well-used to having the Royal Marines and Army green beret members of Commando Forces on board. They therefore assumed that the Welsh Guards would be something similar. However, it had rapidly become clear even to the saltiest of sailors that the Welsh Guards were nothing like as well prepared as they needed to be. After confusions and difficulties, *Intrepid* had put the soldiers ashore, only to be recalled to pick them up again. This entailed a lot of extra work, with the LCs ferrying the troops back on board, and much disruption of a ship that is difficult to operate even under normal circumstances. The sailors were shocked at the condition of the Welsh Guards when they returned after just a night or so ashore: wet, filthy, miserable – and obviously ineffective. Their yardstick was 3 Commando Brigade, who come back on board after arduous exercises in good order – even if we do leave muddy boot prints throughout their freshly cleaned ship. With six hundred demoralised, dirty troops all trying to shower, wash clothing, eat and rest, the ship was in chaos. Then military equipment and personal belongings started going missing. One of my friends complained to the Welsh Guards hierarchy after his military equipment store was raided, to be told there was little that could be done.
>
> Hugh McManners, *Falklands Commando* (Kindle Edition)

B Company was to be at 6 hours' notice with effect from 2100 to provide a troop for the clearance operation for Cape Dolphin which was one of the areas HQ LFFI wanted searched for land-based Exocet. At 1820 the operation was again postponed due to the lack of movement assets.

HMS *Exeter's* Lynx helicopter had to make a forced landing on Sea Lion Island. B Company 40 Commando were asked how long it would take to supply troops to locate and protect HMS *Exeter's* Lynx until it could be recovered.

The Rapier being guarded by Callsign 33/33V was moved and those callsigns were withdrawn to C Company's location.

The section moved back to Ajax Bay to dry out. Whilst packing up at Wreck Point we heard another loud bang from San Carlos and using my binos I watched a Seaslug missile fired from one of our ships arc up over West Falkland, following its smoke trail I saw it hit and blow the wing off the Argentinian Canberra bomber. On arrival at Ajax we found that we were sleeping within 10m – 15m of that 1,000lb UXB. We were accommodated in one of the buildings away from the rest of the company who were up on the hill.

Local Corporal Damian Irving, 9 Troop, C Company

4

Welsh Guards and the Battle for Sapper Hill

08 June

- 38 ranks from Support Company (Milan) 40 Commando are transferred to 45 Commando
- *Sir Galahad* and *Sir Tristram* bombed at Fitzroy

The following 40 Commando Support Company ranks were transferred to 45 Commando for the duration of the Falklands Campaign following the loss of 45's Milans in the air raid of 27 May 82:

- Lieutenant Hughes S.J.
- Sergeants Dooney K., Martin S., Groom R.D.
- Corporals Robinson P., Brown R.P. (noted as L/Sgt), Sullivan D.R., Blackford G.V., Foxley I.
- L/Cpls Pinnington D.J., Parker A.J., Hargreaves K.W.
- Marines Wood S., Sammons K.J., Watt A.C., Houghton R., Adams C.J., Hills G., Evans W.S., Davis J., Snowden J.A., Rogers W.G., Wellings R.M., Moodey N.M., Hushon B.I., Gillingham T.O., Barber M., Brady R.A., Fraser S.S., Clark T., Hollis N., Dunne J.N., Meakin M.D., Hodgson K.R., Scott T.J., Richardson I., Sykes J., Gardiner R.E.

Leaving Teal Inlet, yomping towards the 'Ring of Steel.' Kit check on *Canberra* came to 155lbs, more than body weight for some. Several miles in, that constant and seemingly unending mental torture combined with relentless physical pain must be dealt with, best way is to pick points in the distance, once you have made one, you can do another, then another. The comfort of switching off "Thumb up bum, mind in neutral" was not an option due to the threat of enemy attack.

However, in something of a paradox that continuing intense pain was not wearing us down we continued yomping, the determination not to quit grew, the inner resolve of dealing with the agonising pain was benefiting us and we started growing in strength.

Observing George Houghton trying to squeeze his now enormous trench foot sodden feet back into his boots while men bound open sores and huge blisters with masking tape so as not to let anyone down by dropping out jolted my mind out of its bizarre comfort zone.

A small dose of piss taking from the famed Royal Marines' dark sense humour, and it was back to reality, on with wet kit, and Crack On.

Marine Colin Adams, Milan Troop, 40 Commando (Attached to 45 Commando)

There were a couple of funny events take place on that trip with 45.

"Sykes where's your helmet?" and a voice from the back, said "here you are Eric, you left it in your trench!!" Marine Brum Wellington (RIP) with the biggest grin on his face passed it over to Eric, who then had to carry it the rest of the way.

I was living on rolled oats, and on one occasion I was set up by Cpl Kev Brennan.

He had used a paper clip & rubber bands then tied a packet of rolled oats to them.

"Pinch you like a rolled oat?"

Me thinking it's Christmas ... "Yeah!!"

"Here you are", as he casually tossed the packet towards me only to pull back just as I was about to catch them. Much to everybody's amusement they were all laughing as I was clutching at fresh air.

It was good to see the boys laugh.

Sergeant S. 'Pincher' Martin, Support Company

Whilst 40 Commando was maintaining their daily flexibility for the ever-changing tasks, some of which were cancelled at the last minute due to assets, or manpower availability, this flexibility would now be tested as the attack at Fitzroy had left 5 Brigade weaker thus leaving Jeremy Moore to put more reliance on 3 Commando Brigade. The Welsh Guards had suffered heavy casualties at Fitzroy with the loss of two companies. These were to be replaced by A and C Companies, 40 Commando. Tony Wilson was now somehow of the impression that Julian Thompson was favouring his fellow Royal Marines and saw 5 Brigade being diminished with the transfer.

Tony Wilson had argued for making a breach through the southern outer perimeter at Mount Harriet in an attack directly along the Fitzroy to Stanley track. He suggested that once the breach had been made, all battalions and Commandos could pour through and put the whole weight against the southern inner perimeter. Jeremy Moore took the view that the high ground would need to be taken.

Given that 5 Brigade landed with little or no additional movement assets, and a lot of assets were lost on *Atlantic Conveyor*, it is hard to see Tony Wilson's argument. This is notwithstanding the fact we were 8,000 miles from home and the current moves by the Task Force, which were made before 5 Brigade landed, was why the landing forces of 3 Commando Brigade had the long walk to Stanley.

As this was being discussed on board HMS *Fearless*, news of the *Galahad* and *Tristram* attack came in.

Tony Wilson later observed:

I think we started to suffer to some extent what appeared to be rivalry when it seemed that most of the resources were being allocated to others. Therefore, my people started to feel they were not only deprived but had been shall we say cast into the role of the Cinderella of the Falklands.

Official History of the Falklands, Part 2 (2005), p.620

Sir Lawrence Freedman, in his official history noted:

The reality was that Jeremy Moore had come to share the doubts about Wilson as a commander. He was sure that Julian Thompson could manage three battalions simultaneously, although this would be an enormous responsibility, but he did not want Wilson to be fighting more than one at a time.

Official History of the Falklands Part 2 (2005), p.620

Corporal Damian Irving, and Marine Terry Barnes of 9 Troop, C Company, recall the sight of the Welsh Guards who were brought into the RAP following the *Galahad* attack at Fitzroy:

Around 1600 we heard that *Sir Galahad* and *Tristram* had been hit. Shortly afterwards somebody came running in asking if anyone was medically trained and could help out as the casualties were "incoming". Most of the guys were cooking so I ran out to the HLS and we were told that the Chinook was on its way in with the wounded. It came in, landed with the rear door facing the Red and Green Life Machine. The ramp went down, and I put my head down and ran in. As I ran up the ramp, I was hit by an almost choking smell of burnt flesh. I continued to the front of the helicopter past all the injured and burnt. Looking right and left trying to make sense of what I was seeing amongst the injured very badly burnt guys, not really recognising faces. I stopped near the front, turning to my right and looked straight into the eyes of extremely burnt face who seemed to have some of his leg missing. With all his burnt skin it was difficult to lift him without causing him intense pain and chunks of skin coming off in your hands. In the end with him screaming, me and another guy just picked him up and ran with him off the Chinook into the RAP.

Local Corporal Damian Irving, 9 Troop, C Company

Some of the casevac's, all British, were in a terrible state with burns and limbs missing. When we returned with a gurney, I remember trying to wipe some blood off it before picking up the next casualty. It was extremely hard to hear over the noise of the helicopter's engines, so instructions were mainly given by hand signals. Carrying stretches through the two large main doors into the Red and Green Life Machine I saw surgeons and medical staff huddled around operating tables. We had to bypass all of this to take our injured to a room on the far side.

Mne Ged Herd and I got pinged, with others to pick up stretchers, that had a body bag on them. I remember thinking to myself that it was possibly a dead Royal Marine beneath the rubber veneer did upset me. We carried the deceased past where we had slept the night before and to the temporary grave. I cannot remember Ged or myself saying a word as we walked near the prisoners and up a slight incline above the Red and Green Life Machine buildings and put the stretcher down. I thought that I had just had to get out of there. I did not talk about it to the others in 9 Troop, I just bottled it up and pretended it did not happen. We left the building area and moved up onto the slopes above the buildings in Ajax Bay.

Marine Terry Barnes, 9 Troop, C Company

2 Troop and Company HQ along with a mortar section of B Company, 40 Commando, were to clear Dolphin Point looking for a possible land-based Exocet system which proved uneventful. Malcolm Hunt was concerned with the reason for this task when Division had refused to discuss the matter over insecure means. He asked how Captain Bush, OC

B Company, would brief his men or indeed how he was to be properly briefed. An officer from Divisional HQ visited later in the day but by then it was too late, the operation was already underway. The operation went according to plan and B Company cleared the area and found three rubber aircrew type life rafts.

After repeated requests for detail on the Lynx from HMS *Exeter*, it transpired that 40 Commando should have been told the previous night that the Lynx had been found and there were no longer any plans for the Commando regarding its recovery or securing Sea Lion Island.

Malcolm Hunt spoke to SO2 (Ops) at Divisional HQ and he was advised that the local defence of Port San Carlos was his priority and operations on Pebble Island and/or Mount Rosalie remained possibilities. Both B and C Companies were brought to 6 hours' notice for these tasks at 2301. A Company was to move at 1300 to Estancia House to support 79 Battery. However, at 0045 a signal from Division was sent stating that under the present plan to send a rifle company forward for Phase 1, the attack on the LSLs at Fitzroy had had a dramatic effect. The main upshot was that Phase 1 was now cancelled and there was now no requirement to send a rifle company forward.

The Welsh Guards had lost 2 companies' worth of men in casualties. The men were in a poor state and suffering shock and loss of kit and weapons. A discussion as to the possible location for the Welsh Guards was undertaken and some were initially taken to San Carlos (60) with the remainder destined for HMS *Intrepid*. The Welsh Guards' Commanding Officer, Johnny Rickett, requested that all Welsh Guards were to be located together and as such San Carlos was finalised. They were to be located in the vicinity of the sheep shearing sheds and two companies of 40 Commando were to join the Welsh Guards for the advance to Stanley.

09 June

- General Moore's Operational Order OpO 2/82 was issued
- Argentina Discusses Operation Buzon (Mailbox)
- Planned events for A and C Companies were now not to move forward given the tragic events of Fitzroy

General Daher, Menéndez's chief of staff arrived in Buenos Aires to explain the situation on the islands. Galtieri was still preoccupied with the possibility of an advance from Stanley against the beachhead at San Carlos. Whatever was done had to be done quickly. The plan known as Operation Buzon (Mailbox) was to form the basis of a counterattack on San Carlos and Goose Green areas. The beachhead at San Carlos was to be attacked by the 5th Regiment at Port Howard and supported by 8th Infantry Regiment at Fox Bay who were to take the British position at Goose Green with reinforcements from the 4th Airborne Brigade on the mainland. The recently formed 602 Commando Company, who had been part of the Argentine's initial landing phase would take Wickham Height. The British troops encircling Stanley were to be attacked from Stanley.

To stand any chance of carrying out the plan, the Argentine Navy was told to seize control of San Carlos Water, bombard the British in both San Carlos and Darwin as well as provide transport for the 5th and 8th Regiments in ARA *Monsunen* and ARA *Bahía Buen Suceso*. For its part the air force, fighting at the limit of its capacity was required to achieve local air superiority for the duration of the operation as well as provide transport escort and air support at close range for paratroopers who had to disembark near San Carlos. Possible landing points near San Carlos and Darwin were ill defined. Whatever the decision, they would still have to cross San Carlos Water.

Some decisive flaws of the plan included the capacities of the ships; ARA *Bahía Buen Suceso* could transport the 8th Regiment complete, but ARA *Monsunen* did not have the capacity to transport all of the 5th Regiment, so she would have to make a number of crossings. There was an additional problem in that neither of the ships were capable of a beach landing. All this would require a prolonged period of naval and air control of the area. In any case all discussions were irrelevant since the ARA *Bahía Buen Suceso* was at the time detained at Fox Bay with damage and the ARA *Monsunen* was no longer in Argentina hands since it had been captured by the British a few days earlier. It was due to audacious plans such as this that 40 Commando were left behind to ensure the beachhead remained in British hands, as without it the advance would have simply stopped, and we would have quite likely have lost the Falklands.

Operational Order OpO 2/82 envisaged that 3 Commando Brigade would attack both Mount Harriet and Two Sisters, followed by 5 Brigade's attack on Tumbledown, Mount William and finally Sapper Hill. These attacks would be reinforced by NGS at night with air support during the day. Mount Longdon was still not included but Jeremy Moore gave Julian Thompson discretion on whether to attack it.

Jeremy Moore had gone forward to 3 Commando Brigade Headquarters and told Julian Thompson that he agreed with the plan to attack the north and west as Divisional Headquarters now had intelligence that the Argentines expected the main attack would come in the southwest (Tony Wilson's preferred route) and would be looking in that direction. Mount Longdon would therefore be included in the first phase attacks, but the Commando Brigade would not be reinforced by 40 Commando, which Julian Thompson had again requested. Instead, they would be reinforced by both 2 Para and 1 Welsh Guards – the latter with A and C Companies from 40 Commando who had been moved forward to replace the two companies of the Welsh Guards lost in the horrific attack on *Sir Galahad* and *Sir Tristram*. It can be said that Julian Thompson in a small way had his request fulfilled by seeing two of the fighting companies from 40 Commando forward with the Welsh Guards.

A Company moved forward on 10 June, and C Company on 11 June, to join up with the Welsh Guards for the advance to Stanley. To the relief of A and C Companies, they realised that they were finally about to leave the confines of the hills above San Carlos, not with the rest of the unit as they would have wished, but with the Welsh Guards who they had watched days earlier move through their positions at San Carlos. The company commanders read out a warning order to inform their respective companies that they were to finally move forward to do what they were trained for and complete the jobs they had come to accomplish.

An earlier idea favoured by some at headquarters was to fly forward a battery of Light Guns with protection, which was to have been undertaken by a rifle company from 40 Commando. This battery was to have been positioned north of Mount Low, but the move was eventually cancelled. It was hoped that this battery would be able to bring artillery fire down onto Stanley Airport which the Argentines were still using every night to fly in supplies by C-130 transport aircraft, and presumably to evacuate casualties. The airport was out of range of all the 105 mm Light Gun batteries in both brigades.

The SAS report that there were no enemy troops or OPs between Mount Vernet and Mount Low were taken with a little scepticism by 3 Commando Brigade and as it turned out rightly so. A strong Argentine patrol surrendered to Captain Brown on Mount Round on 15 June having been there since early that month. Helicopters attempting to fly in and then supply a battery along with a fighting company from 40 Commando north of Mount Low would have been seen by the enemy OP on Mount Round and probably shot down by ground fire or Pucaras sent in by the Argentines.

A troop-strength patrol from B Company under the command of Lieutenant Martin was ordered to patrol the area forward of the OPs at Windy Gap, Settlement Rocks and Findlay Rocks. As the patrol reached the crestline of Windy Gap, grid 643935, they noticed an Argentine soldier approaching with a white flag. He surrendered to the patrol and on initial questioning claimed he knew of another two Argentinian soldiers who were injured along with others at Moss Side House. The patrol diverted to the house and checked the surrounding area for enemy hides whilst a cut-off group flew to the high ground southeast of the house. The patrol found nothing other than a freshly killed sheep in the house; the initial Argentinian prisoner had part of this with him, so he seemed to be telling the truth. There was evidence to suggest that his three companions had also taken some of the dead sheep. The prisoner was not armed but apparently his companions were, and he said he had left his weapon with them. The Argentine prisoner began talking in reasonable English, but this deteriorated into a combination of bad English and Spanish. A quick clearance of the area was undertaken but no one was found. The patrol intended to sweep again the following day at first light. The prisoner's belongings included a Royal Marine white belt, cleaning box and medals, so he was clearly more than a medic, and he had been through the former Royal Marine Barracks at Moody Brook, near Stanley.

Signal from LFFI at 2310 passed to A Company suggesting that some sort of Argentine reinforcement may take place tonight either by parachute or by helicopter from West Island to East Island, which would have been the proposed Operation Buzon (Mailbox). Some members of the Argentine command were looking at the possibly carrying out this attack on 12 June. This would, in their eyes, give them time to gain the necessary air superiority around San Carlos.

The Welsh Guards' diary noted that at first light a recce patrol went out to chart the minefield around Mount Harriet which they had found the previous night, assisted by engineers. A navigational error by the Welsh Guards in the coming days would see this minefield cause two men from C Company to be severely injured.

10 June

- A Company left San Carlos for Fitzroy
- B Company continued patrolling around Moss Side House and Elephant Beach House
- C Company remain at Ajax Bay before moving to Fitzroy the next day to join A Company

Sadly, we were not able to take all the Company with us and had to leave some 20 of our marines behind. The very wet conditions on the hill had taken their toll and these men were suffering from trench foot which severely restricted their ability to walk, let alone march long distances.

Peering out of the half-opened door through some dirty Perspex we sighted two LSLs still burning in the bay ... *Sir Galahad* was a black twisted mass of metal and there was a stark look of death about her. *Sir Tristram* looked in better shape save for the aft cabins near the flight deck. We had occupied these at Ascension but now they were no longer there – the stern area had clearly borne the brunt of the damage.

As I retraced my steps to Company Headquarters the shelling switched from the other side of the valley. It now began falling in front of Andy and 3 Troop. One shell fell particularly close, landing less than 40 metres from our forward position. Then the shells began to fall behind us.

We waited, expecting the enemy to decrease their range and the next salvo to hit our position but to everyone's relief the shelling slowly abated. It had not been an intense barrage but was certainly different from being attacked by aircraft. I think given the choice we preferred the latter.

CO commented on the cheerfulness of the company and the professionalism being shown. In reply I explained that all this had been done with little supervision and that war was bringing out the standards imposed on them in training; they were rising to the occasion.

As we waited the arrival of C Company, the sporadic shelling started again in front of our position. This was followed by the sight of 1/7 Gurkha Rifles advancing out of Fitzroy to our rear.

Major Shane Cusack, OC A Company, 40 Commando, *The Summer of 82*

The advance party from A Company mustered on the LS where Malcolm Hunt and RSM noted to Major Cusack, and Lieutenant Buzza, as well as all of the section troop commanders:

Well you've got what you wanted now! I wish you all the best of luck.

It was obvious from the look on Malcolm Hunt's face that he wished he and the rest of 40 Commando were joining the move out from the beachhead. The advance party finally flew out by Sea King at 1230 for the hour-long flight which hugged the contours of the ground and passed the burned hulls of the LSLs *Sir Tristram* and *Sir Galahad* at Fitzroy. The Welsh Guards were to now come under the command of 3 Commando Brigade from the 112359 June. The next phase would be brigade attack on Mount Longdon, Two Sisters and Mount Harriet.

At the drop off point, on the north side of Fitzroy, the adjutant of the Welsh Guards with his bright red gloves met the advance party and positioned the company within grid 215685. The first artillery rounds exploded in the valley to the south at around 1430 and then random shelling, continued until nightfall. One round landed 100m behind Company HQ but everyone quickly became accustomed to the shelling and by the time the company commander had finished his rounds the sangars were just about complete. The Commanding Officer of the Welsh Guards, Lieutenant Colonel John Ricketts, arrived in the early evening to greet the new arrivals.

4 Troop, B Company, 40 Commando patrolled the area around Moss Side House looking for any sign of hides or indications where an Argentine OP may be. 5 Troop were

taken by helicopter to the area of Elephant Beach House to clear that immediate area. Both patrols had negative results for their endeavours.

Captain Andy Pillar, OC C Company, went to HQ LFFI for a briefing on a possible task of raiding Pebble Island. HQ LFFI instructed Andy Pillar to have his company prepared to react to any other tasks contained in the signal detailed by Captain Langford (SO3 HQ LFFI) i.e. operations on Pebble Island for Mount Rosalie, as well as possible extraction of an SAS patrol from West Falkland, and moved to east to Fitzroy to join 1 Welsh Guards. C Company were put on two hours' notice to move and then 30 minutes notice at first light.

11 June

- 3 Commando Brigade battles for Stanley begin
- The injured personnel of the Prince of Wales Company and 3 Company of 1 Welsh Guards, would now come under the Command of 40 Commando, but they were still on HMS *Intrepid* and expected ashore the next day
- B Company, 40 Commando, captured seven enemy in the area of New House (grid 770985) and later at 1432 another three with serious foot injuries were captured. They were all taken immediately to Ajax Bay for treatment and questioning
- C Company left Ajax Bay for their move forward with 1 Welsh Guards at Fitzroy
- A and C Company receive orders to prepare for the move out to Mount Harriet

5 Troop, B Company, 40 Commando, were sent by helicopter to the area of New House (grid 770985) and landed approximately 450 metres from the house in dead ground. Smoke could be seen rising from the chimney, so the troop quickly surrounded the house and gave a quick burst of fire from the GPMG. The seven Argentine soldiers in the house came out with a white flag and hands held high. They were taken prisoner and searched before being taken to Port San Carlos by helicopter, under escort, where they were searched again. On questioning at Port San Carlos, the officer with the group stated that there were three other men who were unable to walk, and they were laying up in a hide close to Moss Side House. He agreed to be taken by helicopter to the location and show the patrol the hide so his men could gain the necessary medical attention. The hide was 1,200 metres from the house and extremely well built and camouflaged.

The three men in the hide had severe frostbite and were taken back to Port San Carlos, then onto Ajax Bay to join the other prisoners. The three men had such severe frostbite there was no choice but to remove their feet. It was noted that despite their injuries, their weapons were in good order, and it is believed that the men were part of a 12-man team, one of whom gave himself up very shortly after the Fanning Head incident. These were not ordinary conscripts; they were professional soldiers who knew exactly what they were doing.

Major assaults on the outer ring of the Argentine defences around Stanley were conducted by 42 Commando at Mount Harriet, 3 Para at Mount Longdon, and 45 Commando at Two Sisters. Some objectives were given codenames so as not to let the Argentines know the plans for the proposed objective. These were Wall Mountain ('Tara'), Mount Harriet ('Zoya'), Goat Ridge ('Katrina'). 45 Commando's attack on Two Sisters also included 40 Commando's Milan Troop who provided fire support for the attack.

Our next task that night was to advance some eight kilometres forward and secure the Forming Up Point for 42 Commando's attack on Mount Harriet and then afterwards to follow 42 Commando onto the feature to clear the enemy positions in daylight.

The Welsh Guards' CO gave some sketchy orders to cover all of this, but a lot of detail was missing – a point that did not escape the notice of Andy Pillar and myself. Alarmingly, no sooner had the orders been completed than it became clear that things had immediately changed. Suddenly, and without explanation, we saw No 2 Company of the Welsh Guards moving off sixty minutes early.

Ignoring this we continued our preparations & deciding to move at "light scales", we put our bergens to one side. Everything of value (sleeping bags and so on) was extricated and strapped to the webbing of our fighting order. We had also broken down the ration packs and were carrying four days' worth of food secreted in various pockets and pouches. With our 'kips' we could provide a semblance of a roof to any hastily built sangar – enough to keep off the worst of the rain anyway.

Just before we moved off at 2000 I sent for the officers and my message was simple – in any attack use fire support, particularly the mortars, artillery, and the anti-tank weapons. Above all else I emphasised that there was no rush, they must take their time and this in turn would avoid needless casualties.

As we dropped our bergens we could clearly see the enemy shells falling on a dirt road some two kilometres to our front. Taking my place in the column I walked through the lines of troops and light-heartedly joked that it would stop by the time we got there. I certainly hoped that would be the case, and fortunately it was.

We advanced quite swiftly until the track fizzled out, we hit a major obstacle of a 600-metre stone run. It was like something thrown up by a volcano. To cross it required leaping from one huge boulder to another which was quite a precarious operation.

The Milan and the Machine Gun Platoons of the Welsh Guards began to have difficulty with their loads. They began dropping valuable ammunition rather than carrying it, which incensed the marines nearby. With choice words they returned it. Eventually the loads became too much, and the platoons were left behind to make their own way.

By the time we arrived at our destination (GR 2769) at 2.30 am, a full moon had appeared creating an effect almost like daylight. We stopped just in time to witness to our immediate front the spectacular display of naval and artillery fire being brought to bear on Mount Harriet. A solitary enemy machine gun continued to fire from the area of the rocks on the top of the feature but was soon silenced with a Milan from 42 Commando. Behind came the assault troops, clearing each position as they made their way to the summit.

Several kilometres away to the east a missile was fired, and a huge illumination was seen out to sea – it later transpired that we had witnessed a land-based Exocet striking HMS *Glamorgan*. Thirteen sailors had been killed.

Major Shane Cusack, OC A Company, 40 Commando, *The Summer of 82*

Orders 1 x bergen between 3, 2 sleeping bags only, the rest was for ammo. No radios on. 20:00 Welsh Guards moved out then we followed. We headed off to secure the start line for 42 Cdo attack on Mt Harriet. I told the guys anything that was dropped by the Guards, and we could use to pick up and carry. 42 had already moved through and started and we moved up behind them and basically watched the assault. As we sat on Harriet in the bay you could see HMS *Glamorgan* giving NGS to 42. While we sat there to our left down on the coastline a white light appeared and seemed to be flying towards *Glamorgan*. As it got near 2 x red lights came up from the ship followed by a bright white flash then a bang. It turned out we had just seen the Exocet hit *Glamorgan*. No more NGS. We were told that we were not needed for the follow up on Harriet, so we spent the night in the snow. The guy without a sleeping bag wedged in between the two that had bags then changing every 30 mins to try and keep warm.

Local Corporal Damian Irving, 9 Troop, C Company

The Company Commander told me to lead the company snake as we were following the Welsh Guards (Prince of Wales Company, I think). The going was getting rougher, and we found ourselves climbing over these enormous smooth stones, like pebbles but about four feet or so high; they were a real swine to get over. We were delayed so much that 42 got there before us and carried on with the battle, for which we had a ringside seat.

Marine Brien Hobbs, 7 Troop, Charlie Company

This period was the start of what I described as the "Yomping stage". I would not at any point compare it to the arduous north route carried out by 45 Commando Royal Marines, but it certainly was physically and psychologically, demanding.

On one hazardous rock runs we came across what was supposed to be the lead group of Welsh Guards in the dark hours, near the base of Mount Harriet. Some of them were sitting down on the rocks. I knew it was the Welsh Guards because, not for the first time, I could hear, as they walked, the noise of their waterproofs. We assisted them by carrying their kit over some of this difficult terrain. I remember picking up an ammunition box and L/Cpl Chris Pretty carrying a spare barrel for a Browning 0.5 he had found lying on the ground near the feet of an exhausted Welsh Guardsman as well as a bergen full of our ammunition on his back. Chris, carried on regardless.

Our new home, south of Mount Harriet, was a little gully, and Chris Pretty took his bergen (almost full of spare 7.62 link rounds for the GPMG) and windproof off to reveal where the straps had rubbed his shoulders due to the weight causing chaffing and abrasions that had bled on to his clothing.

Marine Terry Barnes, 9 Troop, C Company

We were blamed by 45 for the delay starting the flanking attack, but there was another reason they conveniently forgot to mention.

We had 48 missile tubes that need carrying, along with full first line ammunition, in my case I also had two radios, a 350 & 351, granted I had stripped down to the bare essentials, but we were still carrying heavy loads. We began the yomp to the start line and we had not gone 200 metres and had the first casualty. We encountered a sheer drop of 20 feet, one of the rifle company was unconscious, then at the bottom for some reason they turn right and into a stone run, one of the freaks of nature, boulders the size of a bungalow, obstacle course or what? Attempting to pass a message was impossible, so as we walked into the Tri-lux markers of the Artillery position somebody realised they were going the wrong way. Under the orders of Silent Radios until the battle began.

At the end of Goat Ridge, we were ready to fire, too the right of us 42 Commando had started their attack on Mount Harriet unlike 45, they used para-illumination white light from the 81mm mortar, and by illuminating the hillside they were able to use Milan as bunker busters, speeding up the attack, this was the best firework display I have ever seen.

45 Commando's attack did not use white light. Milan at that time had no night capability, so when we began to fire, all we could target was the incoming tracer runs from there machine gun positions. We were credited a gun position. Earlier this year Colin Adams met the Argie officer that informed him we had actually caused a lot more damage than originally thought.

Sergeant S. 'Pincher' Martin, Support Company

[In] our part of the battle for Two Sisters one notable action was Buster (L/Sgt R.P. Brown) RIP throwing 'Jock' Brady (Mne R. A. 'Jock' Brady) behind a rock, he had recognised the sound of that particular incoming as White Phosphorus, I think Ali Barbour (Mne M. Barber) was also pretty close.

Without adrenaline to keep warm the body started to seriously chill, those clothes sodden with sweat from the exertions of battle now posed another serious problem as they started to freeze, wind chill was a huge problem and once again we focused on not going down to the elements. Later talking to colleagues from 42 across the road on Harriet they had to take parkas off dead Argentines and huddle in cover to survive. Whatever it takes, do not go down, remain fit to fight while awaiting further orders

The following morning, I believe 'Nobby' Clarke (Mne T Clarke) was on a task burying bodies and body parts from the previous night, then marking and recording the position, they had not finished digging the graves before they started hitting us with 155s. Certain irony burying enemy dead then they start shelling you for your troubles.

Back up, to the quarry, pretty much hanging our thoughts drifted towards getting a hot wet (drink) and food on, when we were told we had to cross the saddle. There was serious manking and moaning as some had just got the water boiling for that first hot drink, it would have been an easy decision for Roger (Sgt R.D. Groom) to say "Ok 5 mins" but thankfully he remained resolute. Pissed off, we quickly stowed our kit, Thumper (Mne I Richardson) being the Troop Radio Operator had managed a veritable feast of apple flakes mixed with hot chocolate while we were busy and was quite happy lording it over us. All packed ready and waiting he saw a random boot in the rocks and picked it up. Unbeknown to him there was still half an Argentine leg in it. Much to everybody's laughter and amusement he threw up his breakfast. With moral raised, at Thumpers cost, we set about crossing the saddle.

The last person was barely out of the area when a 155-shell hit directly where we were not 2 minutes ago. Luck or good judgement? A cup of coffee and the whole section would have been hit, inspired decision Roger. The next round landed 200m away setting off a secondary explosion. As if being in the open getting bracketed by 155 artillery fire was not bad enough, we were also in a minefield. Certainly, had better starts to the day.

Now sat on the northern peak we watched in the snow as clearance patrols brought in prisoners and the dead. Quite incredulous as we looked at the position we had taken, it was an incredible natural fortress and should really have been impregnable. No time to pat ourselves on the back though as the artillery rained shells in, smashing us for the next 30 (ish) hours between Longdon and Harriet. As long as you can hear it you are OK although Mne Jim Dunne must have been deaf as he got blown up several more times.

Marine Colin Adams, Milan Troop, 40 Commando

The first firing began from the direction of Mount Longdon, and this was the moment 42 Commando decided to activate their deception plan for the initial stages of the attack on Mount Harriet. Watching from our position, on the start line for Mount Harriet and night turned into day as the NGS and 42's mortars eliminated the western end of Mount Harriet. Para-illumination floated down over the source of the enemy fire as several Milan missiles streaked towards their targets and any thought of this system not working against a rocky crag were immediately forgotten. Tracer rounds cartwheeled across the sky before fading away as the weapon systems within those positions were silenced. The devastation to the weapons and personnel who were at the point of impact could only be imagined. Round after round of naval gunfire would drop into a precise area and, considering it was not coming from a shore based 105mm artillery battery but from miles out at sea, this was impressive.

Once 42 Commando were consolidated on Mount Harriet C Company, 40 Commando, were to occupy positions on the mountain while 42 Commando exploited forward towards Mount William. Almost 300 POWs had been taken and it was not realised at the time, but the Argentine commanding officer, Lieutenant Colonel Diego Alejandro Sona was also taken. He was later flown back to Brigade HQ for interrogation.

Overall, the night had gone well as 42 Commando had taken Mount Harriet and 45 Commando had taken Two Sisters. Yet again the plans seemed to have changed and just before first light we withdrew a kilometre to the rear. Here we deployed to a small reverse slope affording us some protection from view. Somewhere though, an enemy observation post had sight of us. Sporadic shelling starting again, and one exploded less than 100 metres away from us. But for the soft peat absorbing the blast this might have had serious consequences. As it was, we were unscathed again.

Then for the first time since we had landed, we saw our own aircraft in the sky. A pair of Harriers flew low over us before climbing high into the sky from where they launched smart bombs onto Mount William. It seemed that we could now forget the constant worry of enemy air attack as the airspace above us was ours. Throughout the rest of the day, we waited for further orders as to where, and when, we would move to next. None came and there was little information available.

Major Shane Cusack, OC A Company, 40 Commando, *The Summer of 82*

12 June
- By sunrise, all attacks had been successful
- HMS *Glamorgan* had been struck by land-based Exocet missile

- Elements of the Prince of Wales Company along with 3 Company of 1 Welsh Guards arrive at San Carlos
- Routine patrol find an enemy hide at Verde House

In the early hours Captain Andy Pillar was called away for orders for C Company, 40 Commando to move back to a new defensive position. This new position was about 3km from Mount Harriet in a shallow re-entrant which afforded reasonable protection and concealment. They were to spend most of the day building adequate defensive positions while the rest of the Welsh Guards and A Company, 40 Commando consolidated nearby. There seemed to be a discussion between 3 Commando Brigade and 5 Brigade as to who should push forward and when.

The attack by the Scots Guards on Mount Tumbledown and the Gurkhas on Mount William would see C Company, 40 Commando, being tasked for another battalion move to occupy 42 Commando's old FUP with a view to exploiting to Sapper Hill after the Gurkhas had gone firm on Mount William. The move was to be at last light on the 13 June and they were to be in position by 2359 . The rest of the day was spent getting food and rest, and guarding POWs taken from Mount Longdon, Two Sisters and Mount Harriet. The night of 12 June was cold and quiet except for the occasional Argentine 155mm artillery round landing sporadically with no real target, more of a harassing fire routine than a deliberate bombardment.

The Welsh Guards, with both companies from 40 Commando, reverted to 5 Brigade to support the coming night attacks, although there was some confusion as 3 Commando Brigade apparently thought that they were staying with them. Julian Thomson had intended to airlift the Welsh Guards and both companies from 40 Commando north of Mount Tumbledown so that they could act as a reserve during the planned rolling advance, and then, in the fourth phase, move to capture Stanley Common to the east of Sapper Hill.

After John Rickett had accepted the latest orders for the next moves, Tony Wilson had an alternative set of plans. The alternative plans would see the battalion act as reserve while the Scots Guards seized Mount Tumbledown, the Gurkhas attacked Mount William, and the Welsh Guards and both companies from 40 Commando would then clear the ground south of Mount William. As John Rickett was about to hold his orders group, his second in command came back with the alternative orders. John Rickett attempted to get some clarifications as to which orders he should act upon and having failed to do so decided to proceed with Tony Wilson's plan.

Just before first light the troops pulled back to a reverse slope defensive position in grid square 2869. A Company, 40 Commando, were left-rear company with C Company, 40 Commando, the right-rear company. The RSM of the Welsh Guards arrived after dawn on his motorbike to deliver rations. Shelling continued throughout the day from both friendly and enemy positions. The shelling unfortunately compromised Marine Wendt when a shell exploded approximately 30 metres away from him whilst he was on a toilet break. Despite much well-intentioned advice from the remainder of the company he still tripped over his trousers several times as he tried to run back to his sangar. The remainder of the night passed uneventfully except for a dramatic drop in temperature and the sight of Harriers dropping smart bombs on Mount William.

Photo Section

Some images in this book refer to Unit Photographer by name or Crown Copyright if it is not clear which of the photographers took the image.

2 Troop A Company Leaving Seaton Barracks. (Photo PO (Phot) Alistair Campbell / ADM_202_930_03_069)

Cpl D Irving, Mne R S Porter and Mne G D Hill at Wreck Point. (Photo D Irving)

O -2

MEMORANDUM

From _____ OC D _____

To _____ CO _____

Date _____ 24 May 82 _____

1. The att letter has recently been sent on to me by DGGRM, to whom it was originally forwarded.

2. Unfortunately we haven't been able to trace the Secretary or organiser of the Reunion, so we haven't got an address to which we can reply.

3. However, I thought you might like it to hang in the CP!

4. Best of luck, but wish we were with you.

Cover note for the letter sent by 40 Commando Reunion, Porchester Hall (see Appendix III).
(National Archives ADM_202_930_03_162 / Crown Copyright)

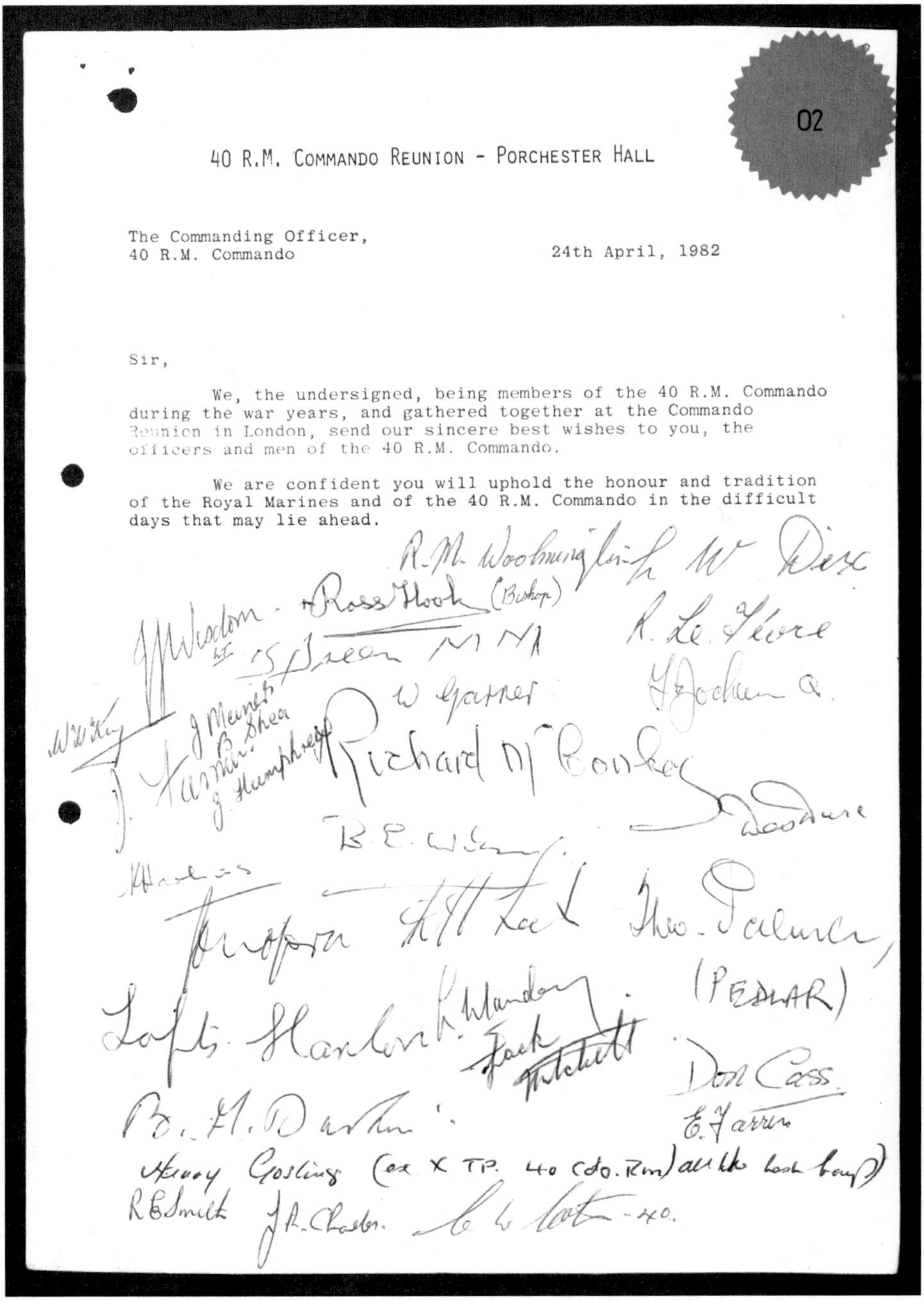

02

40 R.M. COMMANDO REUNION - PORCHESTER HALL

The Commanding Officer,
40 R.M. Commando

24th April, 1982

Sir,

We, the undersigned, being members of the 40 R.M. Commando during the war years, and gathered together at the Commando Reunion in London, send our sincere best wishes to you, the officers and men of the 40 R.M. Commando.

We are confident you will uphold the honour and tradition of the Royal Marines and of the 40 R.M. Commando in the difficult days that may lie ahead.

Letter of best wishes to unit from 40 Commando Reunion, Porchester Hall (see Appendix III). (National Archives ADM_202_930_03_162 / Crown Copyright)

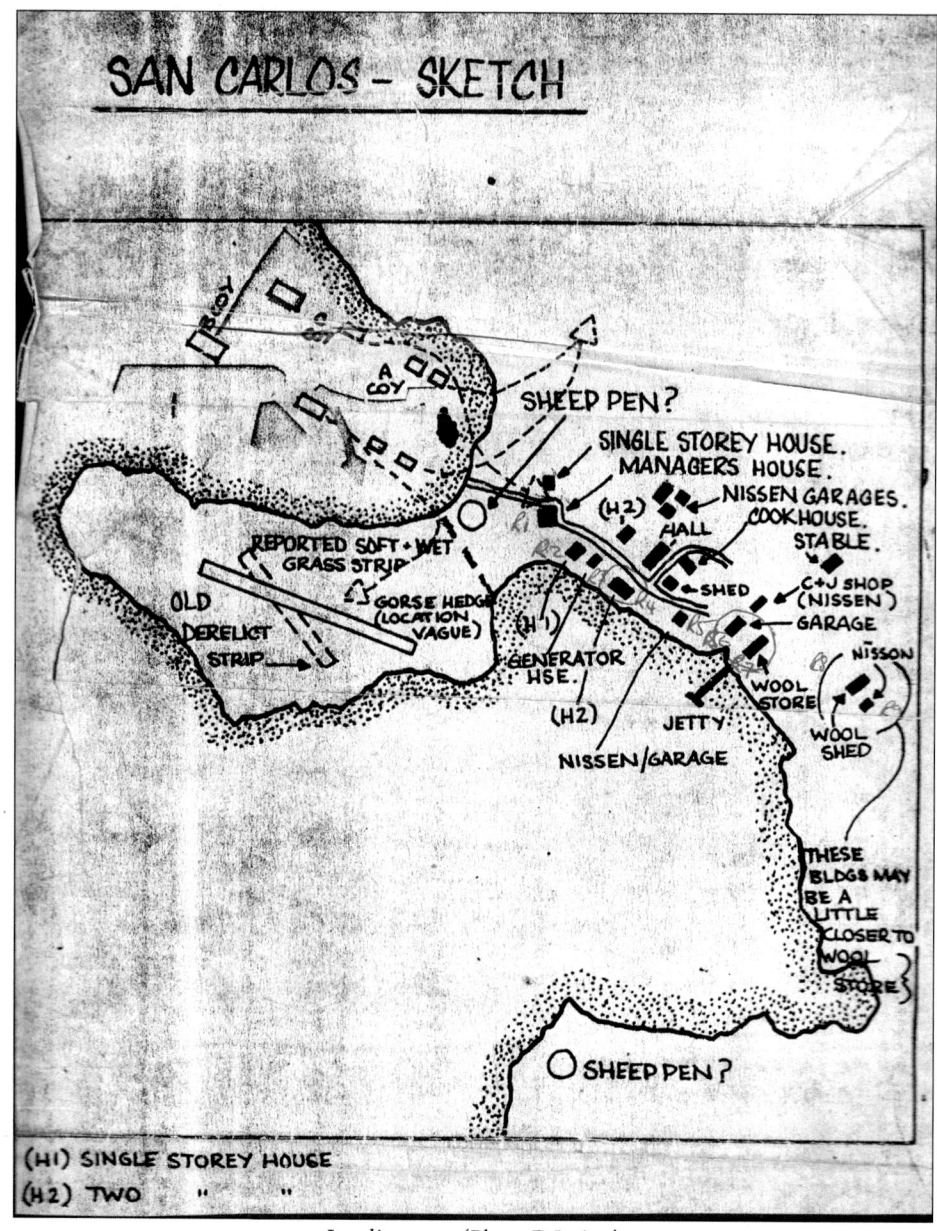

Landing map. (Photo D Irving)

Pete Butcher on West Island. (Photo Pete Butcher)

Keith Littlewood and Taff on West Island. (Photo Pete Butcher)

Mne Terry Barnes of 9 Troop, on Sapper Hill. (Photo Terry Barnes)

Cpl D Irving on the right, Marines Andy Gaunt and Pusser Hill, with Vince Combs under cover in a bag awaiting Casevac following the taking of Sapper Hill. (Photo D Irving)

Stanley Road. (Photo Sgt Ron Hudson – UKLF Collection)

9 Troop, C Company, 40 Commando following the taking of Sapper Hill. (Photo Terry Barnes)

2 Troop, A Company, following the taking of Sapper Hill. (Photo Marine A)

Marine Terry Barnes. (Photo Terry Barnes)

STATEMENT BY COMMANDING OFFICER

1. I have no doubt that during the journey south 40 Commando RM was very well prepared for any task that lay ahead of us in the Falklands. The Commando was fit, well trained, mentally prepared and in a very high state of morale, spirit and motivation. This has shown through in everything that has happened since.

2. Having been the first Royal Marines Commando to land on the Falklands we were disappointed to find ourselves holding the beach head as other units in the formation began the move towards Stanley. Nevertheless every man continued to carry out his comparatively mundane task in a most efficient and well motivated manner largely because Brig Thompson had repeatedly told us that we would be relieved on the arrival of 5 Inf Bde. Sadly this was not to be as on his arrival CLFFI ordered us to remain where we were at San Carlos to defend the FMA.

3. I was most unhappy about this change of plan and went to see General Moore in FEARLESS on 1 June to try to obtain a reversion of this decision. I was concerned about the effect the decision would have on the excellent morale of a good and well motivated unit and on the long term disciplinary effects (vis-a-vis the effect our nonparticipation in the battles to come would have on inter unit relationships in Plymouth). In addition it was not my opinion that the units of 5 Inf Bde would be so well prepared for the task (later proved to be so in my view) and anyway I did not consider that this comparatively static task was making the best use of Commando troops. Having listened patiently to me, not surprisingly, Gen Moore did not change his plans.

4. There was considerable resentment in the Commando at this decision and it was to be reinforced later after 1 WG suffered appalling and sad casualties at Bluff Cove when rather than being relieved by 40 Cdo the unit, in fact, reinforced the battalion with two rifle companies.

5. Given the great disappointment and frustration which these events caused I have nothing but pride in, and admiration for, the way in which the junior leaders in the Commando did their job. Due to this the morale of the Commando stood up very well and every man, in spite of everything, remained cheerful and efficient.

6. Following the surrender of Stanley I drafted a letter to Gen Moore bringing his attention to the feelings in the Commando which were, at that time, running high and which continued for some time thereafter. However, following discussion with Brig Thompson it was decided that nothing would be gained by such action. But it was agreed that my feelings should be recorded in the Commander's Diary.

M P J HUNT
Lt Col RM
CO

30 June 1982

Statement by Commanding Officer following the Falklands War (see Appendix IX). (Photo ADM_202_930_03_144 / Crown Copyright)

Vince Coombs and D Irving at Norton Manor for 25th
anniversary of the Falklands War. (Photo D Irving)

Welsh Guards Sapper Hill Memorial (See Appendix X). (Photo Welsh Guards)

Welsh Guards' Sapper Hill Memorial Plaque (Photo Welsh Guards). (See Appendix X)

The Welsh Guards' C.O. told us to dig in again and we were subjected to random artillery shelling from a 155mm in Stanley. One big lump of earth hitting Elvis who was on top of the gully with a set of binos.

The Wessex started flying some of the POWs to Fitzroy, so I jumped on one with a load of Argie prisoners with the intention of being a point of contact for the rest of the lads as they came in with the Argies. As it got dark the RAF would not fly me + 1 (I can't remember who), back to Harriet. Being a good Bootneck I marched around in the dark and demanded that someone take us back to the front. After a while I was pointed in the direction of the Bde CP. As I approached, I was challenged a couple of times in the dark by the sentry on "Nick" numbers etc, I told him that he could sod off about the "Nick numbers" and codes. So, I end up walking in on 5 Bde commander's briefing, with Brig Wilson. Bright lights, a big map and lots of officer types.

As I entered the CP and lost all my night vision but slowly, I gradually saw a guy with a red beret on stood by the map. His briefing stopped and they all looked at me. "Can I help you" the guy in the red beret asked, and I told them I was a Royal Marine, Corporal Irving, and I needed to get back to the "Front". Brig Wilson just looked at me. He told me that he was sorry, but I would have to wait until tomorrow morning. It suddenly dawned on me where I was and what was going on, in the shit again!! After mumbling some thanks, I walked out past the laughing sentry. We ended up coming back the next morning after sleeping in the prisoner handling area freezing my tits off all night and re-joined the Troop again. The Troop had a bad night, temperatures down to -18c, 4 POWs died and had to make them do a 2km yomp to a gully area.

Local Corporal Damian Irving, 9 Troop, C Company

After Harriet enemy soldiers who had been disarmed made their way to us, we gathered up quite a few, all walking around to keep warm as the weather was getting very cold with the onset of winter, one asked me for something to eat, I gave him some chocolate, but we didn't have much ourselves. Later that day we took turns escorting POWs to Fitzroy by Sea King, two of us and as many Argies as we could fit in. The Argentines looked miserable, no doubt wondering what was in store for them. There were two pilots, one RAF, the other RN; one of them leaned over to me and gave me a fistful of boiled sweets, I got the attention of an Argie officer and handed them over. The change in mood was extraordinary, everyone started smiling and laughing as we made 'For you the war is over' jokes. By the time we landed, we were all best buddies, we told them we had to go back, they almost looked sorry! Quite emotive, I thought about it for a while after. The MPs had to spoil it all by screaming and shouting. I remember saying to my oppo, I think it was Brasso, that we could do with some of that aggression twelve miles east. After a final wave at our new mates, we were off.

Marine Brien Hobbs, 7 Troop, Charlie Company

13/14 June

- 2 Para attack Wireless Ridge
- Scots Guards attack Mount Longdon
- 1/7 Gurkhas attack Mount William
- 9 Troop and a part of 8 Troop, Charlie Company, 40 Commando, undertake a helicopter attack on Sapper Hill which was to be the only daylight helicopter

assault onto an enemy position. This sees them the nearest British force to Stanley when the Argentines surrender

- Patrol from HQ Company find a box of 105mm ammunition, items of kit and trenches at two locations. This may have been part of an earlier intelligence notice of a proposed attack on San Carlos
- 40 Commando advised of SAS Op going in on Fanning Head
- An Intelligence report indicated the Argentines were planning to attack positions on Lafonia and San Carlos areas

At San Carlos a patrol from HQ Company found one box of 105mm proximity fuses at grid 609853, one Argentine water bottle carrier, and one fruit salad tin at grid 615854 and two trenches at the same location. It was thought that this may have been part of an earlier intelligence notice of a proposed attack on San Carlos. Commando HQ sent a troop-strength patrol to Verde House to see if this was being used or had been used by the group associated with the lieutenant commander captured on the 27 May. The house appeared to be in good condition and other than that nothing to report.

The final series of attacks were to be in four phases. The mission Julian Thompson gave to the brigade was for the final push against Stanley, OpO 4/82, which detailed the final night attacks.

Phase 1

3 Para was to advance and secure the Essro building but not to exploit further than the eastern edge of the old racecourse.

Phase 2

45 Commando was to advance and seize Sapper Hill from the start line northeast of Tumbledown and then move via the road northeast to southwest from Stanley.

Phase 3

42 Commando would take Stanley Common stopping 600m east of the objective.

Phase 4

Welsh Guards and both companies from 40 Commando would pass through 42 Commando and attack and seize the positions east of Stanley which would cut the road to the airport.

Tony Wilson objected to joining 3 Commando Brigade and wanted the Welsh Guards and both companies from 40 Commando to remain with 5 Brigade.

The 105 mm Light Gun batteries would be flown as far forward as possible before the attacks to enable the whole objective area and the airport beyond to be well within range.

Brigade Tactical Headquarters was in the middle of a snow blizzard, and nothing could fly. The weather cleared, and as Julian Thompson was about to get off, he was summoned to meet Jeremy Moore at Tony Wilson's tactical headquarters at the rocky outcrop close to Mount Harriet. The plans for the coming night were discussed along with who the Welsh Guards' commander was to be for the forthcoming battle. Tony Wilson stated that he intended taking Sapper Hill with the Welsh Guards and both companies from 40 Commando.

Major Shane Cusack gave orders for the next phase following the Scots Guards' attack on Mount Tumbledown and the Gurkhas' attack on Mount William in which A Company, 40 Commando, were to exploit forward along the south side of the lake and create an FUP in grid square 3169 and await orders to move. The Welsh Guards' Recce Platoon would lead, followed by 2 Company, Welsh Guards, with both companies from 40 Commando with 1 Troop, 59 Independent Commando Squadron, RE. At 2200 we set off, knowing that the south side of the lake would have taken us well clear of the minefield and the whole move should have taken no more than two hours.

Staff Sergeant Smith of the Welsh Guards noted we were heading very close to an area that at the previous night's orders group he had been briefed to be a minefield. In his opinion the ground also lent itself to one with a lake and boggy ground south of the road. His suspicions eased when white mine tape was found. This was later found to have been used by 59 Independent Commando Sqn, RE, to guide 42 Commando to the start line for Mount Harriet.

It quickly became obvious that there was a navigation error, and we were moving on the north side of the lake, which was suspected to be a large anti-personnel minefield, including pop up mines, and not the south side of the lake which was the intended safe route. Questions were being asked as Lt Bob Hendicott, the troop commander of 1 Troop, 59 Independent Commando Squadron, RE, was quite explicit when he briefed the O Group the previous night on the location of the minefield.

Suspicions were confirmed when at approximately 2300 an explosion occurred within the ranks of 7 Troop, C Company, 40 Commando. Marine W 'Mac' McGregor, of 7 Troop's 1 Sec, had stepped on a mine and his foot had been blown off. Everybody's immediate reaction was to freeze, and it dawned that we were in the middle of that large minefield. Calls were passed back which resulted in the company's MAs, LMA Black and LMA Kenny, moving forward to treat 'Mac' just as it started to snow.

Just before midnight there was another explosion and, everyone was ordered to try and keep to the footsteps of the man in front. The AEs of 40 Commando and 1 Troop, 59 Independent Commando Squadron were called forward to clear a path in the minefield. In the distance we could hear the gunfire on Mount Tumbledown and Mount William. One helicopter arrived and departed without the casualties. We were informed that Sunray Callsign 31 was the second casualty. 2nd Lieutenant Paul Allen had received severe injuries to his left leg and foot which required subsequent amputation. The explosions drew mortar and shelling, fortunately inaccurate, but life became distinctly uncomfortable.

A request was made to Brigade Headquarters for a helicopter to evacuate the casualties. At approximately 0030 , 14 June, a 656 Squadron Scout carried out two separate sorties landing in the minefield in an area checked by the Royal Engineers. Lt Bob Hendicott was quite close to the helicopter and the thought of this landing on a mine was not one he wanted to fully contemplate at that time, but the casevacs were the priority at that point.

A small unidentified helicopter, probably another from 656 Squadron, seen collecting casualties from Tumbledown, also flew overhead which drew Argentine machine gun fire. It was likely that the ground was so frozen that the pressure pads on the mines had been loosened as they were walked over until the final pressure of Mac and 2nd Lieutenant Paul Allen finally triggered them. Medics LMA Black and LMA Kenny worked tirelessly to save the lives of these men but in doing so put their own lives at risk, knowing there were anti-personnel mines in the very same ground they were moving over, and these could have gone off at any time.

Now came the problem as to how to extract A and C companies from the minefield without further casualties. Composure and patience in the ranks of 40 Commando were being stretched given the experiences with the Welsh Guards over the last few days. They finally reached the FUP at grid 3169 and laid up for two hours on what was to be a bitterly cold night. A yomp that should have taken two hours had taken an additional five hours after being forced to stand almost motionless in a minefield. It was not known how large this minefield was, but it was decided to continue the advance. 9 Troop, C Company, 40 Commando, were at the front, and they could finally see the 40 Commando's AEs and 1 Troop, 59 Commando Engineers who were sat on a small rocky area towards the end of the minefield. Both A and C Companies, 40 Commando assumed this rocky area was the end of the minefield and as they passed the team of 40 Commando AEs and 1 Troop, 59 Independent Commando Squadron's engineers, most including myself expressed their thanks with 'cheers lads'. Both A and C Companies, 40 Commando were blissfully unaware that the lads were taking a rest from mine clearing and the ground had not yet been completely cleared.

To add insult to injury the return was to be a 180-degree trip by the south side of the lake. The move had taken less than one hour with A Company, 40 Commando, going first guided by Lieutenant Andy Salmon OC 3 Troop. (As it transpired, the now Captain Salmon was to be my OCRM on my forthcoming RM ship's detachment which would see us return to the Falklands and South Georgia in 1984 along with members of 45 Commando and the Ajax Bay team also being part of the detachment.)

Just before dawn we pulled back to our defensive position in low ground 800m south of Mount Harriet and made some hot food in dropping temperatures whilst we watched and listened to the fighting on Tumbledown. Everyone was relieved to see the light of day, with a warning order issued that there would be no move before 1700. However, no sooner had most of A and C Company eaten a meal or were in the process of eating when orders came for a quick move. The enemy was in total disarray and fleeing down from Mount Tumbledown and Mount William towards Stanley. Lieutenant Colonel Rickett issued a warning order for the attack on Sapper Hill as part of Phase 3 shortly after dark on 13 June.

John Ricket was to recall his experiences in the minefield and later stated:

> This was one of the most unpleasant nights that I can remember in my life, being shelled while virtually trapped in a horribly difficult stone run. Eventually we extracted ourselves from this and continued advance with recce platoon now in contact the Argentine minefields on the edge of Mount William.
>
> John Rickett, Welsh Guards' Commanding Officer,
> *5th Infantry Brigade in the Falklands* (2014) p.206

At 0730 John Rickett was advised that the Scots Guards did not require reinforcements for Mount Tumbledown. It may be considered luckily, neither the Scots Guards nor the Gurkhas called for assistance, and we remained uncommitted. If assistance had been called for, how would it have got there with everyone stranded in a minefield? At around 0930, shortly after visiting A Company, 40 Commando, John Rickett received orders from Tony Wilson to attack Sapper Hill as soon as possible, as well as notifying him that a flight of Sea

King helicopters would be with him soon. Not too happy about an attack in broad daylight, John Rickett was assured that the battalion would receive all the support needed, including the bombing of Sapper Hill by Harriers at the moment critique.

Additional support was to include the Blues and Royals who were down to one Scorpion and two Scimitars, having lost a Scorpion during the Scots Guards' diversionary attack. The main force would consist of Welsh Guards with both companies from 40 Commando, a sapper section and a section held in reserve at Battalion Headquarters. John Rickett issued orders over the command radio and within 15 minutes the Welsh Guards with both companies from 40 Commando were ready to move. 9 Troop and part of 8 Troop, C Company, 40 Commando, were instructed to secure the start line.

We had learnt that the 5 Brigade attacks, (the Scots Guards on Tumbledown and the Gurkhas on Mount William), had been delayed 24 . So, we remained where we were for another bitterly cold night and for most of the next day. An announcement was then made informing us that the 5 Brigade attacks were to take place that coming night. Our task yet again was exploitation and on completion, we would possibly then attack Sapper Hill.

Keeping to this plan we set off at 2200 and followed the Welsh Guards' Recce Platoon and their No. 2 Company to our designated start point. We had been told our route would be around the south of a nearby lake (GR 2969) and thence to a position three kilometres further forward to await further orders. To our surprise the direction of travel seemed to be leading us to the north of the lake where alarmingly, our marked maps showed that mines had been laid. Having done a daylight recce we presumed that the Welsh Guards knew what they were doing; but it was not so.

As we marched forward a steady stream of explosions took place all around us as an exchange of fire ensued between the Argentine artillery and our gun batteries. Then just before 2300 a solitary explosion was heard ahead of us and moments later C Company reported a casualty. The single long line of bodies stopped, and the medics moved forward. Then a second explosion and another casualty followed. [A] C Company Troop Commander, who had been organising the treatment to the first casualty, had stepped on another mine.

Quite eerily the moon came out, and it began to very lightly snow. It transpired that the Welsh Guards Recce Platoon, No. 2 Company and the battalion headquarters with the CO, were through the minefield and out the other side. So too was half of C Company. All had climbed onto the next piece of rocky ground and were safe. Among them was C Company OC, Andy Pillar, but without thought for his own safety he then returned to deal with the situation. His action was later to be recognised with the award of a "Mention in Despatches".

At the rear of the battalion column and in the middle of the minefield just behind the casualties was A Company. At first, I deliberated how to extract the Company and wondered whether it might be feasible to do a u-turn and exit that way. For the moment though we needed to sort out the casualties and hopefully avoid any more.

Andy had requested casualty evacuation by helicopter but was told none were available from 5 Brigade, under whose command we now came. On the internal C Company radio net, I was able to have a quick chat with Andy. He was getting very cross particularly as he had also been instructed "to leave the casualties where they were, and they would be recovered in the morning".

I promised Andy to see if I could do any better. Nearby we heard a passing helicopter and by means of the radio found it was from our own 3rd Commando Brigade Air Squadron. What a stroke of luck as before long it had passed the message onwards and another helicopter had been tasked to help and was on its way. An hour or so later, in an exceptional piece of night flying, the casevac helicopter hovered over the mined area and with casualties loaded, flew them off for immediate medical attention.

Standing motionless for the best part of 5 hours in the near daylight conditions of a full moon, we had felt very exposed. We hoped though that everyone else was too busy to take any interest in us and that their minds were elsewhere. This was probably true as by now the fire fight had started on Tumbledown and Mount William and flashes of both tracer fire and exploding artillery shells filled the sky.

Sometime earlier I had moved towards the front of the Company where I had been taken aback at what I saw. A gap of about 30 metres had developed between the rear of C Company and us. When the first explosion occurred, A Company had stopped whilst the rear of C Company had kept going. Now with the casualties gone it was time to close the gap and get moving. I made my way past the handful of marines in front of me and gingerly stepped forward.

Everyone was instructed to walk in the footsteps of the man in front. Expecting an explosion at any moment I madly took a pace forward and then another and another. Then to my joy and certainly to my relief – within 100 metres was a rise up on to higher stony ground. As I reached it, I paused to let Andy and 3 Troop go past. Immortal words were then uttered by Andy: "You really care about people, don't you – you will make a wonderful father someday". In a small re-entrant we deployed using a peat bank as protection and cover from view. It was not long before the marines had hot drinks in their hand and a breakfast meal of sorts was being prepared. We were told that we would not move until 1900 .

Although very tired I began a tour of the company lines to reassure everyone that all was under control. Choice words were being uttered about the Welsh Guards and on several occasions, I needed to remind the marines who the enemy really was. Having spoken to most of my men I ventured towards C Company who too were extremely heated and none more so than Andy Pillar. Again, I did my best to calm them all down and asked their CSM to use his influence to do likewise. I would like to think that my "doing the rounds" had helped diffuse [sic] the situation though many of the marines, with some justification, were still very angry.

At this stage Andy and I reached an agreement that whatever lay ahead, we would lead, and the Guards would follow. We had done with their ways and we would make the decisions.

Major Shane Cusack, OC A Company, 40 Commando, *The Summer of 82*

In the light of the moon we could see a statutory [sic] armoured vehicle across the valley pointing in the same direction as us. Using infrared sites, it was one of the Scorpion[s] supporting the Scots Guards' diversionary attack going on a bit further. Then a quiet 'whump', somewhere down the back of the column there had been an explosion and word then came down the line Lance Corporal Mac MacGregor in Seven Troop had trod on an anti-personnel mine which had blown his foot over the heads of those following him to hit one of the blokes in the face. Lt Paul Allen then walked back down the column [to] see how things were going with Mac when he also stepped on a mine which also blew a foot off. Apparently, he was pretty calm about it.

Marine Chris Pretty, Section Commander with
Lieutenant Carl Bushby's 9 Troop in C Company, 40 Commando

While this was going on you could see the shapes of 40's AEs coming forward and I could see the shape of Barney Barnwell as he walked past, I quietly said to him "your turn Barney."

Local Corporal Damian Irving, 9 Troop, C Company

There was a deep thud from behind us and a message was passed up "mines". It started to snow [and] a scout helicopter arrived, I could only hear, not see it and knowing the injured will get treated and the other notion was quite selfish, "bugger off you're giving our position away".

Mne Craig Brooks standing next to me, swung his bergen around to load on his back. He hit me with it and sent me flying. I just closed my eyes and waited for the bang. Craig was so apologetic I didn't have the heart to shout out what I really thought.

Marine Terry Barnes, 9 Troop, C Company

The soldier who was injured, Mac, a teenager, had been given morphine as he was understandably upset, all the while it was snowing so there was no prospect of seeing where the wretched things were. Suddenly, another bang and Lt Paul Allen went down; after the morphine had taken effect, as he was being evacuated, he said "See you in Hell boys!" I had to laugh, another cliché, he was made of the right stuff!

All this time Capt Pillar and Lt Ken Hames (Company 2IC, formerly a tankie, commissioned in the Queens and on loan to the marines) walked up and down trying to sort things out so that we could get on, a fine example.

Some white tape had been laid in an attempt to mark the route ahead, as I got closer I could see two sappers pointing at what was obviously a popup mine. As they pointed, I nodded and stepped up on an adjacent rock and slipped, I was going straight back on top of it. In a moment, I thought I'd had it, along with the two engineers and poor old Tim Cahill who was right behind me, I could hear his sharp intake of breath as I was falling. All I could think was 'how clumsy', no life flashing before my eyes, just how clumsy. Miracle of miracles, one of the sappers caught me, the others stepping in to help. (Please pardon the amount of detail, this was quite an event for me personally, and for the other three as well I daresay.)

Marine Brien Hobbs, 7 Troop, Charlie Company

As the battles for Wireless Ridge and Tumbledown had a successful conclusion, reports came back to the Brigade Headquarters of an enemy in disarray. At 1225 the Scots Guards reported that large numbers of Argentine troops were retreating from Mount William to Stanley. Large numbers were also seen withdrawing from Moody Brook and possibly a group 300-strong were moving from Sapper Hill to Stanley. It looked as if others are about to surrender.

Julian Thompson spoke to Jeremy Moore over the secure voice radio and suggested that the Welsh Guards, with both companies from 40 Commando, should stay with 5 Brigade as they were still on 5 Brigade's radio net, and they were far easier gathered up by Tony Wilson since speed was now of the essence. Julian Thompson informed Jeremy Moore that he was about to give orders to his brigade to advance and units had been brought to 30 minutes' notice. Jeremy Moore was asked if 3 Commando Brigade should continue advancing, the reply was a resounding yes, but it was to be limited to the 39 Easting.

Jeremy Moore ordered the Welsh Guards, with both companies from 40 Commando, to secure Sapper Hill at 1330 but not to press on until he had firm evidence of any collapse. To this end A and C Companies, 40 Commando, set up an attacking position south-west of Mount William. They then received orders to move forward by helicopter to the FUP southwest of Mount William and attack Sapper Hill. C Company, 40 Commando, moved first to secure the FUP followed by A Company.

The move was to deploy onto the road to Stanley below Mount William with a view to advancing to a position approximately 1km west of Sapper Hill. Included in the orders were possible details of enemy positions straddling the road and it would be C Company's task to clear these, go firm and then A Company, 40 Commando, and 2 Company, Welsh Guards, respectively would further exploit to Sapper Hill with C Company, 40 Commando, acting as fire support company.

The Sea Kings arrived, and John Rickett briefed the pilots to drop the men on the track south of Mount Tumbledown, 3 miles west of Sapper Hill. It had been reported that there was indiscriminate mining everywhere but not, it appeared, on the track itself. The helicopter move went well to a degree, and it seemed that the move had most of the helicopter assets on the Falklands. C Company, 40 Commando, was picked up first with 2nd Lieutenant Carl Bushby's 9 Troop and half of 2nd Lieutenant Ian Webster's 8 Troop.

Unfortunately, the two helicopters carrying 9 Troop and parts of 8 Troop (noted as 7 Troop in most books) flew too far to the east and dropped the marines of C Company, 40 Commando, directly on the track below Sapper Hill in full view of the Argentine positions. The Argentines watched with some incredulity as a Sea King appeared from the west in what was to be an unintended helicopter assault. The Royal Marines in the Sea Kings, upon realising the pilot's error, immediately switched tactics to accommodate the new situation. Marine Chris Pretty remembers that it was broad daylight and his helicopter hurtled along almost at ground level. He thought the flight distance was a little long and then the nose of the Sea King lifted sharply. The Royal Marines braced themselves for the heavy battle landing and a rapid debussing.

This fundamental error was to result in two casualties being taken by 9 Troop, who found themselves under direct enemy fire before they had even left the helicopter. In the following firefight, Marine V.I. Combs received a bullet wound to the arm and L/Cpl A.C. Hepburn a shrapnel wound to the head. The final shots of the war had been fired.

The aircrew had received word at the last minute that the planned landing zone on the road to Stanley was too dangerous, not least because of the minefields, so moved the LZ back a few miles. On the ground, the Royal Marines of 40 Commando received word that the track was possibly mined on both sides, so it was to be slow progress up the Stanley Road, with everyone staying clear of the mined verges and adjacent fields, especially given their experiences the previous night. C Company, 40 Commando, made their way up the Stanley Road only to find that they were not to go into Stanley because of the confusion over the surrender and other units heading for Stanley. The last thing anyone wanted now was a blue on blue.

Meanwhile the Company Commander, Andy Pillar was bewildered to see to the Sea Kings returning from well forward of his location by Mount William, and Carl Bushby's request for artillery fire confirmed his worst fears. At this time, the Argentines were in the throes of surrendering so no fire support was available for the Royal Marines of C Company, 40 Commando, however it appeared that they had the situation under control. The rest of the company was still static on the road and as the message came over the radio that there were white flags over Stanley all one could see was rifles raised in the air in a proclamation of victory.

On my way back to my own lines Simon radioed and told me of fresh orders to move without delay. The enemy were reportedly in total disarray and fleeing from both Tumbledown and Mount William towards Stanley. There was however one last defended position on the outskirts of Stanley – Sapper Hill.

We were told helicopters were on their way and would lift us nearer to the objective. The plan was for the two Royal Marine companies (A Company left and C Company right) to assault Sapper Hill. No. 2 Company and Battalion Headquarters would be to the rear and in reserve. I recall that for once we were to be given artillery in direct support.

The plan suited Andy and I – we knew where we stood – it was the two Royal Marine companies who were together in this. Each of us gave swift orders to our troop commanders. In turn and with little time available they briefed their men – 3 Troop left assault, 1 Troop right assault, followed by my element of Company HQ. Simon and his element of Company HQ would be a bound behind as would 2 Troop.

In those final moments there was huge emotion running. Knowing that some of their chums would not be there when it finished, marines were giving each other a final hug or pat on the shoulder as they moved towards the incoming helicopters. I too was giving last minute instructions to the troop commanders. They had come of age and knew the severity of the task ahead.

I reminded them that no matter what (and we knew the area had been mined), they had to keep the momentum going and reach the objective; anything less and the casualties would multiply.

Our helicopter ride was brief. We hugged the terrain flying very low before dropping beside the road just past Mount William. The firing had already started as we disembarked behind C Company. A brief fire fight was ongoing with some nearby Argentines, and C Company had some minor casualties.

Suddenly we heard a radio message "There are white flags flying over Stanley" – as we paused, a further message came saying our imminent attack had been cancelled.

As we glanced around, we saw for the first time numerous small anti-personnel mines scattered all around the area. We needed no second invitation and carefully made our way onto the hard surface of the road.

We paused for a moment to take stock of what had just happened. Sapper Hill would have been a tough nut to crack as it had been defended by a company of enemy dug in with machine guns, to their front, barbed wire and mines. We were indeed fortunate to have avoided carrying out that last task; the cancellation had come not a moment too soon.

The news of the Argentine surrender brought smiles to everyone's faces and there was huge relief that it was over. But we knew though, that we could not relax yet as no-one was sure that every single Argentine would hear, let alone obey, the orders to surrender. Nearing Sapper Hill twenty minutes later, we passed a dead Argentine soldier lying beside the road – there was a twinge of sadness that he had not made it to the end as it was not his fault he was here in the first place.

Then it was up onto the feature itself with panoramic views all around. As we looked towards Stanley, we could see the "shanty town" appearance of correlated [sic] iron roofs on the houses. Many marines were heard to say, "is that it, is that Stanley, is that what we were fighting for?"

It was the 14th of June; we had been ashore for 24 days and the fighting was over.

Major Shane Cusack, OC A Company, 40 Commando, *The Summer of 82*

Both helicopters that landed 9 Troop had to be taken out of service for extensive repairs. One of the helicopters in that stick of three was to later report the damage they had found after shutdown: one bullet through the main spar of a rotor blade, one bullet through the left engine exhaust above the pilot's head, and one bullet through the electrical bay beneath the pilot's feet. It was a testament to the Sea King that this aircraft flew several more hours that day with the damage undiscovered with no ill effects. If that blade had subsequently broken in flight, the aircraft would have self-destructed in the air, and we would likely never have known why.

Before we had the chance to land properly the whole of the left side of the helicopter came blasting in, bits and pieces flying everywhere. The noise was deafening. The helicopter flared onto the deck and the guys started spitting out immediately trying to find cover and identify where they were. We had landed on a small light-coloured track in the middle of nowhere and helicopters are still being shot up. Someone suggested it was the Gurkhas on Mount William. The helicopters then revved up and bound over to the south leaving 9 Troop under heavy fire. The road might be mined on both sides, but it seemed better to be in the middle of the minefield than in the open without any cover. The Argentines were only a short distance away on a small hill. With the 17-year-old marine Vince Coombes giving covering fire by spraying the hill with his GPMG, I stood in the middle of the road and pushed guys off the road into cover afforded by a bank.

The firefight rolled backwards and forwards as each side opened heavy fire and then to cover and the inevitable retaliation. Lt Bushby's tried to radio for help, but, since he was using a trailing antenna opposed to a whip aerial, he was unsuccessful. Marine Coombes was badly wounded in the arm and a number of Royal Marines went over to treat him. Another Royal Marine suffered a head wound, another thought that he had been hit in the backside until it turned out his rear pouches had been shot off. The Argentines attacked 9 Troop's right flank, but this was defeated by heavy sustained machine gun fire. The firefight continued with neither side making any headway. Firing gradually slowed down and then the Argentines simply evacuated Sapper Hill. Lt

Bushby again gingerly raised the trailing antenna and learnt from C Company that the Argentines had surrendered.

Marine Chris Perry, Section Commander with
Lt Carl Busby's 9 Troop, C Company, 40 Commando

2 x ASW helicopters, not our usual Commando Junglie Sea Kings, came in and picked us up. We loaded the troop into the Sea King and I moved to the front and give a grid reference to one of the pilots, I noticed his name on the side of his helmet "Bucket" – (turns out that is his actual name, and he is still about). Flight time was about 2 minutes, so after about 4 minutes I looked out of the window I could see the road beneath us. I wondered if something changed with our orders, as this was a fluid situation? the helicopter finally flared to land. As I looked back down the helicopter shafts of light began appearing to a sound like pebbles in a coke tin. As the helicopter landed, we all jumped out and the aircrewman was laid on the floor screaming "Argies on the hill" with a surprised and horrified look on his face, I shouted back "we know".

The body of the Sea King had blocked our view of Sapper Hill on the road. We then started seeing some tanned faces, somebody mentioned don't worry they're Gurkhas. At that the hillside exploded in noise and light. We had no choice but take what limited cover there was in the minefield. One of the GPMG gunners, Vince Combs, had ran across the other side of the road, towards the enemy, laid down and started returning fire, as we all did.

Unfortunately, I was also about to learn why we didn't fire 66mm laid down in the prone position. I tried to sight the 66mm, with its naff cross sight, sweat in your eye, with incoming rounds and that pusser's helmet, slipping down every time you lifted your head up. I took aim, I fired, and I nearly burnt the back of my f**kin leg off with the back blast! I shouted to one of the guys (possibly Terry Barnes) and got a second 66mm, it flew out and hit a group of rocks that I thought the enemy were.

By this time everyone was shouting for Vince to come back over to our minimal cover, smoke was thrown to help him and shield him. Vince got up, turned, and started to run back towards us amongst all the incoming rounds when he was hit and spun round.

I crawled across to Vince and whilst laid down, I didn't want to get shot now so I got my knife out and cut his webbing off and tried to find out where he had been hit. As I moved up his arm his bicep came away in my hand and as he came round, he looked at me with a bloody knife and his bicep with a look of horror on his face thinking I had cut his arm off. Good job Doc Black came along and sorted it properly. By this stage Andy Gaunt, Pusser Hill and Elvis were there. I gave Vince some morphine and marked his head and left him in the hands of Doc Black before going back to the section/troop.

Lt Carl Busby said that the white flag had been seen and they had surrendered. He gave the order to "make safe" and ammo and casualty reports were asked for, it all sounded surreal. I was always crap at maths so just threw some numbers out but mentioning the 2 x 66mm and Vince. Slowly we all stood up and the rest of the company came down the road.

Local Corporal Damian Irving, 9 Troop, C Company

My Section, 33C, loaded onto the first Sea King helicopter and the aircraft followed the contour of the land, at one point when it banked at such a steep angle and speed, I looked out of the door and could almost touch the foliage/heather. Suddenly the engines screamed, and the nose of the craft almost pointed vertical then came down to land with a bump, port side facing up hill. I could hear cracking noises and crumps but thought nothing of it. The navigator seemed to be in a bad mood, he grabbed me by the arm pointed up the hill and then almost kicked me out – I thought what's his bloody problem! I was third or fourth person out of the leading Sea King. With my SLR, I took up a firing position looking up the hill. We had been dropped off almost on top of the enemy's positions, not, as briefed some 5 km back for an advance to contact! We were also very conscious each side of the track had been laid with anti-personnel mines and our previous night's experience in the minefield.

Cpl Dee Irving on my left, Mne Mick Thoburn AKA 'Elvis' was laying on my right in the same position. I looked up the hill and saw three Argentine soldiers in their grey uniforms, hoods up, at about 100 – 150m, three quarters of the way up the hill. One of the Argentine soldiers always sticks in my memory because, unfortunately for him he was fat, had a huge black moustache and therefore made a bigger target. During this part of the firefight, I can recall Dee Irving asking me to pass the 66mm, so I did and thought nothing of it. A few seconds later Dee fired the 66 mm at a target. I was not so much as annoyed with him but what really pissed me off was the fact that I had carried and slept with that 66mm from day one and never got to fire it.

I can also recall a deep thud of a 0.5 gun being fired at us from a position off to our left. Then I heard a thud and a crack, looked up and saw Vince had been knocked back and was, with sheer determination and courage, trying to crawl back to his gun. It was obvious he was in pain. Dee told Elvis and me to help. Elvis was slightly closer to Vince; with some effort Vince had moved closer to where we were laying. I crawled up on to the track and recovered Vince's GPMG. I placed the tripod on the top of the track and fired at anything or anyone on the hill to the left. I was conscious that I was running out of link and shouted for more. At this stage I looked down to my right and saw Elvis and Dee patching up Vince.

The injury on the top of his arm was oozing deep red blood like a sponge being squeezed and soap suds pushing out. Dee cutting cartilage, muscle, and clothing away with a pusser's knife. Out of the corner of my eye, I noticed some Argentines jumping through a heavily foliaged area, taking cover every so often and firing FNs at us. I could see by my tracer rounds that my fire was slightly too low, so I raised the sights and continued firing burst of three – five rounds, stopped, looked up over the sights, seeing that the target had disappeared. Dee asked me if I had seen them to the right and I replied, "got them".

At this stage I believe I saw a very brave act. L/Cpl Chris Pretty, taking his gun team, made up off Mne Ged Herd and Mne Brian Edmunds, to the furthest right flank of 9 Troop under fire with absolutely no cover, facing away from the main enemy. This action was carried out without any direction from a superior and showed an excellent awareness of tactical importance while under fire and leadership qualities unique to the Royal Marines. At this stage there was a call from the right where our troop commander Lt Carl Bushby RM and Troop Sgt Nick Holloway to cross the track moving up hill towards the enemy.

I can remember seeing a guy (later identified as marines Clive Lucking and Dave Sturgess) from another troop's gun team in C Coy, on the track a few hundred metres away to our left completely exhausted swearing because he had run but missed the fighting. One of the lads to my left (Mne Griffiths I think) pulled out a tiny Union Flag and started to sing God Save the Queen followed by others joining in. After this I can recall a Blues and Royals Scorpion light tank with a couple of Welsh Guards' Officers arriving and saying something about taking over from here using the tanks to their advantage and getting to the top of Sappers Hill first.

Lt Carl Busby and Mne Ged Herd gave them a few thoughts along with those of the rest of 9 Troop. So, we ignored them and continued advancing forward along the track towards Port Stanley, passing a dead Argentine body close by. We were told not to advance on into Port Stanley but stay put, I'm pretty sure that if we had 9 Troop would have been the first to reach the capital.

Marine Terry Barnes, 9 Troop, C Company

Bill Howie was there dishing out some enthusiasm "Go on, Hobbsy!" and Taff Lloyd was encouraging people to get moving quickly and not to go off the track because of mines if we could avoid it. I was hoping the air strike would hurry up as the road would surely be part of an Argie DF plan. We discovered the reason for all the rush, 9 Troop had been dropped actually on the objective and 9 Troop got themselves sorted out and returning fire.

We shot off up the track to catch up with the others followed by a Welsh Guards' GPMG gunner, I don't recall seeing any other Guards at this stage. A short while later, we joined the rest of the Troop at the crest of the hill; there were a couple of dead Argentine soldiers, I thought it was very sad, if they had kept their heads down for another 10 minutes!

A couple of journalists, from the Observer I think, showed up with a Welsh Guards officer informing them that:

"Gentlemen, the Welsh Guards have taken Sappers Hill."

I ended up with a Colt .45 somehow, (now at the bottom of Southampton Water) and a steel helmet, which I still have, thanks to Dee Irvine of 9 Troop who noticed I had forgotten it during one of our moves. We were pretty hungry as there had been no time to get any rations up. Eughy Reed found this enormous tin of corned beef which he opened, and we all tucked in.

Marine Brien Hobbs, 7 Troop, Charlie Company

Implements of war and dead Argentines were strewn about all over the place. It appeared that the Argentines had abandoned their positions in great haste and left most of their equipment behind. As if ordered, the weather changed dramatically over the next few hours with an ice-cold wind interspersed with snow. We spent quite an uncomfortable night on Sapper Hill with the wind howling around the bivvys most of which were exposed in the baren hillside that was Sapper Hill, but we were consoled by the fact that the day was won, and it was all over. The Welsh Guards with both companies from 40 Commando were to return to Fitzroy where we were all crammed into a shed for the night before A and C Companies re-joined 40 Commando on 17 June.

Extremely anxious to link up with C Company, 40 Commando, John Rickett stated:

Just as we crossed our start line my battery commander held this radio to my ear as Tony Holt, the gunner CO, wanted to speak urgently to me. Suffice it to say that we were out of communications with 5 Brigade, but the gunners always seem to get through. I was told that white flags were up in Stanley, that we were only to fire if fired upon first and the Brigade Commander wished me to hasten with all speed for Sapper Hill. By this time, we could hear firing from the area forward troop which had been dropped off too far forward. Captain Pillar duly reported that they were under fire from Argentine positions on Sapper Hill. He appeared rather reluctant to move his company forward. He wasn't totally in the picture on my last radio transmission with 5 Brigade, so together we all moved best possible speed down the track firstly to link up with his troop and second to get to Sapper Hill fast. I had already summoned the Blues and Royals' troop, but it seemed to take an awful long time to catch up with us! Undaunted we linked up with 9 Troop where one Royal Marine had been shot. We hurried past them and at last, the Blues and Royals arrived. Jumping on the lead vehicle with my command group and telling Andy's company to follow on at best speed we occupied Sapper Hill from the rear i.e. from Stanley side … There was no resistance as Argentine soldiers had already withdrawn to Stanley leaving their dead behind them. The remainder of the battalion soon joined us, and I gave out positions for the companies to man.

John Ricketts, Commanding Officer Welsh Guards,
5 Infantry Brigade in the Falklands (2014) p.216

This helicopter assault on Sapper Hill seems to have convinced Brigadier General Jofre that further resistance was pointless. He recalls:

As predicted, British helicopters-borne infantry, 40th Commando Battalion, lost no time in following up until checked with a bloody nose at Sapper Hill. After that things went from bad to worse. No sooner had Major Jaimet reached Sapper Hill than Colonel Dalton, the Brigade Operations Officer, told me, "Many soldiers are in a strange state and the kelpers are bound to get hurt. One 3rd Regiment platoon has been told to go into the houses by a fanatical lieutenant, who has also ordered the men to kill the kelpers – something awful is happening." I'll never forget that moment. It was like a lightning bolt hitting me. It was becoming evident to me that I was no longer in control. We've had it. "The lives of the kelpers are being risked", I told General Menendez and he realized that there was no question of fighting any further. Menendez told me that he wished to talk to Galtieri to arrange a ceasefire. I agreed. It was all over. Fighting on Sapper Hill was out of the question.

Brigadier General Jofre, Argentine Forces,
5 Infantry Brigade in the Falklands (2014) p.217

At 1657 Battalion HQ reached the summit of Sapper Hill. The final advance up Sapper Hill was made in the tracks of the Scorpion commanded by Lt Correth (RHG/D). Recce Troop, 45 Commando, reached Sapper Hill from the north-west. The day was generally cold and dry but there were high winds and hail throughout the night, but morale remained high as the job was not done.

The Welsh Guards' War Diary records that hope become certainty as more and more deserted enemy positions were passed. Backed by a troop of the Blues and Royals, apparently the Welsh Guards secured Sapper Hill at 1657Z without opposition. There is no mention of 40 Commando or 8 and 9 Troops' firefight or the two casualties. This was to be a point of contention years later when the Welsh Guards erected a memorial for Sapper Hill.

While the Welsh Guards, with both companies from 40 Commando, were reorganising on Sapper Hill, Lieutenant Colonel Whitehead of 45 Commando appeared from the west and the two commanding officers divided the hill between them. John Rickett ensured that the Welsh Guards were on the leeward side, which seemed a little ungallant considering 45 Commando had just spent the last 16 days exposed to the most awful weather and conditions whilst yomping across the Falklands. Lieutenant Hendicott of 59 Independent Commando Squadron, RE, and his men from 1 Troop were the first Royal Engineers to reach the hill and later probably wished they had not bothered. The night was capped by an extremely cold southerly storm from the Antarctic. Tony Wilson arrived on Sapper Hill and he was elated that the 'Welsh Guards' had arrived so quickly.

The first night on the hill we put together a makeshift sanger [sic] made of tarpaulin and oil barrels attached to an Argentine position. It was freezing with a blizzard blowing and we had no sleeping bags or refinements (something we had grown accustomed to by now anyway), only our battle order. Finding some Argentine long-sleeved t shirts, still in their plastic wrappers, we put them on under our windproof tops and laying close to someone to keep warm from their body heat. Although it was a very cold, bitter night and I can recollect shivering, I did get some sleep. Some Argentine ration packs we found were a god send; I can clearly remember eating some biscuits that were very similar to TUC Crackers and finding cigarettes and a box of matches that I placed into my mess tins and stored back into my kidney pouches (I still have these today).

Marine Terry Barnes, 9 Troop, C Company

We watched the Jock Guards hard fought effort taking Tumbledown and the Para's on Wireless Ridge the following night, I believe we were supposed to follow through to Sapper Hill, but Charlie Company took it so maybe brain fog, anyways the order came through that "the Argies have surrendered move to Stanley". On the way we were redirected to Sapper Hill, during this time on the old track just before Moody Brook Pete Holdgate (40 Commando's RN Photographer) took that famous Yomper picture of Robbie (Cpl Peter Robinson, but not sure if he was the best looking, or the least ugly? but an excellent choice). Shortly after, and miraculously, our bergens caught up with us just in time for another cold night on a mountain and a weird anti-climatic feeling to deal with.

Our NCOs had been building us up for the prospect of hand to hand fighting in Stanley. It was time to switch the mindset off and try and humanise again. We yomped into Stanley with ridiculous weight on our backs [and], rather ironically for Anti Tanks, halted beside a row of AML 90 armoured cars outside the Globe Pub and took our packs off. Not sure who the sentry was but most of us went into the pub, a tin of Tom Thumb cigars was produced (Pincher or Kenny Hargreaves) that went very well with a couple of beers that seemed to be free, (although I later found out that Robbie had a fiver on him [and] may have paid for them). We went outside, to find 45 had abandoned their attached Milan Troop ranks of 40 Commando and had marched off to the airfield.

Marine Colin Adams, Milan Troop, 40 Commando

That evening, having heard the news, I went to the House of Commons to announce the victory. I could not get into my own room; it was locked and the Chief Whip's assistant had to search for the key. I then wrote out on a scrap of paper I found somewhere on my desk the short statement, which I would have to make on a point of order to the house. At 10pm I rose and told the house that it had been reported that there were white flags flying over Port Stanley. The war was over. We all felt the same and the cheers showed it. Right had prevailed. And when I went to sleep very late that night I realised how great the burden was which had been lifted from my shoulders. For the nation as a whole, though the daily memories, fears and even the relief would fade, pride in our country's achievement would not.

Prime Minister Margaret Thatcher, Memories of the Falklands (2002) p.4

Soon after last light the Welsh Guards, with both companies from 40 Commando, received their bergens courtesy of some logistical magic by Regimental Sergeant Major Davies of the Welsh Guards. The next day we were withdrawn to Fitzroy and linked up with the Scots Guards, Gurkhas and other elements of 5 Brigade. Denied the triumph of entering Stanley, at least the Welsh Guards, or more accurately 9 Troop and part of 8 Troop, C Company, 40 Commando, had the satisfaction of being the nearest to Stanley when the Argentines surrendered and carrying out the only daylight helicopter assault onto an enemy position of the whole of the Falklands War.

The moment of surrender provided mixed feelings and a vast eye-opener for every marine as they had experienced an opportunity to compare standards of professionalism directly between the Royal Marines and those of the Welsh Guards, and there was no comparison.

40 Commando was instructed to deploy HQ elements as necessary plus one rifle company to Port Howard by first light on the 15 June via landing craft from HMS *Intrepid* to supervise the evacuation of the Argentine garrison.

At 1505 on 14 June the Argentine garrison indicated a willingness to talk. At 1530 orders had been given to British ground troops to fire in self-defence only. At 1715 Admiral Sandy Woodward signalled to his ships that the situation was very delicate as the mainland reaction to the surrender negotiations was not known. No naval attacks were to take place without further orders, but the Argentine air threat remained and had to be countered. At 1810 Jeremy Moore signalled Sir John Fieldhouse at 3 Commando Brigade. Large numbers of Argentines were putting their weapons down and surrendering.

Once the administrative details were finalised it was agreed that the formal surrender would be low-key with no press present. At 2030 Colonel H. M. Rose, the Commanding Officer of 22 SAS, and General Moore sent the following message:

General Menendez has agreed to a ceasefire in the West and East Falkland. DTG ceasefire effective now. 1 PNG hel deliver surrender document to Fitzroy at 2200 and the General will arrive at Stanley the sign at 2330. Menendez has reservations about Argentine Navy and Air Force will speak to General Galtieri. Troops are moving to the airfield and leaving their weapons at the W End of the Isthmus. W Falkland – no further action till first light. The Argentines will cooperate in the admin of PW. They will also give a deep-water harbour and RE Sp with the minefield and loc of mines. Do you accept?

Jeremy Moore arrived in heavy snow at 2230 . Sometime after midnight GMT he signed the instrument of surrender with General Menéndez. However, to avoid any further misunderstanding over dates and time zones it was dated 2359 on 14 June 1982 and was effective from that time. Even without the word 'unconditional' it was a total and comprehensive surrender with regards to Argentine personnel and equipment on East and West Falkland and all the outlying islands. At 0200 on 15 June Moore signalled back to London:

> Major General Menendez surrendered to me all the Argentine Armed Forces East and West Falklands together with their impedimenta. Arrangements are in hand to assemble the men for return to Argentina to gather their arms and equipment and to make safe their munitions. The Falkland Islands once more under the governments desired by the inhabitants.
> God save the Queen.

The Argentine military personnel did not like the Paras and frequently complained of unduly rough treatment, but they spoke well of the Royal Marines. Brigadier General Jofrey stated that the clearance process went much smoother when the Royal Marines took over completely from the Paras after he complained. He described his own relations with British officers he had to deal with as courteous but cold.

After Jeremy Moore had received the formal conditional surrender from General Menéndez, 40 Commando HQ and B Company were tasked to move to Port Howard, West Falkland, and raise the Union Flag. They were also to evacuate all the Argentine troops from the settlement and surrounding areas. On the night of the 14 June Malcolm Hunt received orders to move B Company by landing craft from Port San Carlos to an RV off Fanning Head. From there they would meet up with a third landing craft where Malcolm Hunt was to be given final orders before setting off to Port Howard.

Details of the surrender can be found in the appendices.

5

Post-Surrender and the Trip Home

15 June

The following FLASH signal was sent at 141715Z:

OP CORPORATE
1. WHITE FLAG REPORTED OVER STANLEY. LAND FIGHTING AROUND STANLEY CEASED, SURRENDER NEGOTIATIONS BEING ARRANGED WITH ARG LAND FORCES COMMANDER
2. SITUATION THUS VERY DELICATE. ARG MAINLAND REACTION NOT KNOWN. OUR GUARD MUST NOT BE REDUCED BUT WE MUST NOT JEOPARDISE RESULTS SO FAR ACHIEVED
3. NO NAVAL ATTACK ON FALKLAND ISLANDS TO TAKE PLACE WITHOUT FURTHER ORDERS. NGS SHIPS PROCEED INSHORE BUT DO NOT OPEN FIRE ON LAND TARGETS UNLESS SPECIFICALLY ORDERED
4. ARG AIR THREAT (OVERLAND) REMAINS AND MUST BE COUNTERED
5. THE THREAT AT SEA HAS NOT CHANGED

- All OPs in the San Carlos area were now withdrawn
- Argentine Forces Surrender at Port Howard
- Port Howard Beach is found to be a daisy chain of AP and AT mines up to 2,500lb
- Six Argentine bodies and one British officer buried in local cemetery and the Argentines wish to know what was to happen with their dead

The Task Force Commander Sandy Woodward was anxious about the fate of the men and captured enemy in weather conditions that had deteriorated badly. Winter had arrived with a vengeance with sleet, snow, howling winds and bitter cold making the troops' lives miserable in the extreme. The men had lived rough and exposed for four weeks and eaten compo rations the whole time. They had fought their way across terrain that the Argentines thought to be an impossible task, and the stocks of food and ammunition were low it was imperative that they were given maximum support as quickly as possible.

It was confirmed that the Argentine forces on West Falkland knew about the surrender. One of HMS *Intrepid*'s LCUs carrying the Commando Tactical HQ left San Carlos for an RV with two LCUs carrying B Company off Chancho Point. In appalling sea conditions, Captain Bush, OC B Company, 40 Commando, transferred from one LCU to another to receive his orders from Malcolm Hunt. The sea state was judged too high for the LCUs to safely cross Falkland Sound and it was decided that all landing craft would head for Port San

Carlos and disembark their passengers. It looked at that point as if the task would have to be cancelled as HQ LFFI were unable to provide any alternative movement assets.

Malcolm Hunt spoke to the commander of the Argentine 5th Infantry Regiment at Port Howard on the civilian two-meter band radio, and arrangements were made for the surrender and handing over of weapons and equipment. Local efforts produced two Sea Kings, one Lynx and one Wessex which were used to deliver the Tactical HQ and part of B Company, 40 Commando, to Port Howard at 1315 . As they approached the football field, everyone was feeling a little apprehensive as to the reception and wondered if all the Argentines forces would agree to the surrender. Whilst on the approach, the pilot came up on the radio to say that any fear anyone had may be unfounded. The Argentinians were marshalling the helicopters in and had already started piling up their weapons.

B Company, 40 Commando, immediately organised themselves and started to search and process the prisoners as well as disarming the few remaining prisoners who had not already voluntarily surrendered. To everyone's amazement, there was also a steady stream of Argentine soldiers coming down from the hills. There were occasional bouts of temper, from those who felt affronted by defeat and wanted to make their feelings known stating that this was Argentine land and not British land. B Company could now see that the constant threats of counterattack from West Falkland were very much a real possibility and one that thankfully had not materialised. They would wonder why the men and equipment on West Falkland had not been used to harass and even attack the main supply depot at Ajax Bay, or San Carlos and how the outcome may have been different.

The remainder of B Company moved over to West Falkland later that evening, having crossed the Sound by trawler and made the final part of the journey by landing craft. For the remainder of the period at Port Howard, the company cleared all the enemy positions, weapons and ammunition and started filling in the trenches. The Argentines were extremely cooperative, and the evacuation proceeded apace using HMS *Intrepid*'s LCUs. Approximately 750 Argentines, with the exception of a few special category prisoners of war, and those who knew the layout of minefields, were evacuated by first light. It was intended to centralise the company positions, marking minefields and clearing them where possible the following day.

Company Sergeant Major Les Gordon was informed that one of the prisoners had revealed that the entire beach had been mined in a daisy chain configuration. That was the beach where B Company would have come ashore on the initial attempt to land at Port Howard. The devastating effect of this discovery and close call for B Company and Malcolm Hunt was not lost on anyone. If one anti-personnel mine had been set off, it could trigger the whole chain which would have been set off along the entire length of the beach, resulting in many fatalities or severe injuries, including Malcolm Hunt.

The garrison commander was immediately summoned and through an interpreter was asked where the layout map for the minefield was to allow our assault engineers to begin to dismantle the beach boobytrap. To everyone's amazement he said he did not have one and he had no idea where or how many mines there were. This was not only totally irresponsible towards the local population, but also his own troops and the engineers who now had to defuse them. It was also against the Geneva Convention.

Along the beach, anti-tank mines were laid with tripwires for use in the anti-personnel role, with some command detonated, the largest of these being 2,500lb. The AE Troop, augmented by 10 men from 9 Royal Engineer Squadron, lifted 714 anti-personnel mines and 475 anti-tank mines by hand, which was an outstanding achievement. Sadly, in the process of destroying the mines Cpl Trevor Lee, together with four other men, was moving up a steep bank from the beach area when he stepped on an anti-personnel mine and lost his foot. It is thought that this mine had fallen down the bank as they were being laid.

B Company were to spend nine days clearing up the mess at Port Howard. The medics, particularly Surgeon Lieutenant Andy Prosser, had been appalled by the blood spillages not cleared up, and dirty medical instruments left lying around at the abandoned field dressing station.

Malcolm Hunt was seen sitting outside beside an enormous pile of weapons, bayonets, steel helmets and clothing with a large grin, having taken the surrender of Port Howard with HMS *Cardiff* lying offshore. Malcolm Hunt remained in Port Howard until 19 of June. B Company remained in Port Howard until 23 June when they returned to San Carlos prior to re-embarking on *Canberra* on 24 June.

Within Port Howard, a British grave was found which belonged to Captain Gavin Hamilton, SAS, who was part of a four-man OP on the high ground of a ridge called Many Branch Point, 2,500 metres from the Argentine positions at Port Howard. Late morning on 10 June, Captain Hamilton and a radio operator, Cpl Roy Fonseka were discovered by a four-man Argentine patrol from the 1st Section of 601 Commando Company, from Port Howard. Captain Hamilton was unfortunately killed, and Cpl Fonseka was taken prisoner. Captain Hamilton's body was buried with military honours by the Argentinian garrison. When the Argentine commander of Port Howard, Colonel Juan Ramon Mabragana, was interrogated he stated that Hamilton was '*the most courageous man I have ever seen*' and recommended that he should receive a gallantry decoration for his actions during the firefight. Captain Hamilton was later posthumously awarded the Military Cross.

With some relief we were flown off the hill by helicopter to Fitzroy, where we were put in a barn, cramped like factory chickens, but at least out of the appalling weather. The toxic fumes from so many cookers going at the same was sometimes nauseous. The smell of over forty men that hadn't showered for weeks could have been overwhelming if it had not of been for the familiar aroma of rations being cooked; the air had a tinge of chicken curry and bacon burgers.

Marine Terry Barnes, 9 Troop, C Company

It was snowing again, and we were told to get our kit ready as we were going to be pulled out. By accident or design, the Welsh Guards company were pulled out first, despite having spent only a few days in the field and having nice, comfortable DPM parkas. We were in a barn with the Guards, they started to give us some stick, it was meant to be funny I daresay, but it fell on stony ground and there was quite a bit of flak returned. After all we had put up with, not once were we spoken to by 1WG officers, no greeting, no thanks for our assistance, especially helping with their kit. Enough said.

Marine Brien Hobbs, 7 Troop, Charlie Company

16 June

- Plans were made for HQ and Support Companies, 40 Commando, to be deployed to Fox Bay settlement to deal with the 8th Regt and finish a clearance operation started by HMS *Avenger*

- Both A and C Companies, 40 Commando, returned after their move forward with 1 Welsh Guards. They did not reoccupy a former defensive position as an effort was made to put everyone under cover to enable them to get some much-needed rest and recuperation
- All stations were advised that captured Argentine helicopters would be flying with friendly pilots and all weapons to be tight

There was time to speak to the men of A Company. I gathered them round me near the shearing sheds at San Carlos.

I told them that they had not been found wanting and had done all that was asked of them extremely well and with great professionalism.

I told them that in years to come they would be proud that they had taken part in the Falklands War and of their many achievements.

Above all else I told them I was proud – proud of them and proud to have commanded them.

Major Shane Cusack, OC A Company, 40 Commando, *The Summer of 82*

17 June
- Argentine Junta collapses
- Callsign 7 were instructed to take four days' rations and water with them to Fox Bay with the first wave leaving San Carlos at 1849
- Mail arrives at Port Stanley, and it is requested that it is redirected to San Carlos
- A composite company of 40 Commando moved to Fox Bay on the east side of West Falkland to commence the post-war clean-up operation. The company was commanded by Captain Alan Berry RM comprised of the following:
  Lt Mike Woolley as 2I/C
  Company HQ
  The Rev Godfrey Hillard RN
  POMA Watts
  4 Signallers
  1 Section of AEs
  Lt Mark Richards IC Mortar Troop
  Lt Mike Acland IC Survey Troop
  1 Section B Echelon
  1 Section MT Troop
  1 Section Defence Troop
  Lt Alan Thompson and Recce Troop joined the company on 19 June 82

Fox Bay had previously been occupied by a battalion of the Argentine 8th Regiment on the west side and a squadron of engineers on the east side. The bay was well defended from attack from the west but had little defence to the north. Most of the trenches were full of water and the minefields were tactically well cited but were largely surface laid with no defined boundaries, and the records did not correspond to the actual minefields.

Prior to 40 Commando's arrival, HMS *Avenger* had taken the surrender and organised the removal of all prisoners except for 28 (three officers and 25 other ranks) who were to be used as working parties. The Navy had stated that it had sorted out all the arms and ammunition and declared the settlement safe, although this was not found to be the case.

The first task in Fox Bay West was to evaluate the size of the problem and a list of priorities.

A. All weapons cleaned and catalogued
B. All ammunition inspected segregated and dumped in a safe area with all unstable ammunition and other materials to be blown up by the Royal Engineers
C. Minefields identified and main tracks cleared to give civilians access to their livestock
D. The settlement was cleared and cleaned up with trenches filled in by the Argentine POWs

The Argentinians had left Fox Bay West in an appalling mess and had no regard for personal hygiene in or around the buildings they lived in. This was also found to be the case in all the locations throughout the Falklands that the Argentines had occupied. One example was the bunkhouse where they had gutted sheep in the rooms, leaving the remains inside. Human excrement was everywhere and so the prisoners' first task was to clean the bunkhouse where they would live. There were other buildings, including ones previously occupied by Falkland Islanders, in a similar state. A composite troop from A Company, 40 Commando, was to move to Fox Bay East on 20 June to conduct a similar operation.

18 June
Signal received from C in C as follows:

```
Z 181016Z  JUN82  ZPW  NA  Z
FM CTF 317
TO TF 317
RBDAPW/CBFSU  ASCENSION
BT
UNCLAS
SIC 19F
PERSONAL FROM CINC
```

1. I HAVE HAD THE HONOUR TO RECEIVE THE FOLLOWING MESSAGE FROM HER MAJESTY THE QUEEN AND PASS IT TO YOU ALL WITH GREAT PLEASURE. QUOTE
2. I SEND MY WARMEST CONGRATULATIONS TO YOU AND TO ALL UNDER YOUR COMMAND FOR THE SPLENDID WAY IN WHICH YOU HAVE ACHIEVED THE LIBERATION OF THE FALKLAND ISLANDS. BRITAIN IS VERY PROUD OF THE WAY YOU SERVED YOUR COUNTRY. SIGNED ELIZABETH R. UNQUOTE
3. CTG 317.1 ENSURE THIS IS PASSED TO SUBORDINATE UNITS

Stamped M.V. Lycaon
O.N.   364438
Liverpool

C Company, 40 Commando, were embarked on HMS *Intrepid,* and it was proposed to embark Tactical HQ, HQ Main and B Echelon the following day, but HMS *Intrepid* considered she did not have enough room. It was then intended to embark only Tactical HQ and HQ main with B echelon remaining in San Carlos.

19 June

At Fox Bay there were over 25,000 rounds of 7.62mm blank ammunition, which suggest that some of their soldiers did not know how to use a weapon in the first place, or possibly some of them really did think they were on an exercise. A lot of their 105mm ammunition was in such poor condition that it was unstable, and it is doubtful whether some of it would have fired.

The following is a list of the equipment and ammunition found at Fox Bay and again one would wonder why, if they had this stock, the Argentines did not at least try a counterattack:

> 31,800 rounds of 12.7mm
> 126,600 rounds of 7.62mm ball/tracer
> 10,100 rounds of 7.62mm link
> 211 hand grenades
> 138 Energa anti-tank grenades
> 74 x 3.5-inch anti-tank rockets
> 430 x 105mm [artillery shells]
> 33 x 120mm mortar
> 733 other rounds
> 500 mortar fuses
> 3 x Blowpipe
> 38 handheld flares
> 37 cartridge flares
> 62lb TNT
> 107 all types of anti-tank mines
> 577 all types of anti-personnel mines
> 1,057 9mm rounds
> 99 x 0.45-inch rounds
> Weapons – 23 GPMG, 8 x 12.7mm, 7 x 81mm mortars, 3 x 120mm mortar, 4 x 120mm RCL, 18 x 3.5-inch rocket launchers

The overall clearance operation proceeded slowly and was hampered by the available assault engineer support and the considerable quantities of unstable and potentially dangerous explosives. The ammunition dump was in an area which would pose a hazard to the settlement. The possible transfer of the ammunition dump to a safer location was not viable due to its unstable nature and the possibility of napalm being present within the dump. Some of the minefields were unmarked, and again, the few minefield registers that were available bore little resemblance to what had been found. Two more mixed minefields, both unmarked, remained to be checked and cleared. Considerable manpower was required to accelerate the progress when further minefield assistance was available, but it was thought the minefield clearance would take months to complete. In actual fact the final minefield was cleared from the Falklands only in late 2020. Over the weekend of 16 November 2020, residents flocked to see the final mines left by Argentine forces at Gypsy Cove and Yorke Bay.

20 June

- The arrival at North Arm of the Gurkhas entailed a change of plan and A Company was now to deploy to Port Stephen on 21 June by helicopter with four days' rations, after recovering the troop undertaking the guarding of POWs at Ajax Bay
- C Company, 40 Commando, were ordered to take responsibility for the guarding of POWs at Ajax Bay via HMS *Intrepid*
- A planning meeting was held to start unit transfers to *Canberra* and home

A composite troop along with Company HQ, 40 Commando, moved to Fox Bay East to conduct a similar operation to that on the west side. The settlement was clean, and the equipment and ammunition were in a safe condition and smaller quantities. All weapons and ammunition were catalogued, and the settlement area tidied up. An Argentinian ammunition ship, *The Successor*, was run aground alongside the jetty; it contained 5,000 rounds of 120mm and copious quantities of food and Spanish wine, most of which was taken by civilians. The ship was put out of bounds to Royal Marines.

The 28 prisoners left behind in Fox Bay West looked very young, undernourished and not capable of looking after themselves, let alone fighting, and as luck would have it, they were commanded by an English-speaking captain. The captain had been the community relations' officer and as such was little help in identifying the minefields, except where the Argentines had blown themselves up, as one had recently done when driving a civilian tractor. The civilians told stories that the Argentinians would shoot at their own aircraft, although without confirmed success, and on the one occasion when attacked by a Harrier they did not shoot at it.

21 June

Very early in the day, 40 Commando was directed to cancel the move to Port Stephen and to send an advance party to HQ 3 Commando Brigade for an embarkation meeting with a view to their embarking later in the day, with the remainder of the Commando possibly on 23 June. The Commando was ordered to congregate in San Carlos prior to embarkation.

A Company's advance party at Port Stephens was recovered to San Carlos.

Malcolm Hunt ordered that C Company should still move to Ajax Bay, but this was later cancelled and only 8 Troop deployed there.

B and HQ Companies, at Port Howard and Fox Bay respectively, were ordered not to clear any mines except where they prevented essential civilian movement. Other minefields, including those newly discovered, were to be marked and left.

Four special category prisoners were held by B Company, 40 Commando:

> Captain Albert Erno NIETO, NI 105032 (Comms)
> Lt Gustav Adolf CALDERINI, NI 208392 (Engineer)
> Lt Lucio MARIO CANDIA, NI 212495 (Infantry)
> Sub Lt Robert Henry HERRERA, NI 203 (Infantry)

22 June

Captain Bush, OC B Company, was given permission to blow three panels of anti-personnel mines outside the settlement at Port Howard. He had asked that a Para engineer stay with him, but Divisional HQ decided there were higher priorities in Stanley.

Captain Bush was ordered to withdraw his subunits by last light 23 June and to be prepared to move any time after first light on 24 June.

All ammunition was withdrawn from all ranks and weapons secured.

Following numerous trench filling and clean-up operations the unit was starting to relax and finish its tasks in readiness to return home.

Callsign 85B complained that the promised 80 cases of beer were six cases short. An investigation found five were missing from C Company loading lines and one had gone missing en route, possibly on an LCVP. As a result, that call sign only paid for 74 crates to the PRI representative arriving at that location.

Canberra would embark 40, 42 and 45 Commando which was disappointing for some of the crew. Given the individual units' experiences in the Falklands the unit commanders greeted the decision with a degree of relief that any potential flashpoints with Paras would be avoided.

23 June

Michael Clapp and staff move ashore to Stanley.

B Company flew back to San Carlos prior to embarking on *Canberra* for the trip home.

The only surviving Chinook (Bravo November) was provided to lift B Company and HQ Company to San Carlos ahead of schedule. Captain Bush requested that his engineers be moved later in order that they could dispose of the final mines which was agreed. He was to leave details of minefields cleared or awaiting clearance with the settlement manager. This would give later units a good indication as to what had and had not been completed.

24 June

Trip home and ready for a tour of South Armagh, Northern Ireland in January 1983.

40 Commando re-embark onto *Canberra* for the trip home.

0740 flying stations on *Canberra* started the embarkation of 40 Commando Royal Marines. Nos 7, 14, 16 and 24 boats were put in the water to assist. It was thought embarkation would take all day. Lunchtime came and everyone was on board. There were no delays, no last-minute hitches, and everything went smoothly. Those in the boats were scrambling up the nets and through the sea doors battering delightedly through the familiar passageways towards allotted cabins, laughing and greeting the crew, hiding their anxiety as they passed familiar faces. The crew members were hoping that those with whom they had become friends on the trip down, and they now classed as family, were not among the dead or injured. When they saw familiar face come on board the crew members would just look and emotionally say *"it's good to see you"*. The crew thought of the lads as their own children coming home. Return of the Royal Marines of 40, 42, and 45 Commando further lifted the crew's spirits, and it was good to hear the chatter in the bars. Throughout the day *Canberra's* showers were in constant use as men washed away the stench of almost five weeks of the trenches.

The Commanding Officers of 40, 42, and 45 Commando decided that the units were to run a relaxed routine during the trip to the UK, numerous activities would be arranged, and everyone would be required to do at least 30 minutes PT per day. They were conscious that there had to be a certain discipline because otherwise the whole thing would unravel very quickly. It was decided to have a minimum number of restrictions on what the men could not do. This was also to say 'you have done an excellent job, relax and enjoy the voyage home'. All that remained was a quick trip to Port William to pick up Brigade HQ and then head for home.

As we landed on the flight deck and then stepped off, Cpl George Porthouse knelt down, kissed the floor and muttered something like "you beaut" in his Geordie accent. It was almost like a priest genuflecting on holy ground. As I entered my new cabin it felt bizarre, no wind or rain and clean bed sheets. It felt irreverent to dirty the place up with my filthy clothes, boots and kit. I stripped off, wrapped a towel around me, grabbed some soap and dived under, my first shower for weeks. I could feel my body warm up and go pink as the blood flow increased to my extremities.

We were in a hurry to get things stored away asking what are we going to do with our pile of dirty dhobi stacked in the centre. I think it was Mne Simon Poole that found out that we could send it to the ship's laundry.

I would not have touched someone else's garments in that condition. I was amazed that two days later I found my clothes returned, laid on my bed, immaculately clean and ... pressed, what luxury.

Marine Terry Barnes, 9 Troop, C Company

As for the islands themselves, the British Government was now committed to their defence in a policy referred to as 'Fortress Falklands'. A first step came on the 24 June when an extended-range Hercules landed at Stanley airfield. Then in October, after its lengthening and re-designation as RAF Stanley, the airport could be used by Phantom fighter jets. A major airfield, and associated installations, completed in 1985 and named Mount Pleasant Airport, was able to handle wide-bodied, long-range aircraft capable of reinforcing the Falklands at short notice.

As a 19-year-old in the Falklands War all sense of time was lost as days seemed to blur into one, hours seemed like minutes and minutes might have been hours. Our urgent recall from ranges in the North West of England, sailing on the *Canberra*, landing at San Carlos, my actions on land which include being stranded in a minefield, left by helicopter by mistake in the direct line of fire, a rarely recorded firefight by 9 Troop Charlie Company 40 Commando Royal Marines.

There were numerous occasions that deserve mentioning and were just as frightening as these "final days" such as leaping across from the SS *Canberra* to Landing Craft during a large swell in the South Atlantic, spotting sharks while swimming in English Bay at our stop off on the Ascension Islands on the way down. And of course, the more emotional aspect of carrying injured personnel off helicopters at Ajax Bay and entering the Red and Green Life Machine with a colleague (Ged Herd) viewing operations on the go and carrying body bags via the captured prisoner's enclosure to a temporary grave site.

I did witness some exceptional soldering such as Chris Pretty taking his gun section made up off Ged Herd and Brian Edmunds to the furthest right flank of 9

Troop under enemy fire with no cover, facing away from the main enemy. Captain Andy Pillar's walk through a minefield in pitch black to check the injured were being dealt with and that the path was clear. I know that there is a great deal of other examples witness by other members of 9 Troop and I apologise for not recalling them all. I must mention one other before I get to the main event. I am afraid it was a certain Lance Corporal, again, that offered aid to a struggling Welsh Guardsman (crying out "I can't go on!") on a particular hard going rock run when advancing in the dark hours, near Mount Harriet even though Chris had his own particular problems of his own. When it was daylight Chris took his shirt off to reveal abrasions still bleeding on his shoulders from carrying his bergen almost full of spare 7.62 link rounds for the General Purpose Machine Gun (GPMG).

At Wreck Point on or around the 2-06-82 where our section 3.3.C was based, relieving members of 45 Commando guarding a Rapier site. The sanger [sic] was surrounded by our new arctic two-man tents. After taking my "medicine" to relieve the pain of trench foot during the day, I woke in the middle of the night with stomach cramps. I had no option but to run outside in the pitch black and relieve myself as quickly and quietly as possible of what I can only call a large amount of diarrhoea. I then returned back to my tent, a satisfied marine, fell asleep contented and forgot about the event.

On returning back to our two-man tents to prepare some "wets and scran" all that could be heard was a flurry of expletives from Cpl Dee Irving (section commander) "What the fuck" and then "who the fuck" continued with "which one of you cunts took a dump right outside my tent". I recall a raucous of laughter, especially from Big Ged who has never stopped recalling and laughing about the story of who defecated outside the section commanders' tent. At the time of Dee's allegations of who the culprit was, I had completely forgot about my night's events and therefore have been and still am, in complete denial of the charge and therefore the pointing fingers are still wagging as to "who took a dump outside Dee's tent!"

Marine Terry Barnes, 9 Troop, C Company

25 June
- Michael Clapp appointed Chief of Staff to Command British Forces Falkland Islands.
- *Canberra* sails for UK with Bulk of 3 Commando Brigade.

1722 *Canberra* weighed anchor and quietly got under way for home. *Canberra's* course was eastward and a final precaution against the extremely unlikely possibility of attack taking her beyond the reach of even the longest-range Argentine aircraft before heading north.

The *Canberra* crew smiled as they heard the feet pounding the promenade deck, but this time it was a gentler and more relaxed running during the training sessions. The Royal Marines onboard were keen to stay in shape when they got back and looking fit for their wives, girlfriends or possibly future acquaintances when they go home.

In the coming weeks recreation expanded to fill the time available and allow the men onboard to decompress steadily after their intense experiences of war. The commanding officers had made an excellent decision to bring the men back slow-time to deal with any psychological consequences which would include post-traumatic stress. The men would have a chance to chill and chat to each other and let everything go by the time they got home.

The benefit of sharing memories and recalling emotions honestly, in the company of those who had been through the same experiences brought with it an understanding that your reactions were entirely normal. The people with you knew what you wanted to say and what you were thinking. They made an excellent ear for listening and shoulder to cry on if the need was there. They were also your family, your Royal Marine family and you can guarantee they will look after you no matter what, now or in the future.

It is apparent that CGRM and others in London/Northwood do not understand the feelings of us all out here in the Task Force. The Brigadier finally clinched it with a signal to C in C Fleet to the effect that a remarkable affiliation has grown up between the ship and 3 Commando Brigade and we all wanted to arrive back in Southampton together, from whence we sailed in April.

Onboard, the mood remains euphoric, not surprisingly, but at present the celebrations are generally under control. It is not too easy however, as we have in the ship something near 2,000 teenagers who have just won a war.

Canberra – The Great White Whale Goes to War goes on to note:

Perhaps this, our last day, was the busiest yet. Helicopters came and went. More and more people came aboard, and *Canberra* was almost bursting at the seams. Now that we had completed loading, we were anchored a long way out in Port William. The weather was cold and blustery, and our boats had a long run to and from Port Stanley. After an hour or two at the wheel, the cox'ns had to be brought back on board and warmed through they were chilled to the bone. Then it was over. Our boats were hoisted; the last helicopter departed.

"Weigh anchor" ordered the Captain.

Darkness had fallen. It was pitch black and a bitterly cold night. The wind had risen, and sleet squalls lashed across the ship. Far away the lights of Port Stanley twinkled as though in farewell.

On the fo'c'sle, the anchor cable rumbled as the Chief Officer weighed. Slowly, *Canberra* turned away and the lights astern faded. We left the Falklands and were on our way home.'

Canberra – The Great White Whale Goes to War
The Peninsular and Orient Steam Navigation Company (1982) p.112–113

03 July

As we passed Ascension, the rumour mill was in action and said we were to get entertainers for the rest of the trip home. Speculation included names such as Frankie Howard and Anita Harris, but a cheerful lively group of singers, comedians and players turned up. They had come out to brighten the last days of the journey, and they did.

The following signal was received and transmitted to everyone onboard:

030300Z
CTF 317 TO SS CANBERRA
UNCLAS SIC 19F OP CORPORATE

PERSONAL FROM COMMANDER IN CHIEF

WELCOME BACK TO THE NORMAL ATMOSPHERE IN YOUR
HOME PASSAGE
  YOUR MAGNIFCENT AND UNIQUE CONTRIBUTION TO THE
FALKLAND ISLAND OPERATION IN THE MANNER IN WHICH YOU
HAVE ACCOMPLISHED EVERY TASK REQUIRED HAS BEEN FOLLOWED
WITH THE HIGHEST ADMIRATION I MYSELF AND ALL UNDER
MY COMMAND
  PLEASE, TAKE MY PERSONAL THANKS TO YOUR CREW AND MY
BEST WISHES FOR A MOST HAPPY TO RETURN TO THEIR FAMILIES

04 July

Sandy Woodward prepared to send his last signal to be transmitted to authorities in the
South Atlantic under the Command of Jeremy Moore and himself. It was to be sent to all 31
ships, 20 Royal Fleet Auxiliaries, five minesweepers, 43 merchant ships and 13 air squadrons
directly involved. It read:

AS I HAUL MY SOUTH ATLANTIC FLAG DOWN, I REFLECT SADLY
ON THE BRAVE LIVES LOST, AND THE GOOD SHIPS GONE, IN THE
SHORT TIME OF OUR TRIAL. I THANK WHOLEHEARTEDLY EACH
AND EVERY ONE OF YOU FOR YOUR GALLANT SUPPORT, THROUGH
DETERMINATION AND FIERCE PERSEVERANCE UNDER BLOODY
CONDITIONS. LET US ALL BE GRATEFUL THAT ARGENTINA DOESN'T
BREED BULLDOGS AND, AS WE RETURN SEVERALLY TO ENJOY THE
BLESSING OF OUR LAND, RESOLVE THOSE LEFT BEHIND FOR EVER
SHALL NOT BE FORGOTTEN.

Arrangements for our reception were being planned and a family connection was for
Plymouth as two of the three Commando units were based there. 42 Commando at Bickley
Barracks and 40 Commando at Seaton Barracks across from 59 Independent Commando
at Crownhill Fort. (40 Commando was soon to move to Norton Manor Camp in Taunton
following their Northern Ireland tour and a major exercise in the Mediterranean in 1983.)
There were other elements at Stonehouse Barracks close to Plymouth. However, for *Canberra*,
a Southampton-based vessel, this would mean not finishing at her home port and the
chances are that she would not be able to get alongside, let alone get inside the breakwater
at Plymouth. If she were to dock in Plymouth, the various elements would have to be landed
by boat or helicopter to separate locations. Stores and equipment would subsequently have
to be recovered from Southampton later.

Canberra's Captain, Dennis Scott Masson and his crew indicated that the passengers
should decide where to dock and offload her new family. Despite everyone's loyalty to the
West Country, there was an overriding loyalty to Captain Scott Masson, his crew and the
Canberra whose home was Southampton. It was decided that Southampton it would be.

The band played night and day after fulfilling what were numerous different roles. Music
filled the ship as it gave concerts and small groups split off to tour the decks and bars getting
men who got up to sing and generally perform alongside the band. Captain John Ware

produced a piece of music entitled *The San Carlos March*, And the composition was very well received. Onshore there were people on the headlands there were people everywhere all along the south coast.

10 July

Position as at 0700 47° 46' north and 6° 57' West

       71 nautical miles south by west of Lands' End

       Course 024° – 070°

       Speed 19.58 knots – 470 nautical miles

       1520 Land Ho! England

       1615 off Mounts Bay

       1700 off the Lizard. The Earl of Inchcape and 40 members of the press came onboard from RNAS Culdrose

       2030 off Start Point

       2315 off Portland Bill

Canberra's last full day at sea was calm and sunny. Mid-afternoon the hazy shape of land could just be seen. The chairman of the Peninsular and Oriental Steam Navigation Company, the Right Honourable Earl of Inchcape, was now on board. He was accompanied by Dr R Leach, Chairman of P&O Cruises; Mr L Scott, Managing Director of P&O Cruises; and Mr P Thomas, Director of Information. An RAF Nimrod flew overhead and did a creditable imitation of a fighter as it roared in salute and went into an almost vertical climb.

At lunchtime Captain Scott Masson drew two winners of P&O's grand raffle. P&O had donated two luxury cruises; a three-week cruise for two and a two-week cruise for two which were to be taken sometime in 1983. The prizes were drawn and broadcast to the ship with the second-prize winner Sgt Mick Northfield, HQ Coy, 40 Commando being first on the bridge to collect. It took a few more minutes to get the first-prize winner to respond as he was below in his cabin and did not really believe what he had heard. However, Cpl Jones of A Company, 40 Commando, finally made it to pick up his prize.

The raffle was the biggest money-spinner for the South Atlantic Fund on board. All the money from ticket sales went to the fund with £2378.66 raised. Throughout the whole voyage the ship was raising money in a variety of ways, and one can of beer fetched £78.00.

Other endeavours raised the following amounts:

       Collection of spare change before 21 May £109.78 1/2p

       Junior rates horseracing night £55.10

       Band concert collections £463.14 1/2p

       West Leeds Boys' High School (cheque) £16.00

       Donation from Miss P.E. Lambe (cheque) £30.00

       Swear box (in the Bureau) £3.60

       Donation from Christopher Hawke (Book – Rick Jolly) £15.00

       P&O Petty Officers' and Leading Hands' Mess £222.00

       P&O Crew Bean Competition £183.20

       Crew donation £828.00

       Crew collection for HMS *Ardent's* ship's company £164.00

       Military Force Officers' Mess monies remaining £170.28

45 Commando bar rebate £245.84
Second swear box (more successful than the first) £27.75
Military Warrant Officers', Senior NCOs', Senior Rates' Mess £322.94
45 Commando raffle £58.82

It was a brilliant evening the best that England had to offer, calm and peaceful. Boats came out to greet us, pilot boats, coastguards, tourists, private boat owners they all waved, sounded their horns and cheered. The officer of the watch sounded the ship's horn, cameras flashes were seen everywhere. On the flight deck the band gave its last performance with all the ceremony they could muster. The noise was deafening; it was like a Roman amphitheatre around the flight deck where more than 2,000 men cheering the band on. They were clearly taken aback they had not expected a welcome like this.

In the polished performance that is always given by the Royal Marines Band, with perfect timing as the sun set, the Union Flag was lowered as the last note of sunset faded away. There was a moment of silence and then 2,000 voices cheered. Those who criticise the existence of military bands should have been there that night. They should have been there when the bandsman were offloading ton after ton of compo and stores San Carlos Water. They should have been there to help them carry stretchers of British and Argentine wounded and seeing some horrific sights of men's bodies torn apart, let alone the stench of the dying and gangrenous limbs. They should have seen the response of men whenever the band performed. One last night at sea; what a finale and with the outline of the south coast as a backdrop.

11 July

0530 *Canberra*'s passengers were woken none too gently by a Royal Marines bugler broadcasting reveille. This was immediately followed by a somewhat lengthy traditional Royal Navy awakening:

> Wakey, wakey, wakey, rise and shine, the sun is burning your eyes out. Show a leg, show a leg, show a leg! Heave ho, heave ho, heave ho, lash up and stow – don't turn over – turn out.
>
> *Canberra – The Great White Whale Goes to War*
> (The Peninsular and Orient Steam Navigation Company, 1982) p.128

Then came the gentle tones of Lois Wheeler, who had been prevailed upon to give his last and more characteristic P&O passenger awakening:

> Good morning ladies and gentlemen. It promises to be a fine day, with every prospect of a warm welcome when we dock. Now if you would care to make your way to the dining halls you will find an early breakfast awaiting you. We hope you have enjoyed your cruise and that we might have the pleasure of your company again. Good morning.
>
> *Canberra – The Great White Whale Goes to War*
> (The Peninsular and Orient Steam Navigation Company, 1982) p.128

0626 off Bournemouth
0630 of St Catherine's Point off the Isle of Wight

Canberra loitered off the Isle of Wight with the mist promising a perfect day. A few small craft were seen in the water coming out to welcome her home, next the aircraft that were circling were getting ever lower, some of them so low we could clearly see the pilots. Then more boats joined, the water turned white from the wakes of the sailing boats, motorboats, big boats, small launches. Then to a roar of applause from all in *Canberra* as children in canoes with their safety boat close behind paddled against the stream of hundreds of boats and everyone made way for them. Every point of land every vantage point was full of people. Overhead there were helicopters and light aircraft darting about the rapidly clearing skies.

0800 off the NAB tower.
0900 HRH the Prince of Wales flies on board, joining the Commander in Chief, Admiral Sir John Fieldhouse, G.C.B., commander of the Task Force operations in the South Atlantic, the Commandant General Royal Marines, Lieutenant General Sir Steuart Pringle KCB and the Medical Director General of the Royal Navy, Vice Admiral Surgeon Vice Admiral Sir J. A. B. Harrison KCB, QHP, FRCR.

I must apologise to the Company Sergeant Major of A Company, 40 Commando, WO2 Nolan, at this point. He informed me earlier in the day that I was to be part of a group who would meet HRH Prince of Wales. However, at that time I decided to be with everyone else on the rails of the *Canberra* watching the small craft and in particular a couple of young ladies. I am sure he would let me have this little indiscretion upon our welcome home.

I was to later, in a small way, make up for this when my ship's detachment, in 1984, with the now Captain Andy Salmon (former OC 3 Troop, A Coy) as my OC RM, when we escorted Prince Andrew from Ascension Island to St Helena before returning him to Ascension Island, whilst we made our way to South Georgia and the Falkland Islands. During one patrol in the Falklands, we did give the inhabitants of Weddel Island a fright when they noticed the detachment patrolling across the island and they thought it was all about to start again. We worked from the settlement for a short while, especially given the hospitality of the settlement manager and his family, before moving onto the east island. At one point we were overflown by a Phantom near Goose Green who was checking that the patrol was friendly. You have to consider this was only two years after the invasion, so everyone was still a little anxious.

1045 Prince Charles and other visiting VIPs depart by helicopter.

As the *Canberra* left the Solent and turned towards Southampton, the 400-strong ship's company, all volunteers, had never seen such a homecoming. The *Canberra* was pitted with indentations, her paintwork flaking from salt, the hull streaked with rust; she looked like she had been through the wars, and she had, quite literally.

As the channel narrowed and the sea room decreased, the craft became concentrated and were sometimes virtually touching. Fire Service tugs pumped plumes of water a hundred feet into the air, drenching boats. More pleasure-craft kept appearing and it was turning into a perfect summer's day. Some of the craft were slow and could only just keep up, others went racing round the ship hooting and waving and small family boats pottering along. One small craft kept coming in very close to throw cans of cold beer and lager up to the troops lining the rails above them, most of which fell into the sea. There were welcoming banners everywhere, some with people's names, others simply '*To the Task Force*'. Space along the rails of the *Canberra* had been allocated according to units and these were packed with very happy Royal Marines.

Any boat that came by with women on board was subjected to good-natured cries of *'Get your kit off for the boys!'* One of the small craft had two young ladies standing on its bow and so when they heard this, they raised their tops for the boys. Several ladies who seemed too respectable and sensible for this sort of thing were also following the young ladies' example. This must have been the greatest moment for the Queen of the Seas, First Lady of the Merchant Navy, heroine for the day announced the commentators.

Not a spot of jetty floor could be seen for the mass of people, family, friends and public who just wanted to show their thanks and appreciation. On board, the Commando Forces Band stirred emotions for the last time while on the jetty the Royal Marines Band from Portsmouth responded. Instinctively the Director of Music began to synchronise the music until both bands played as one. The Royal Marines Band and their musical emotion was felt by all of those present alongside those of the occasion.

From the dockside the crowds cheered the Royal Marines who had draped sheets and canvas over the rails with *'WE WENT WE FOUGHT WE CONQUERED', 'LOCK UP YOUR DAUGHTERS THE BOOTNECKS ARE BACK'*, and *'MAGGIE RULES OKAY'*. The comments at the threatened stoppage of the railways *'CALL OFF THE RAIL STRIKE WILL CALL AN AIRSTRIKE'*, and the most personal of all those who had sailed 25,245 nautical miles on its epic and hazardous voyage *'CANBERRA CRUISES WHERE QE2 REFUSES'*. Safe at last *Canberra* was looking so forlorn; this normal pristine white cruise ship looked worn out, but she was a mother figure bringing her children safely home.

The last 50 yards seemed to take an age as the tugs pushed *Canberra* onto the jetty and the conclusion to what was an extraordinary trip for such a vessel. By now individuals could recognise each other and frenzied waving and shouting were the order of the day as they tried to attract the attention of their loved ones. The climax of this collective and emotional time was the releasing of a cloud of balloons as the bands prompted hundreds of voices into singing *Land of Hope and Glory*. It was a fairy tale ending this extraordinary of adventures for a ship that had become a second home for many. For once those who had borne the brunt of danger and adversity now shared in the glory.

Just after 1100 , *Canberra* secured alongside Southampton, after 94 days 25,245 nautical miles at sea. *Canberra* and the crew along with her passengers had arrived home safely. The Port Police said that they lost count at 35,000 people flowing through the gates. Banners, flags, flowers, bunting, singing mass of people and families.

Julian Thompson was the first to leave *Canberra*, to cement the final stages of this trip. The various units landed, with the crowds cheering troops in green berets bearing Naval, Royal Marine and Army cap badges, alongside the whitecaps of the Royal Navy and the Merchant Service for without whom we could not have succeeded in our task to retake the Falklands and South Georgia and the South Sandwich Islands.

I came down the gangway behind Corporal Jones of A Company, 40 Commando, who knelt down and kissed the ground thankful to be back in UK. I have hunted for a copy of this photograph as I am sure some of the press took a picture, but to no avail. Shortly after, I was walking through the shed only to be surprised to see my parents who had driven down from Wirral. I was not aware they were coming, and this was a great surprise.

We were only expecting to get off the liner, put our kit on four tonners, and jump in the back or if lucky get onto civilian coaches and head southwest back to Seaton Barracks, Plymouth. As we passed the Isle of Wight the number of vessels was up in the hundreds.

The *Canberra* sounding her whistle in response to others and warning the little boats that she was not going to stop for any craft. I can remember one buxom young lady, on a small boat being asked to "show us yer tits" and she kindly obliged. When she pulled her top back down cover herself up there were boos and calls of "show us some more". She then casually, totally removed her top to a rapturous response from us on board; what a wonderful sight!

On board, someone from Charlie Company ran back inside, down a stairwell into a cabin, grabbed a white bed sheet, scrolled something, just legible on it, "Charlie Company 40 Commando Royal Marines". This makeshift banner was hung over the promenade deck safety rails.

Despite what we had been told there had been absolutely no customs checks, just a few Military Police in uniform hanging around undercover of the dockside shed standing next to tables. I dumped my kit down on the floor in the shed and found my family. I had some mixed emotions when I hugged my mother, I didn't feel that tearful, just pleased to see them.

The trip from Southampton to Plymouth was memorable, in every town or village we passed through the coach was stopped by people wanting to jump on and either give us some form of alcohol or a kiss and a hug. People had lined the streets and were waving banners and flags; it was as if each town was trying to outdo the other.

Several weeks later back at Seaton Barracks I heard a noise, looked up and saw a fellow marine I recognised, hopping past on one leg, a stump where the other foot should have been. I suddenly remembered the night in the minefield.

Marine Terry Barnes, 9 Troop, C Company

Next stop, a well-earned leave and then NI training ready for our tour in January 1983 to South Armagh.

Roll of Honour

It is always sad to lose someone, but when that someone is part of a close-knit team or unit, it can be said that the loss is felt even more by those that are left. During the Falklands 40 Commando included 59 Royal Engineers, with whom we shared our geographical locations of Seaton Barracks and Crownhill Fort and with whom we worked closely. We sadly lost the following personnel in an Argentine bombing raid at San Carlos on 27 May 1982:

Marine D G McAndrews	San Carlos Bombing	27 May 1982
	(Died of wounds on board HMS *Intrepid*)	
Sapper P K Gandhi	San Carlos Bombing	27 May 1982

Casualties

Mne W Derrick	San Carlos Bombing	27 May 1982
	(Shell Shock – Remained at San Carlos)	
Mne S M Jeffrey	San Carlos Bombing	27 May 1982
	(Leg Wound – Casevac to Ajax Bay)	
Sapper McGuinness	San Carlos Bombing	27 May 1982
Mne W 'Mac' McGregor	Anti-Personnel Mine	13/14 June 1982
2/Lt Paul Allen	Anti-Personnel Mine	13/14 June 1982
Lance Corporal Hepburn	Wounded Sapper Hill	14 June 1982
Mne V I Comb	Wounded Sapper Hill	14 June 1982
Cpl Trevor Lee	Anti-Personnel Mine	15 June 1982

LCU F4

LCU F4 was one of the Landing Craft which transferred 40 Commando from *Canberra* to HMS *Fearless*. The crew saved Dave Sturgess from 40 Commando who had fallen between *Canberra* and the landing craft. They were also the home to Recce Troop onboard HMS *Fearless* prior to the landings in San Carlos:

C/Sgt B R Johnston QGM RM
Sergeant R J Rotheram RM
Marine R D Griffin RM
Marine A J Rundle RM
Mechanical Engineering Artificer (Propulsion) 1 A S James
Leading Marine Engineer (Mechanical) D Miller

Returning the Fallen

The question of return of British fallen is always a sensitive one and the families of the fallen were given a choice. The servicemen killed in action could either be buried in a military cemetery at San Carlos on the Falkland Islands or be repatriated for burial in the UK. Families of those who were buried on the Falkland Islands or had died at sea would be offered the opportunity of visiting the Falklands at public expense. Most of the families elected to have their loved ones returned to the UK for burial. In late October John Knott attended a ceremony at a new permanent cemetery for the 16 fallen whose family had chosen for them to remain on the Falkland Islands, at a site in San Carlos overlooking 3 Commando Brigade's landing point. After a helicopter salute and a pipers' lament another 65 fallen sailed for home onboard RFA *Sir Bedivere* (one to Hong Kong). A wreath was thrown into the sea in memory of the 174 who had died at sea.

In February 1983, the cemetery for the Argentine dead was consecrated at a site close to Goose Green. It took until 1991 before the first significant visit of Argentine relatives to the site. In the Falkland Islands several memorial sites mark lives lost in the conflict. In Port Stanley a Liberation Monument was erected just outside Government House and unveiled on 14 June 1984, exactly 2 years after the Argentine surrender.

The South Atlantic Fund was established for donations to meet the needs of the armed forces, associated civilian personnel and respective dependents who had suffered distress during the conflict. By the time it was closed at the end of 1992 it had received £15.25 million, made up of more than 400,000 separate donations, and as a result of investments had been able to disburse £16.6 million leaving a residual sum of £3 million to be handed over to the single service benevolent funds to meet future needs.

Appendix II

Updates

Mention in Despatches

Captain A. R. Pillar, 40 Commando RM
On the night of 13 June 1982 on the Island of East Falkland, 40 Commando Royal Marines were advancing on the Sapper Hill feature, 3 kilometres to the west of Port Stanley. Captain Pillar was commanding the leading company when they became entrapped in an unmarked anti-personnel minefield and subjected to sporadic enemy artillery fire. Despite a danger to his own person from continuing explosions, Captain Pillar returned through the minefield to organise the evacuation of casualties from the rear of his Company. His presence and calm example gave the Company confidence throughout a long dangerous night. For his fine leadership, courage and resolve, Captain Pillar is recommended for Mention in Despatches.

London Gazette Supp. 49134, page 12842
National Archive file WO373/188/198

LMA G. Black
On the night of 13 June 1982 on the Island of East Falkland, 40 Commando Royal Marines were advancing on the Sapper Hill feature, three kilometres to the west of Port Stanley. Leading elements became entrapped in an unmarked anti-personnel minefield and a number of casualties were incurred. Showing a complete disregard for his own safety, Leading Medical Assistant Black, Royal Navy, went into the minefield to treat the wounded. His calm professional manner and bravery inspired and calmed the men around him. His actions undoubtedly saved lives. Leading medical assistant Black is recommended for Mention in Despatches.

London Gazette Supp. 49134, page 12843
National Archives file WO373/188/213

Liberation Day in the Falkland Islands
14 June has been a public holiday in the Falkland Islands since 1984, officially called "Liberation Day".

Wood for the Fallen
On Portsdown Hill, a chalk ridge that overlooks Portsmouth harbours and the Isle of Wight, opposite the Churchillian pub, there is a small, wooded area. In December 1982, to commemorate the British War Dead from the campaign, a Falklands Memorial Plantation consisting of 258 Beech trees – one for each serviceman and civilian killed – was planted near the top of Portsdown. The dedication ceremony was carried out on 6 December 1982 by Lt. Col. Sir James Scott Bt. Lord Lieutenant of Hampshire. The trees were donated by the Tree Council.

Landmines

The Argentines laid around 25,000 mines in approximately 119 minefields, covering a total of 12 square miles of the Falklands. In early November 2020, the Falkland Islands were finally declared mine free. Over the weekend of 16 November 2020, residents flocked to see the final mines left by Argentine forces on Gypsy Cove and Yorke Bay being detonated, ridding the islands of a key reminder of the conflict. Efforts to remove the mines in the Falkland Islands had been underway since 2009. Demining teams from Zimbabwe were recruited to assist UK companies with the disposal, working in the challenging weather conditions of the windswept islands.

HMS *Hermes*

It was announced on 6 October 2020 that HMS *Hermes* had reached her final destination – the breakers' yard. Construction of HMS *Hermes* began when the Second World War was still raging, and she launched in the year the Queen was crowned. HMS *Hermes* had been on the verge of retirement when she was suddenly called into service, facing threat of Exocet missile attacks as she led the Task Force in the South Atlantic in 1982.

Four years after the conflict, HMS *Hermes* was sold to the Indian Navy, renamed INS *Viraat* (*Giant*) and helped mount a blockade against Pakistan in 1999. Now, 67 years after her launch, the elderly aircraft carrier was sailed to the ship's graveyard in Alang, Gujarat, to be broken up for scrap. Schemes to make her a museum or a sunken diving centre came to nothing, and a crowdfunding bid to bring her home to England failed.

Sir Tristram

Immediately following the end of the conflict, *Sir Tristram* was towed to Port Stanley, where she was used as an accommodation ship. *Sir Tristram* then returned to the United Kingdom in 1983 on the heavy lift ship, the MV *Dan Lifter* and was extensively rebuilt. Following the rebuild, *Sir Tristram* re-entered active service in 1985, and saw service in the Gulf War, and the Balkan conflicts of the 1990s. *Sir Tristram* supported relief operations for Hurricane Mitch off Central America. In 2000 *Sir Tristram* was deployed to Sierra Leone in support of British operations there, followed by a cruise to the Baltic Sea in support of MCMVs. Early 2001 saw *Sir Tristram* return to Sierra Leone to take over from *Sir Percival* as the ship supporting British forces ashore there. In 2003 *Sir Tristram* was deployed as part of the largest British fleet for 20 years in support of the invasion of Iraq. *Sir Tristram* was decommissioned on 17 December 2005 but continues to be used for training purposes by UK Special Forces Group.

Sir Galahad

On 21 June, the hulk of *Sir Galahad* was towed out to sea by the RMAS Tug *Typhoon* and sunk by HMS *Onyx* using torpedoes; it is now an official war grave, designated as a protected place under the Protection of Military Remains Act. *Sir Galahad*'s bell has been placed in The Falkland Islands Memorial Chapel, Pangbourne, Berkshire.

A replacement ship entered service in 1988, carrying the same name and pennant number.

San Carlos Today

Today, the settlement does not look that different except for the cemetery. The site of 3 Commando Brigade Headquarters bunkers gouged out of a bed of gorse, can be clearly identified. Settlement farm buildings still show many signs of the military presence. The floor of the shearing shed has hundreds of small black circles where troops had used their hexi cookers. Pat Short, the settlement manager, had previously said that he will never paint over the signs, nor will he fill in the large pits nearby once occupied by 79 Battery's guns. These will be left partly for the interested visitors and partly because the pits are the right size and shape to provide shelter for sheep at lambing time. The Short household still has a strong interest in the war and four kittens were called Harrier, Lynx, Wessex and Tibbitats – though at the time Sea King and Vulcan were under consideration for Tibbitats

Appendix III

40 Commando Reunion Letter

The following letter was sent to the Commanding Officer with the following Memorandum:

From OC D
To CO
Dated 24 May 82

1. The att letter has recently been sent on to me by DCGRM, to whom it was originally forwarded.
2. Unfortunately, we haven't been able to trace the secretary or organiser of the reunion, so we haven't got an address to which we can reply.
3. However, I thought you might like it to hang in the CP!
4. Best of luck, but wish we were with you.

Signed MJM

40 RM COMMANDO Reunion – Porchester Hall

The Commanding Officer
40 RM Commando   24th April 1982

Sir,
We, the undersigned, being members of 40 R.M. Commando during the war years, gather together at the Commando Reunion in London, send our sincere best wishes to you, the officers and men of 40 R.M. Commando.

We are confident you will uphold the honour and tradition of the Royal Marines and of the 40 R.M. Commando in the difficult days that may lie ahead.

[The letter is signed by several members of the unit present at the reunion]

Appendix IV

Op Order 1/82

Op Order 1/82, issued in May of 1982 should not be confused with LFFI Op Order 1/82 issued by hand in San Carlos on 01 June 1982. Noted below are two options for the retaking of the Falklands, one in Berkley Sound just north of Stanley, and the actual one at in San Carlos.

OpO 1/82 issued May 1982 from HQ 3 Commando Brigade RM HMS Fearless

Friendly Forces
Land: 5 Brigade to reinforce by May 82
Sea: TF 317.8 and TG 317.0 support the land force until May 82
Air:
(a) Twenty Sea Harriers embarked HMS Hermes and Invincible for air defence, maritime attack and ground attack
(b) Eight Sea Harriers and Six GR3 replacement aircraft in Atlantic Conveyor

Execution
a/ General Outline:- 2 phases, Phase 1 land one Commando by LCU, secure COW BAY and VOLUNTEER BEACH and established a beach head. The Landing Force (LF) moves ashore by LCU and helicopter into beach head. Phase 2 launch successive cdo/btn hel assaults from the beach head to secure JOHNSON HARBOUR SETTLEMENT (JHS), PORT LOUIS SETTLEMENT (PLS), URANIE BAY BEACH and LONG ISLAND – MOUNT LOW ridge line.

40 Cdo RM
Phase 1:
(a) Land by LCU and secure COW BAY and VOLUNTEER BEACH. Establish a beach head and prep def posns
(b) Clear MOUNT BRISBANE and secure fire base for 79 Battery in area grid 3695
[Handwritten note]:
Secure? Or defend? See RHG/D Ph2 (a)
Phase 2:
(a) Continue prep of def posns
(b) Provide one company at 30 minutes notice as Brigade Reserve.

42 Cdo RM
Phase 1:
Secure fire base for 8 with one company helicopter in area grid 3691
Be prepared 30 minutes notice to move helicopter to reinforce initial M & AW Cadre screen on LONG ISLAND – MOUNT LOW ridge line

Phase 2:

(a) on order land by LCU over VOLUNTEER Beach. Move to LS ... . including company from 8 Battery fire base.

(b) On order moved by helicopter from LS ... . to reinforced screen on LONG ISLAND – MOUNT LOW ridge.

45 Cdo RM

Phase 1: In reserve

Phase 2:

(a) order land by LCU over VOLUNTEER Beach and move to LS ... .

(b) On order secure URAINE BAY, LONG ISLAND Mountain, and HORSESHOE PADDOCK by helicopter assault.

(c) Establish defensive positions in same area.

2 Para

Phase 1: On order land by LCU over COW BEACH and move to LS ... ...

Phase 2:

(a) On order secure PLS by hel asslt

(b) Est def posn around PLS.

3 Para

Phase 1: On order land by LCU over VOLUNTEER BEACH and Move to LS ... .

Phase 2:

(a) On order secure JHS by hel asslt

(b) Est def posn around JHS

(c) Secure fire base for 29 Battery and 7 Battery in areas grid 2894 and 2895

RHG/D

Phase 1

(a) Land by sea at COW BAY and VOLUNTEER BEACH

(b) Provide initial fire sp to Cdos during beach assault operations

Phase 2

(a) Exploit forward from beach head and sp screen in areas grid 3495 and 3498

[Handwritten note has been added to the document] *Bad Going?*

(b) Be prepared to sp subsequent helicopter assault ops on order

29 Cdo Regiment

Phase 1

(a) 79 Bty deploy to area grid reference 3695 and sp 40 Cdo RM

(b) T Battery provide AD cover for beach head with two tps

(c) Deploy 8 battery in area grid reference 3691

Phase 2

(a) 79 and 8 Battery provide fire sp to 3 PARA during assault on JHS

(b) When JHS secure deploy 7 and 29 Bty to area grid reference 2894 and 2895

(c) 7, 8, 29 and 79 Battery provide fire sp to 2 PARA during assault on PLS. [on the document 8 & 79 are crossed off]

(d) 7, 8, 29 and 79 Battery provide fire sp to 45 Cdo RM during assault on URANIE BAY area. [on the document 8 and 79 are crossed off]

(e) 8 Battery [79 Battery also pencilled in later] provide fire sp to 42 Commando RM whilst Ops estb on LONG ISLAND to MT LOW RIDGE line

(f) T Bty provide AD cover with one tp over URAINIE BAY, JHS and PLS. Redeploy tps with 40 Cdo on order, to re-join bty and provide add AD cover to URAINIE BAY complex.

59 Independent Commando Squadron

Phase 1

(a) Clear beach area of obstructions and explosive devices

(b) Clear and mark route off beaches for CVRT

(c) On order withdraw from beach head

Phase 2

(a) Be prepared to clear and mark routes at URANIE BAY beach

(b) Clear mines, obs and explosives as required

(c) On order be prepared to set up bde sp facilities including water pts, Harrier/Hel Pads, EFHE and preparations of def posns.

3 Cdo Bde Air Sqn

Phase 1

(a) A Flt to provide two 2 Gz (SNEB) in DS of 29 Cdo Regt and one Gz (SNEB) in DS of 612 TACP for fire sp direction and coord, and GPO recces.

(b) B Flt to provide one Sc (recce) in DS of Bde Comd, two 2 Sc (ATGW) in DS 40 Cdo RM and three 3 (ATGW) at 15 mins notice to move.

(c) On order C flt to provide two 2 Gz (N+SNEB) in DS of 846 and 848 NAS for escort and protection.

(d) M flt to provide two 2 Gz (SNEB) in DS of 40 Cdo on order, one GZ (SNEB) in DS of 42 Cdo for move ashore.

(e) On order, 656 Sqn AAC det to provide one Sc (recce) in DS of 2 Para and 3 Para respectively for mov ashore and to be prep at 30 mins notice to mov for ATGW ops in sp of B flt.

Phase 2

(a) A Flt to provide two Gz (SNEB) in DS of 29 Cdo regt for fire sp direction and GPO recces, and one Gz (SNEB) in DS of 40 Cdo RM coy in res.

(b) On order, B flt, M flt, and 656 Sqn AAC det to provide ac in DS of unit ops as follows

i.   Bde comd – One Sc (recce)

ii. 3 Para hel asslt on JHS two 2 Sc (ATGW), two 2 Gz (SNEB)

iii. 3 Para secure fire base at GR2894 and GR2845 – two 2 Sc (ATGW/recce)

iv. 2 para hel asslt on PLS – two 2 Sc (ATGW), two 2 Gz (SNEB)

v.   2 Para to estb def posn at PLS – two 2 Sc (ATGW/recce)

vi. 45 Cdo hel asslt URAINE BAY, LONG ISLAND Mt and HORSESHOE PADDOCK – two 2 Sc (ATGW), two 2 Gz (SNEB)

vii. 45 Cdo estb posn in same area as 'vi' above two Sc (ATGW)

viii. 42 Cdo hel asslt to renifice screen on LONG ISLAND Mt LOW ridge line – two Sc (ATGW), two Gz (SNEB)

(c) C flt – no change Phase 1

(d) All flts be prep airborne FAC and AOP tasks

(e) All flts be prep to estb FARPS (ATGW and SNEB) ashore

(f) B flt and 656 AAC det to maintain between then two Sc (ATGW) at 30 mins notice to move throughout.

1 RSRM

H – 12(?) provide 10 x RRC at … … … … . Beach. Pick up M&AW Cadre and 42 Cdo Recce Tp and insert at … … … … Beach

Phase 1 – Nil

Phase 2

Be prepared for exfiltration tasks on order

M & AW Cadre

H – 12 Land at … … … … . Beach by RRC with Recce tp 42 Cdo move to LONG ISLAND – Mt LOW ridge line and est Ops to cover likely en approaches fm the South.

Phase 1

Mark and secure two LS for 42 Cdo

Phase 2

Provide sp to 42 Cdo during hel landing and mov to def posns on LONG ISLAND – Mt LOW ridge line.

AD Tp

Initially provide coord AD with five sects for beach head. As Cdos/bns pass through beach head deatch sects in accordance with Task Org and provide AD as ordered.

Sects are to move by hel.

846 NAS (SK)

Phase 1

(a) Lift 79 Bty to GR3695 with six SK

(b) Lift AD Bty (-) to bridge head with four SK

(c) Lift Coy 42 Cdo to GR3691 with six SK

(d) Lift 8 Bty to GR3691 with ten SK

(e) Deploy MACT as required

Phase 2

(a) Lift 3 Para fm LS … … … … .. to JHS with ten SK

(b) Lift 7 Bty fm LS … … … … .. to GR2894 with ten SK

(c) Lift 29 Bty fm LS … … … … to GR2895 with ten SK

(d) Lift 2 Para fm LS … … … … … . To PLS

(e) Lift 45 Cdo fm LS … … … … … .. to URANIE BAY LS

(f) Lift remainder AD bty LSL to URANIE BAY complex with four SK

(g) On order lift 42 Cdo (-) fm LS … … … … .. to LONG ISLAND MT – Mt LOW ridge line with ten SK

(h) Lift AD Bty (-) fm bridge head to URANIE BAY Complex

848 NAS (Wx)
Phase 1
(a)   Provide four Wx to sp two SKs back-up
(b)   Provide two Wx for casevac ammo resup
Phase 2 – No change

Option 2 is San Carlos

Port San Carlos / Ajax Bay Option
Execution General Outline. (Four Phases).
Phase 1 secure PORT SAN CARLOS by helicopter and beach assault with one Cdo.
Phase 2 secure SAN CARLOS Settlement by hel and beach assault with one Commando.
Phase 3 secure AJAX BAY complex by hel and beach assault with one Cdo.
Phase 4 estb def pon with one Commando on reverse slope SUSSEX mt.
After a series of detailed tasks as to who and what is to be deployed where there follows a
description of the AJAX BAY and SUSSEX Mountain areas.

Op O 2/82

Issued 12 May 1982 from HQ 3 Commando Brigade RM HMS Fearless
Mission
To land at PORT SAN CARLOS / AJAX BAY complex and establish a beach head from which to launch the offensive operations.

Execution General Outline
Silent landing in 3 phases.
Phase 1
Simultaneous beach asslt by two Cdos to secure SAN CARLOS settlement and AJAX BAY complex.
Phase 2
Land two bns concurrently to secure PORT SAN CARLOS settlement and a defensive position on the reverse slope of SUSSEX Mt.
Phase 3 heli move ashore of arty and AD to cover beach
[Notes scribbled on documents vary as follows]

'As quick and silent as pos'
'Landing not end in itself – merely the beginning'
'Press on past enc as fine discipline in def don't allow en draw fire'
'NP8901 Paca [illegible]'

40 Commando RM
Phase 1
a)   Land by LCU over BLUE ONE beach and secure SAN CARLOS settlement
b)   Estb def pos on reverse slope of VERDE Mts GR 6086 and ROCKY Mts GR 6183
c)   Clear position or 79 Bty GR5985 and LITTLE RINCON GR 5884
d)   Provide one coy to secure blocking posn and FUP/SL area for 2 PARA in valley bottom GR 6080 until completion of Phase 2
e)   Estb Bde OP screens with recce tp as detailed in annex C
f)   Limit of exploitation (less screen positions) 62 Easting
Phase 2 and 3
No change

45 Commando RM
Phase 1
a)   Land by LCU over RED Beach and secure AJAX BAY complex
b)   Clear gun posn for 8 Bty area GR5684 and NW quarter GR 5683
c)   Establish def posn on reverse slope high ground West of AJAX BAY
d)   Estb Bde OP screen with recce tp as detailed in annex C

e)   Limit of exploitation (less screen positions) 54 Easting
Phase 2 and 3
No change

2 Para
Phase 1 Nil
Phase 2
a)   Mov ashore by LCU across BLUE TWO beach and mov to FUP/SL GR 6080
b)   Clear gun posn for 29 Bty area GR 6082
c)   Clear fwd to SUSSEX Mt ridge. Limit of exploitation (less screen positions) 78 Northing
d)   Estb def posn reverse slope SUSSEX Mt feature GR 5978
e)   Estb Bde OP screen with ptl coy as detailed in annex C
Phase 3
No change

3 Para
Phase 1 Nil
Phase 2
a)   Land by LCU you over GREEN beach and secure PORT SAN CARLOS settlement
b)   Clear gun posn for 7 Bty area GR 6092
c)   Estb def pon reverse slope SETTLEMENT ROCKS GR 6293 to WINDY GAP GR 6493
d)   Estb BdeOP screen with ptl company as detailed in annex C
e)   Limit of exploitation (less screen positions) 95 Easting Northing
[Easting has been scrubbed out and Northing added on documents. Not clear if this was a change in plan or typing error]
Phase 3
No change

42 Commando RM
Phase 1-3
a)   Remain as res afloat
b)   Cdo to be at 30 minutes notice to mov from H hour
c)   Be prep to reinforce the beachhead or other tasks by hel and craft on order

B Sqn RHG/D
Phase 1
a)   Land one troop by LCU with 40 Cdo over BLUE ONE beach
b)   Provide fire sp from LC during assault if required
c)   Exploit fwd in beach head and provide fire sp if required and obsn to 40 Cdo incl coy blocking posn GR 6080
Phase 2
a)   Land one tp by LCU with 3 PARA over GREEN Beach
b)   Provide fire sp from LC during asslt if required
c)   Exploit fwd in the beach head and provide fire sp if required and obsn to 3 PARA

29 Commando Regiment
Phase 1 Nil
Phase 2 Nil
Phase 3
a)   Deploy 79 Bty by hel to gun posn GR 5985
b)   Deploy T Bty by Hel to provide AD cover to beach head (detailed locations in annex C)
c)   Deploy FDC by hel to area GR 5683
d)   Deploy 29 Bty by Hel to gun posn GR 6082
e)   Deploy 8 Bty by Hel to gun posn GR 5684
f)   Deploy 7 Bty by Hel to gun posn GR 6092

59 Independent Commando Squadron
Phase 1
a)   Clear beach areas of obs and explosive devices
b)   Clear and mark routes off BLUE ONE and GREEN beaches for CVR(T)
c)   Assist cdos/bns with clearance of obs and explosive devices in def areas
d)   Advise and assist prep cdo/bns def posns
Phase 2
No change
Phase 3
No change to phase 1 and 2 except on order to be prep to set up bde sp facilities incl WP, hel/Harrier pads and EFHE

3 Cdo Bde Air Sqn RM
Phase 1
a)   Provide one Gz (SNEB) in DS of Bde Comd and one Gz (SNEB) in DS of 29 Cdo Regt for fire sp direction and co-ord
b)   Provide one Sc (Recce) in DS of Bde Comd, two Sc (ATGW/Recce) in DS of 40 Cdo from first lt and two Sc (ATGW/Recce) in DS of 45 Cdo from first lt
c)   On order provide two Gz (SNEB) in DS of 846 NAS and 848 NAS for escort and protection from first lt
d)   Provide two Gz (SNEB) in DS of 42 Cdo from first lt
Phase 2
No change except
(a) Provide two Sc (ATGW) in DS of 2 PARA from first lt and two Sc (ATGW/Recce) in DS of 3 PARA from first lt
Phase 3
No change except
(a) Provide one Gz (SNEB) in DS of 29 Cdo regt for GPO recces from first lt
(b) On order provide one (ATWG/SNEB) FARP in 40/45 Cdo TAOR and one (ATGW/SNEB) FARP in 2/3 Para TAOR
(c) Be prep for airborne FAC AOP tasks
(d) Be prep to estb FOB's ashore when ordered

1 RSRM

Phase 1 and 2

Nil Change

Phase 3

(a) Estb FOB ashore in area SAN CARLOS settlement GR 5984

(b) From first lt provide four RRC each to 40 Cdo, 45 Cdo and 3 PARA for ptl, liaison, resup and casevac tasks as required

(c) From first lt provide 4 RRC to 2 PARA for liaison, resup and casevac tasks as reqd
     [This section is handwritten in orders and not part of the original order]

M & AW Cadre

Phase 1

(a) Land LCU with 40 Cdo RM

(b) Remain in 40 Cdo's TAOR and prepare for future tasks

Phase 2-3

No Change

On Completion of Phase 3

(a) At last lt move four teams by hel to drop off point GR UC 9079

(b) Move to LUP and estb mobile OP's in area WHITES Mt GR UC 8779, Mt SIMON GR UC 9478, EVELYN HILL GR UC 9782, BULL HIL GR UC 8583

(c) Observe and report all en ground and air mov, incl DOUGLAS Settlement GR UC 8899, and TEAL Inlet GR VC 0087

(d) Ptl duration seven days. Extraction after last lt on D+7

AD Tp RM

Phase 1-3

(a) Provide co-ord AD cover for beach head in accordance with task org and as ordered

(b) Sects are to mov by LCU with support unit, resup of msls by hel at first lt.

846 NAS (Sea King)

Phase 1

Nil

Phase 2

HMS Hermes det be prep to disembark on order

Phase 3

(a) Resup Blowpipe msls and mor ammo to each cdo/bn LS

(b) Lift 79 Bty to GR 5985

(c) Lift FDC to GR 5683 (on call serials)

(d) Lift T Bty to designated locs

(e) Lift RRB to GR 5395

(f) Lift 29 Bty to gun posn GR 6082

(g) Lift 8 Bty to gun popsn GR 5684

(h) Lift 7 Bty to gun posn GR 6092

(i) Lift addl cdo/bn mor ammo as required

(j) Deploy MAOTs as required

(k) On order fly pers bde Tac HQ ashore

(l) On order fly D Gp ashore

848 NAS (Wessex)
Phase 1-2
Nil
Phase 3
(a) Provide one Wx for casevac and one for ammo resup
(b) On orders fly BAS FARPs ashore
(c) Provide two Wx in gunship role

3 Cdo Bde HQ and Sigs Sqn RM
Phase 1-3
(a) Estb HQ B in the AOR HMS Fearless
(b) Be prep to deploy TAC HQ by Hel and BV 202 by LCU
(c) Be prep on order to deploy recce party ashore for HQ B
(d) Be prep on order to deploy HQ B by LCU over BLUE ONE beach

Cdo Log Regt
Phase 1-2
Nil
Phase 3
(a) Provide second line sp from log LSLs as required
(b) Estb FDS ashore
(c) Be prep to estb fwd BMA ashore
CINCFLEET issued the Operational Order 3/82 (Operation SUTTON.) The mission was *to repossess the Falkland Islands as quickly as possible.*
Operations were to be in the following phases:-
Phase 1
CTG 318.8 to maintain a blockade within the TEZ (Total Exclusion Zone)
Phase 2
CTG 317.8 to conduct SF recce and direct-action tops prior to the main landing
Phase 3
CTG 317.0 (COMAW) with TU 317.1.1 (3 Commando Brigade) embarked conduct main amphibious landing (including MCM Ops) (Mine Counter Measures)
Phase 4
Landing Ops by TU 317.1.1 prior to arrival of CTG 317.1 (Commander Land Forces Falkland Islands) (CLIFFI) and TU 317.1.2 (5 Infantry Brigade)
Phase 5
Establishment CTG 317.1 (CLIFFI) in HMS Fearless and Landing of TU 317.1.2
Phase 6
Repossession of the Falkland Islands by TG317.1 (Landing Forces) supported by TG 317.8 and TG 317.0
The plan for the main landings was now set for the retaking of the Islands from the Argentine Occupiers.
The criteria affecting the choice of beach were
(a) Good approaches for landing craft helicopters with an easterly position to minimise the air threat

(b) An area in which ships were least vulnerable to submarine attack. This is the reason that had led to the choice of San Carlos over Mare Harbour which offered good, sheltered landing but little cover. This would be used for the deception plan, and Berkley Sound would be a bold move and would shock the enemy, but it was high-risk because of the energy deployments and minefields laid off the Sound.

Appendix VI

Capture and Questioning of Captain De Corveta 27 May 1982

A report into the incident is located within the official papers for 40 Commando. A shortened version of this seven-page document is as follows:

It was not long after objectives had been secured and company positions sited, that the FOO party attached to B Company, 40 Cdo RM, moved further east and established its OP position of the forward, eastern slope of the San Carlos feature. The four-man FOO party commanded by Captain R Jenkins of 29 Ind Cdo Regt RA, recorded his position as grid 610844. To the east lies the low undulating ground of the inner Verde while to the south a large re-entrant attempted to divide the ridge line. To the rear, and to the west, were the defensive reverse slope positions of B Company.

It was about mid-afternoon on the 27 May 82, one of the FOO party moved in rear of their position to find a suitable toilet area. On moving through a small rock outcrop, he thought he caught sight of a lone figure, and he immediately went back for assistance. Capt Jenkins returned with the member of the FOO party and caught sight of the lone figure and challenged him. On hearing their voice, he froze and threw down his weapon.

The incident was logged as 1735 hours and at the same time a pickup patrol led by Sgt P Kay of B Coy, was dispatched, with orders to make a search of the area then deliver the prisoner to Cdo HQ in San Carlos Settlement. The patrol checked the prisoner in silence and general area and noted that the unprepared position which had been occupied by the prisoner, there was a clear view stretching from Sussex Mountain through west to Ajax Bay, and closer to him a view of the San Carlos settlement and the area occupied by 3 Cdo Bde RM. He could not see the company positions on the reverse slope.

The prisoner tied and blindfolded was led pace for pace to Cdo HQ where, after a confused press reception the prisoner handling procedure was allowed to continue. On completion of the handover the Int Sect removed the prisoner to a small, corrugated iron shed alongside the jetty at San Carlos. A strip search was instigated and on finding his badge of rank confirmed that he held the rank of Lt Cdr in the Argentine Marines. A PRISREP was sent to Bde HQ with a reply that a rigid raider would be sent over to collect the prisoner for an interrogation at Ajax Bay. Meanwhile, a detailed search was made of his equipment but revealed nothing, likewise his initial questioning, in English only led to misinterpretation.

The rigid raider arrived at 1930 hours and the prisoner was escorted to the rigid raider at 1936 hours. En-route to the jetty the prisoner and escorts were forced to take cover as the scream of a Skyhawk aircraft filled the air, their target being the ground forces at San Carlos and Ajax Bay. Due to the air attack the situation was chaotic with exploding ammunition everywhere. The prisoner was eventually turned over to the RM Police and he took the journey to Ajax Bay.

Later that evening the following contact report was passed from C/S I to O

> 22:32 Contact 22:20 Hrs
> 3 people seen within my location at grid 612859.
> They were challenged and ran away in a SW direction.
> Three shots were fired at them one believed hit.
> The sound he made when hit was not English.
> 22:42 Possible enemy movement between C/S 2 and us engaging now.
> 22:45 We believe we flushed the enemy back over the saddle at grid 612857.

The follow up patrol at first found nothing to answer any of the obvious questions. A further piece of the puzzle came in the interrogation report which made no connection between the prisoner and the contact report. Doubts were thrown on the fact that the first positive air attack on the ground forces came shortly after his capture. Was this a coincidence or was he a FAC?

On the 08th June, during a routine clearance patrol a missile tailfin at grid 616843 was noticed. This was considered to be an Energa type projectile from an Argentine FAL. C/Sgt Stubbings (AE1) and Marine Jones were sent to look at and destroy it. Before destroying the projectile, they discovered, in the same hide a 9mm pistol, loaded, and made ready, and wrapped in 4x2. They also found 45 x 7.62 rounds, 6 x 9mm rounds and an Argentine chocolate bar wrapper.

A search of the area within a 300m radius of the find, discovered, very near, a curved hole in the ground caused by water action, about 3ft deep, 5ft long 3ft wide with diddle dee (red crowberry). The hole had not been modified but had obviously been used as a hide by 2-3 occupants. Was this hide used by the Lt Cdr who was captured on the 27 May 82 or by a patrol to gain information on the landings? The condition of the pistol strongly supported the first conclusion.

The final two pieces of the puzzle came from the Intrep and a signal. The Intrep dated 22 June 82 stated that a group of 5 marines, previously under the command of the Lt Cdr captured at San Carlos were apprehended walking back to Stanley. The signal made reference to the C/S I in San Carlos on the 27 May 82 read "On afternoon of 23 June 82 patrol by A Coy found 2 graves at stream junction 627862. One body in bank on south side, second on top bank, both badly decomposed, believe these dead as result earlier contact"

Both pieces of information fit but are they all from the same puzzle? Did Lt Cdr send six men back to Chata Hill, or did they lose one man to become the five captured walking back to Stanley. Why send the remainder of his patrol back whilst he continued alone? Was it the five who formed the OP party which brought in the air attack, between C/S I and 2's positions whilst looking at the Lt Cdr or possibly a second group of men probing our forward defences? Without more information the picture cannot be completed and doubtfully ever will.

Document relating to the questioning of 004082 CAPTAIN DE CORVETA (Maj / Lt Cdr) CAMILETTI

PERSONAL DETAILS

1 – DANTE JUAN CAMILETTI, born 31 Aug 1946 at MARIA TERESA, SANTA FE. Went through officer cadet school and has served 19 years in Marine Inf. Presently serving with Marine Det Stanley as 2I/C Det. Arrived 7/8 April aboard civilian FOKKER frm Puerto BELGRANO, where he had held an admin post for 2 ½ years. Married 3 children (2 M 1 F), family in PUERTO BELGRANO. PW and Capt MOERMANS are from ESTADO MAYOR (Staff HQ) BUENOS AIRES originally.

INFORMATION

2 – Left Stanley about dawn on Sun 23 Apr. 2 x HUEY helicopters carried eleven-man patrol to CHATA HILL. When they arrived, spent all day there then set off after dark for BOMBILLA HILL (10-11 Km distance). Arrived there 8-9am. Spent all day mon there observing but saw NTR. Left shortly after midday Tue heading 240 deg and arrived at location facing CERRO MONTIVIDEO about 0700 Wed. PW plus on Cpl then travelled along dorsal and remained some 2 hours, saw nothing, but when returning noted heli movement, carrying underslung loads (arty) at about 1230 hours, south to north of SAN CARLOS. After re-joining of patrols, sent 6 men, with SNCO in charge, with written report. These men were to descend to river, heading 180 deg then head 90 deg to eventually reach CHATA HILL. At about midnight he sent the other four members of the patrol back the same way. He himself then headed 240 deg, using the stars to guide him (Los Gemelos / Twins) and arrived at place of capture (VERDE RIDGE) about 0730. Remained there until caught (approx. 1700) observing ships but said he could see no troops.

3 – Had Night-vision aids (pragmatic) twin-visor type Swiss make. Said they went back with the others, as they had moisture between the lenses, and batteries almost exhausted. Range only about 50M, says he volunteered for this mission because he had little to do at Stanley. Used his rank to get the job! Radio carried was operated by Cpl (radio specialist). Type – RACAL 4031 HF coverage 2-30 MHZ, using nicle – Cadmium batteries. Freq used 3353 KHZ (day), 2242 KHZ (night 1700 – 0800). C/Ss VOLVO (Stanley Marine Det), CAMILO (patrol). Neither C/S nor freq changed. No authentication used. Reported direct to Captain De NAVIO MOERMANS. Whilst crossing RIO SAN CARLOS at about 1430 on Tue patrol buzzed by Harrier ac. Causing eqpt, including two radio batteries to be lost in the river. The one remaining battery, which was attached to the radio, lasted only for the next report (Tue), since when they had no comms with base. Comms not carried out at specific times, but once at night and once during day. Radio weighs about 4kg. All patrol members, inc PW take turns carrying it.

4 – All members were armed with FAL rifle and most had a pistol also. PW had 9mm Luger. Says he had not seen any Brit troops during travels, and only a few friendlies retreating from SAN CARLOS, but did notice some vehicles Wed heading 030 deg from SAN CARLOS.

5 – PW said he believed 10,000 to 12,000 troops in and around Stanley. Also, that there are 155mm (Hoffman)? Arty pieces. Harriers afraid to fly below 5,000 and in

consequence bombing haphazard, with civilian casualties, including some dead. Says Harrier pilot presently being held at hospital in Stanley after ejecting.

6 – Despite reporting by capturing troops, that PW had mentioned a car, he denies this (probably just misinterpretation, as he was only questioned in English initially).

7 – PW is still very fit and self-assured, I personally do not believe much of what he has said but require time to confirm this impression. He is very different from other PW taken up to now. Reckons he will return home disgraced, confident we have far too few troops to gain victory. Made several points about our treatment of him being considerably poorer than theirs to us. Generally, a tough nut to crack.

8 – Search of capture area, might, I feel, result in discovery of radio / night vision aid / extra equip. Desperately wants to smoke, and feels the cold badly.

9 – At about 0120 complained of irregularities in his heartbeat. Took him to doctor, who diagnosed palpitations / slight exposure. Continued questioning, at about 0200 having made him warmer.

10 – Other two PWs had surgery, unfit for questioning apart from basics. Did try a bit of 601/EC "GUEMES", but neither appeared to recognise the terms. Will pursue ASP.

PWs are

a.   Sgt PEDRO GALVAL (218302)
b.   Pte GERADO MORALES (16238902)
Both of 121 R Cdo Coy, Recce Sect

11 – Due to attack and presence of UXB, questioning had been erratic, to say the least. Have been unable to even consult notes / maps as working from dug out. Will "fill in" and expand info soonest. Please let IO 40 Cdo RM see this report or have a copy.

ADDITIONAL NOTE

PW denies all knowledge of Maj MARIO CASTAGNETO – likewise any notion of how to operate as FAC. As for extraction of patrol, this only possible, he says, CHATA HILL. Any trouble they ran in to from there on in was their own problem.

Says he was told when he left that he was the only patrol in that sector. He was to observe and report anything and everything, twice a day. Agree there has to be more to it than that, but PW wet, cold, miserable and sullen. Possibilities of improvement in results when we can improve conditions a bit.

Appendix VII

Official Account of San Carlos Bombing

An official document noting the Bombing of San Carlos is as follows:

At 1935 Hrs on 27 May 1982, Lt J B Dutton RM sent the following message from 40 Commando Command Post to the 3 Commando Brigade Headquarters: 'My location has just been bombed. There are casualties from 59 Commando Squadron Royal Engineers and B Echelon'. It transpired that the report was accurate.

Two Argentine aircraft were responsible for the raid. Their approach route was made at a very low altitude from the West. They appeared above the ridge which runs North and South to the West of Ajax Bay. Stooping low they continued across the water from a direction almost due West. The aircraft were flying on a similar bearing in close proximity to each other, almost wingtip to wingtip. Neither aircraft was more than 50 feet above the water.

The two Skyhawks released their payloads of two bombs each when very close to their target which appears to have been the prominent sheep shearing shed at San Carlos. The release of the bombs carried out simultaneous to the aircraft commencing their escape ascents.

The first bomb landed near the jetty, in the water, and failed to explode. The next bomb did explode and fell some 20 meters from the water on a bank which rises up from the beach. The third bomb landed between the sheep shed and the shore and caused the death of Mne McAndrews, 40 Commando Royal Marines. Finally, the last bomb fell some 50 meters beyond the shed and caused the death of Spr Gandhi of 59 Independent Commando Squadron Royal Engineers.

The bombs were accurately described by eyewitnesses as being some 4 feet in length, predominantly white in colour with a red nose cap and yellow band. They also possessed tail fins and were artificially decelerated in flight by trailing parachutes. On post incident investigation of the unexploded bomb, they were found to be a standard 250lb high explosive with impact fuses.

On completion of the raid, the aircraft continued heading West and disappeared beyond the Verde Ridge which is some 1000 meters from the settlement of San Carlos.

The attack on San Carlos was coincident with a raid of larger proportions on Ajax Bay to the West which caused five deaths and twenty wounded (Cdo Log Regt RM and 45 Cdo RM). The San Carlos attack caused five casualties, two deaths, those of Mne McAndrews and Spr Gandhi and three lesser injuries to Mne Jefferies, Mne Derrick and Spr McGuinness. The air attack occurred without warning.

Operation Order 1/82 (LFFI)
Issued June 1982

Written Front Page from Lt Col Stevenson HQ LFFI to 40 Commando

Delivered by Hand

Warning Order
1.   One company to fly tomorrow 9 June at 1200 hrsZ to GR 3881
2.   TASK – To defend 79 Battery Position
3.   79 Battery will start to fly in as soon as company lift is over
4.   LS will be secured by G Squadron SAS
5.   Length of task indeterminate – take rats for 3 days
6.   Coy to be placed under command of 3 Commando Brigade, to be nominated upon arrival on LS
7.   Sea Lion Island task now cancelled (handwritten note stating 'Nothing There')

[Actual movements and task came in a typed document which has been copied below]

2 MISSION
TO CAPTURE PORT STANLEY
3 EXECUTION

A. <u>GENERAL OUTLINE</u>. 3 PHASE ATTACK. PHASE 1 – 4 COMMANDO/ BATTALION NIGHT ATTACKS SECURE MOUNT HARRIET AND 2 SISTERS. PHASE 2 – 2 BATTALION ATTACKS TO SECURE TUMBLEDOWN MOUNTAIN AND MOUNT WILLIAM. PHASE 3 – SECURE SAPPER HILL. NGS BY NIGHT. CAP AND CAS BY DAY.

B. <u>3 CDO BDE RM – TASKS</u>
(1) PHASE 1 – SECURE MOUNT HARRIET AND 2 SISTERS IN 4 COMMANDO/BATTALION NIGHT ATTACKS. COMMAND HAS DISCRETION TO SECURE ADDITIONAL OBJECTIVES AS HE SEES FIT.
(2) PHASE 2 – SUPPORT 5 INFANTRY BRIGADE ATTACK ON TUMBLEDOWN MOUNTAIN AND MOUNT WILLIAM
(3) PHASE 3 – BE PREPARED ORDER TO SECURE SAPPER HILL.

C. <u>5 INF BDE – TASKS</u>
(1) <u>THROUGHOUT</u> MAINTAIN ONE COY IN DEF GOOSE GREEN / DARWIN

(2) <u>PHASE 1</u> SP 3 CDO BDE ATK MOUNT HARRIET AND 2 SISTERS

(3) <u>PHASE 2</u> SECURE TUMBLEDOWN MOUNTAIN AND MOUNT WILLIAM IN TWO BTN ATK

(4) <u>PHASE 3</u> BE PREP ON ORDER TO SECURE SAPPER

D. <u>40 CDO – TASKS</u>

(1) REMAIN RESPONSIBLE FOR COORDINATING GROUND DEFENCE OF FMA

(2) DET TO COMD 1 WG TWO RIFLE COYS

(3) MAINT ONE COY IN DEF PORT SAN CARLOS AIRSTRIP.

(4) UNTIL DEPLOYMENT 1 WG COY (NOT BEFORE 11 JUN) CDO LOG REGT AND FRHU TAKE OVER DEF AJAX

(5) MAINT ONE COY AT 12 HRS NTM TO ESTB UK PRESENCE ON WEST FALKLAND

E. <u>36 ENGR REGT – TASKS</u>

(1) PROVIDE CBT ENGR SP TO 3 CDO BDE AND 5 INF BDE. ONE FD SQN EACH

(2) PROVIDE ENGR SP TO FORCE.

F. <u>CDO LOG REGT RM – TASKS</u>

(1) CO-ORD LOG SP FROM FMA

(2) PROVIDE SP TO 3 CDO BDE RM

(3) USING FRHU AND OWN RESOURCES TAKE OVER AJAX

G. <u>SB SQN – TASKS</u>

(1) AS ALREADY TASKED IN WEST FALKLAND

(2) REATIN TWO PTLS AT 6 HRS NTM FOR FORCE TASKS.

B. <u>C SUPS TO BE HELD ASHORE AND AFLOAT</u>

(1) <u>UNIT FIRST LINE</u>

    (A) TWO DAYS AMMO LESS MOR AND ARTY. MAX MOR, ARTY TO BE CARRIED

    (B) TWO DAYS RATS

    (C) FULL TAMKS AND 2 CANS

(2) FWD BAAS – TWO DAYS STOCKS PHASE 1

(3) TWO DAYS STOCKS FOR THE FORCE FOR OP LESS PHASE 1

(4) FMA – FOUR DAYS STOCKS FOR THE FORCE

C. <u>MOV</u>

(1) <u>FMA TO FWD BAA'S / FWD FMA</u> – BY LSL, LCU AND HEL

(2) <u>FWD OF FWD BAA'S / FWD FMA</u> – BY HEL, CRAFT, VEH

(3) <u>HEL NETS</u> – ALL HEL CARGO NETS AND SLINGS ARE TO BE RETURNED TO FWD BAA'S / FWD FMA IMMEDIATELY UPON RESUP

D. <u>MED</u>
(1) ADS 3 CDO BDE FWD BMA TEAL CLOSES ON COMPLETION PHASE
1 . TO MDS FITZROY ON ORDERS THIS HQ
(2) MED 16 FD AMB OPENS FITZROY SETTLEMENT H HR (-24) PHASE 1
(3) MDS LOG REGT RM REMAINS OPEN AJAX BAY
(4) FMED – REMAINS FMA LESS DET ESTB FWD FMA H HR (-24) PHASE 1

E. <u>CASEVAC</u>
(1) <u>PHASE 1</u>
    (A) <u>3 CDO BDE RM</u> – THREE WX 5 AT ADS 3 CDO BDE FWD BMA
        TEAL FOR H HR (-4). EVAC TO ADS OR DIRECT TO MDS
        FITZROY SETTLEMENT OR AKAX BAY WHEN NEC.
    (B) <u>5 INF BDE</u> – THREE WX 5 AT MDS FITZROY SETTLEMENT
        FROM H HR (-4)
(2) <u>PHASE 2</u>
    (A) <u>FWD FMA</u> – THREE WX 5 AT MDS FITZROY SETTLEMENT
        FROM H HR (-4)
    (B) <u>FMA</u> – TWO WX 5 AT AJAX BAY FROM H HR (-4)
(3) PHASE 3 – AS FOR PHASE 2

F. <u>AVN FUEL</u>
(1) ALL LSLS TO DEPART FMA FULLY TOPPED UP
(2) MAX APFC's DEPLOYED TO DP ESTANCIA HOUSE PHASE 1.
THEREAFTER TO FWD FMA

G. <u>FUELS</u> – RESUP FROM FWD FMA BY UBRE AND CAN. FWD FMA
RESUP FROM AO

H. <u>REPAIR AND REC</u>
(1) <u>REPAIR</u>
    (A) PHASE 1 FRT 3 CDO BDE RM FWD BAA. FRG FWD FMA
    (B) PAHASE 2-3 FRG FWG FMA
(2) <u>PRI REPAIR</u>
    (A) LT GUNS
    (B) COMD VEH
    (C) CVRT
    (D) OTHERS

J <u>PW</u>
(1) AS HQ LFFI SOP 701
(2) MAIN CAGE FWD FMA OPENS PHASE 2 H HR
(3) INITIAL GD PROVIDE BY RM POLICE TP AND RMP

5 <u>COMMAND AND SIGS</u>
A <u>LOCS</u>
    (1) MAIN HQ REMAINS IN HMS FEARLESS

(2) TAC HQ (DORMANT) ESTB FWD AT FITZROY FROM 102359.
OCCUPATION BY CLIFFI ON AS REQUEST BASIS.
(B) <u>CEI</u> – ALREADY ISSUED AS ANNEX S TO OP/O 1/82
(C) <u>PASSWORDS</u>
[There followed a list of passwords and timings for the operation]
(D) <u>CODEWORDS</u>
[There followed a list of codewords and timings for the operation]
(E) <u>NICKNAMES</u>

<u>LOC</u>	<u>NAME</u>
WALL MT	TURBINE CIGAR
MT HARRIET	STILL CONCORN
TWO SISTERS	ROCK TRUNK
MT LONGDON	RECORD BILL
WIRELESS RIDGE	CHOP LINE
BEAGLE RIDGE	ABBEY SON
MT LOW	FLIGHT GLOW
TUMBLEDOWN MT	LEAF VEIN
MT WILLIAM	STRING CREASE
MOODY BROOK (THE STREAM)	RUBBER DUCK
SAPPER HILL	MIXED TREE
STANLEY COMMON	TWIN APART
STANLEY	MOTOR DROP
STANLEY AIRPORT	ATOM LUCK

6. <u>INSTRS</u> – ACK

Appendix IX

Surrender Document

The surrender document is on display at the Imperial War Museum in London. It is worth noting that the time of surrender was backdated three hours in order that both Zulu time (UTC) and the local time were recorded as 14 June even though technically it was already 15 June in London. This was to prevent possible confusion by Argentine troops who might have mistakenly thought that the surrender took effect the following day, 15 June 1982 and they would therefore still fight until that time.

Present at the signing of the letter of surrender were:

Captain Melbourne Hussey, Argentine Navy Translator
General de Brigada Mario Menéndez, Argentine Army
Vice Comodoro Carlos Bloomer-Reeve, Argentine Air Force
Vice Commodore Eugenio J Miari, Argentine Air Force, Senior Argentine legal advisor
Captain Rod Bell, Royal Marines Translator
Lieutenant Colonel Geoff Field, Royal Engineers
Colonel Brian Pennicott, Royal Artillery
Major General Jeremy Moore, Royal Marines
Colonel Mike Rose, Special Air Service
Colonel Tom Seccombe, Royal Marines
Staff Sergeant Glenn Harwood, Royal Signals

The letter of surrender read:

Headquarters, Land Forces
Falkland Islands

INSTRUMENT OF SURRENDER

I, the undersigned, Commander of all the Argentine land, sea and air forces in the Falkland Islands [Menéndez's signature, scribbled over the crossed-out word of "unconditionally"] surrender to Major General J.J. MOORE CB OBE MC as representative of Her Britannic Majesty's Government.

Under the terms of this surrender all Argentine personnel in the Falkland Islands are to muster at assembly points which will be nominated by General Moore and hand over their arms, ammunition, and all other weapons and warlike equipment as directed by General Moore or appropriate British officers acting on his behalf.

Following the surrender all personnel of the Argentinian Forces will be treated with honour in accordance with the conditions set out in the Geneva Convention of 1949. They will obey any directions concerning movement and in connection with accommodation.

This surrender is to be effective from 2359 hours ZULU on 14 June (2059 hours local) and includes those Argentine Forces presently deployed in and around Port Stanley, those others on East Falkland, [Menéndez's signature] West Falkland and all outlying islands.

[Menéndez's signature] Commander Argentine Forces
[Moore's signature] J. J. MOORE Major General
[Pennicott's signature] Witness
2359 hours 14 June 1982

Telegram Sent for notification of an Argentine Surrender:

FM TPS HEREFORD
TO CTF 317
         CTG 317.8
         CTG 317.0
         CTF 317.9
INFO   CTU 317.1.1
         CTU 317.1.2
UNCLAS
SIC 19F

THE FOL IS THE TEXT OF A MSG FROM 317.1 PASSED VIA HEREFORD TO ADDRESSEES ABOVE. MSG BEGINS

HQ LFFI PORT STANLEY. IN PORT STANLEY AT 9 O'CLOCK PM FALKLANDS ISLANDS TIME TONIGHT THE 14 JUNE 1982, MAJOR GENERAL MENENDES SURRENDERED TO ME ALL ARGENTINE ARMED FORCES IN EAST AND WEST FALKLAND, TOGETHER WITH IMPEDIMENTA. ARRANGEMENTS ARE IN HAND TO ASSEMBLE THE MEN FOR RETURN TO ARGENTINA, TO GATHER IN THEIR ARMS AND EQUIPMENT, AND TO MARK AND MAKE SAFE MUNITIONS. THE FALKLAND ISLANDS ARE ONCE MORE UNDER THE GOVERNMENT DESIRED BY THEIR INHABITANTS.
     GOD SAVE THE QUEEN

SIGNED J J MOORE
MSG ENDS

Relations between the UK and Argentina were not restored until 1989 and then it was only under a formula which states that the islands' sovereignty dispute will remain aside.

Appendix X

Sapper Hill Plaque

The following article has been reproduced by kind permission of Major Graham Adcock RM, (Retd), Editor of the Royal Marines Globe and Laurel Magazine:

The Welsh Guards had a Plaque placed upon a stone cairn on Sapper Hill in 2018, to commemorate the final part of the Falklands and to establish their part in removing an invading force from the islands. The plaque reads:

> At 1230z hours on the 14th June 1982, 1st Battalion Welsh Guards received orders from HQ 5 Infantry Brigade to attack Sapper Hill, the final ill overlooking Stanley. After a helicopter move forward the Battalion, with two companies from 40 Commando, Royal Marines under command, advanced on foot. Whilst C Company, 40 Commando came under fire, sustaining two casualties, the rest of the Battalion pressed on eventually seizing Sapper Hill at 1657z. Just after this, word came through that the Argentine forces had surrendered, and the war was over.

The memorial was funded by the Welsh Guards Charity, a memorial to commemorate the capture of Sapper Hill by the 1st Battalion Welsh Guards during the Falklands War was unveiled by His Excellency Mr Nigel Phillips CBE, Governor of the Falkland Islands on Wednesday 11th April 2018. Brigadier Rickett gave a short résumé of the Battalion's actions after the bombing of the *Galahad* and explained the reason for the memorial. He pointed out the part played by the Battalion in the final battles for Stanley culminating in the seizure of Sapper Hill, the nearest hill to Port Stanley itself.

However, this wording and what I saw as an embellishment on behalf of the Welsh Guards, also struck a chord with the remainder of 40 Commando in that the description of the events is incorrect. The then Company Commander of Charlie Company, 40 Commando, Captain, Now Brigadier, Andy Pillar thought it only right to put the record straight and he took it upon himself to address the matter with the Welsh Guards. Later, in the Royal Marines Magazine, the Globe and Laurel of September / October 2018 he wrote an article entitled '*Sapper Hill, 14 June 1982 – For the Record*' In this article he detailed the exact events of the day as well as briefly describing his discussions with the Welsh Guards and their then Commanding Officer, now Brigadier Johnny Rickett CBE. I have reproduced the article in full below:

Sapper Hill, 14 June 1982 – For the Record
Brigadier A Pillar OBE, former Coy Cdr, C Coy, 40 Cdo RM

On 11 April this year a Welsh Guards Memorial was unveiled on Sapper Hill. Commissioned and funded by the Welsh Guards Charity, the memorial is in the form of a cairn that features a plaque bearing the crest of the Welsh Guards, an inscription and Celtic across. The inscription relates to the action on Sapper Hill on 14 June 1982.

Whilst it is very positive to see important events marked for posterity, it is essential that they are described accurately and honestly and reflects the contributions of those involved. The action on Sapper Hill was a comparatively minor event that was nonetheless important, particularly to those involved. It was also noteworthy as the last engagement between British and Argentine forces before the declaration of a ceasefire. Unfortunately, no Royal Marine, serving or retired, as far as I can establish, was consulted or involved in the design and wording of the memorial and there was no Royal Marine representative at the unveiling and dedication of memorial. This is not just disappointing but offensive giving that at the time the action occurred more than half the Welsh Guards' Battalion's fighting strength comprised Royal Marine Commandos in the form of Alpha and Charlie companies of 40 Commando who had been placed under command after the Welsh Guards effectively lost 2 companies in the bombing of *Sir Galahad* at Bluff Cove. Furthermore, the only troops to engage with the Argentines and both inflict and sustain casualties during the action on Sapper Hill were Royal Marines, members of 9 Troop, Charlie Company, 40 Commando.

That aside, the real issue here is that the impression given of the events relating to Sapper Hill on 14 June 1982 by the wording on the plaque is largely erroneous. What follows in the next 3 paragraphs is a very brief account of what actually happened.

By 14 June the pace of events was accelerating rapidly, and British forces were closing in on Stanley. Sapper Hill was one of the few remaining objectives between them and the capital. At about midday on 14 June the Welsh Guards were ordered by HQ 5 Infantry Brigade to capture Sapper Hill. Charlie company was to be the first company flown forward to a point some 2.5 kms short of Sapper Hill with orders to spearhead a battalion advance and to exploit any opposition is encountered. Quick orders were given and 9 Troop on the 2Lt Carl Bushby was first to employing with orders to secure companies LS. 9 Troop was to be followed by C Company HQ and attachments and the balance of the company. The remainder of the battalion would subsequently be flown forward as helicopters become available. 2Lt Bushby's troop embarked in two Mark 5 Sea King helicopters, the normal role of which was ASW but given the pressing need for helicopter support, they had been stripped out to act as troop carriers. The LS was on the track which all had been briefed was mined on either side. Due to a map reading error by the leading pilot, the 2 aircraft flew to for forward landed at the foot of the objective, Sapper Hill. Whilst disembarking 9 Troop, both aircraft were hit by small arms fire but remained airworthy and flew back to pick up more troops. In plain view and within a few hundred metres of at least 2 companies of Argentine Marines and infantry dug in on Sapper Hill, 9 Troop took what cover it could and engage the enemy using all available firepower including two 66 mm shoulder launched anti-tank rockets. During the ensuing firefight, Mne Vince Comb, a GPMG gunner who was laying down suppressive fire received the GSW to the bicep and forearm and L/Cpl Alex Hepburn, a Sec 2ic sustained a shrapnel wound to the head.

Whilst 2Lt Bushby desperately tried to radio for artillery support, C Company HQ had been landed at the correct LS and realising what had happened, raced forward to join up with 9 Troop. 9 Troop's engagement, short but intense, lasted about 15 minutes in total after which firing from the Argentine positions petered out and troops on the hill could be seen disappearing over the crest and out of view down the reverse slope in the direction of Stanley. It was subsequently recorded in several different Argentine accounts that 3 Argentine soldiers were killed by incoming fire from 9 Troop and there were an unrecorded number of wounded. Providentially, the 'accidental' landing on Sapper Hill by 9 Troop and the aggressiveness in which they engage the Argentine positions not only appears to have this lodged the Argentine defenders but also convinced Brigadier General Joffre, the commander of the Argentine 10th Infantry Brigade (responsible for Sapper Hill) that further resistance was pointless. He apparently spoke to General Menendez and shortly after reports started trickling through of the appearance of white flags and an Argentine surrender.

By the time C Company HQ married up with 9 Troop, the firing had ceased and the casualties were being treated and prepared for evacuation. At this point the rest of the Battalion including Alpha Company and 2 Scimitars from the Blues and Royals, all of which had moved hastily along the track, joined with Charlie Company and together the unit pressed on the short distance to the summit of Sapper Hill. The vacated Argentine defensive positions were cleared without a shot being fired or any POWs being taken. Defensive areas were assigned, and the Battalion occupied Sapper Hill as 45 Commando arrived from the direction of Two Sisters. At about this time, reports came in confirming the Argentine high command had capitulated. The war was over.

So, contrary to the impression given by the wording on the memorial, the Battalion did not move forward by helicopter as a composite unit and then conduct an advance on foot. Nor did the Battalion press on to seize Sapper Hill whilst Charlie Company was under fire. As the above account makes clear, the only subunit to have contact with the Argentine defenders on Sapper Hill was 9 Troop of Charlie Company as a consequence of a pilot map reading error. The rest of the Welsh Guards Battalion including the balance of Charlie Company were geographically dislocated from 9 Troop's firefight. By the time the Battalion had made up the ground between its LS and 9 Troop's location, the fighting had ceased and the Argentines had fled their positions on Sapper Hill. Finally, Sapper Hill was not seized, it was merely cleared, occupied and secured.

Unsurprisingly therefore, when the memorial came to the attention of Op Corporate veterans of Charlie and Alpha Companies of 40 Commando there was reaction ranging from incredulity and indignation to unbridled anger at what some interpreted as an attempt to rewrite history. As the Company Commander of Charlie Company at the time, I took it upon myself to address the matter. I spoke with a number of close colleagues to confirm my own recollection of events. They included my fellow Company Commander of Alpha Coy, Shane Cusack, my erstwhile CSM, Bill Howie and Nick Holloway who had been troop Sergeant in 9 Tp. They all corroborated my version of events and were able to add some important detail. In May of this year, I wrote to the Regimental Adjutant of the Welsh Guards and was subsequently put in touch with Brigadier Johnny Rickett CBE who had been the CO of the Welsh Guards during the war and was, I learned, very much involved in the design and construction of the memorial. I made my case regarding the memorial and the plaque in particular and I insisted the wording should be changed, offering to help with any cost this might necessitate. There followed an exchange of emails as a result of which and undertaking had been given that the plaque will be replaced and the Welsh Guards would accept responsibility for this. The new plaque will bear the inscription shown below:

> At 1230z on 14 June 1982, the 1st Battalion Welsh Guards with A and C Companies of 40 Commando Royal Marines under command, received orders from HQ 5 Infantry Brigade to attack Sapper Hill, the final hill overlooking Stanley. During the Battalion's move forward by helicopter, 9 Troop of C Company, who had been landed to for forward, was involved in a sharp firefight and sustained two casualties. The Battalion pressed on rapidly linking up with this troop and secured Sapper Hill at 1657z. Just after this word came through that Argentine forces had surrendered and the war was over.

Despite the fact that this situation was totally avoidable, those responsible for the memorial have had the good grace to recognise a wrong has been done and have agreed to put it right. The new wording is not exactly as I would have wished it and although the difference is subtle, it is now a brief but accurate summary of events on 14 June 1982. Most importantly is recognises the involvement of 9 Troop specifically, even if it does not do sufficient justice to the courage and bravery with which it fought and the impact of this action on what was effectively the last line of Argentine resistance.

D Irving, Globe and Laurel September/October 2018

Appendix XI

Statement by the Commanding Officer

1. I have no doubt that during the journey South 40 Commando RM was very well prepared for any task that lay ahead of us in the Falklands. The Commando was fit, well-trained, mentally prepared and in a very high state of morale, spirit and motivation. This has shown through everything that has happened since.

2. Having been the first Royal Marines Commando to land on the Falklands we were disappointed to find ourselves holding the beach head as other units in the formation began the move towards Stanley. Nevertheless, every man continues to carry out his comparatively mundane task in a most efficient and well-motivated manner largely because Brig Thompson had repeatedly told us that we would be relieved on the arrival of 5 Inf Bde. Sadly, this was not to be as on his arrival CLIFFI ordered us to remain where we were at San Carlos to defend the FMA.

3. I was most unhappy about this change of plan and went to see General Moore in FEARLESS on 1 June to try to obtain a reversion of this decision. There was concerned about the effect the decision would have on an excellent morale of a good and well-motivated unit and on the long-term disciplinary effects (vis-à-vis the effect are nonparticipation in the battles to come would have on inter unit relationships in Plymouth). In addition, it was not my opinion that the units of 5 Inf Bde would be so well prepared for the task (later proved to be so in my view) and anyway I did not consider that this comparatively static task was making the best use of Commando troops. Having listened patiently to me, not surprisingly, Gen Moore did not change his plans.

4. There was considerable resentment in the Commando that this decision and it was to be reinforced later after 1 WG suffered appalling and sad casualties at Bluff Cove went rather than being relieved by 40 Cdo the unit, in fact, reinforced the battalion with 2 rifle companies.

5. Given the greatest disappointment and frustration which these events caused I have nothing but pride in, and admiration for, the way in which the junior leaders in the Commando did their job. Due to this morale of the Commando stood up very well and every man, in spite of everything, remained cheerful and efficient.

6. Following the surrender of Stanley, I drafted a letter to Gen Moore bringing his attention to the feelings in the Commando which were, at that time, running high and which continued for some time thereafter. However, following discussion with Brig Thompson it was decided that nothing would be gained by such action. But it was agreed that my feelings should be recorded in the Commander's Diary.

Signed M P J Hunt
Lt Col RM
CO
Dated 30 June 1982

Appendix XII

Letter to Relatives on Homecoming Arrangements

Headquarters
40 Commando Royal Marines
Seaton Barracks
Tavistock road
Plymouth
July 1982

Dear Everyone

Thank you all for being so patient, here at last is the answer to all your questions though unfortunately final confirmation will not be possible until Monday 12th July 1982!

In this letter I will attempt to summarize the arrangements which have been made to help you, the relatives, welcome 40 Commando Royal Marines home from the Falkland Islands. I have also taken the opportunity to include some news of the wife's club which is at the end of this letter.

I apologise to anyone who receives this letter but knows that their relative is not on the *Canberra*. By the time that you receive this letter I hope to have contacted all this involves and fortunately we are expecting all the members of the Commando back with the week – 10 – 17 July.

By now you all know that the RMS *Canberra* is due to dock back in Southampton at 1100 hours on the 11th July 1982 at berth 106, we are well aware that many of you will want to be there and the following arrangements have been made to help you.

We have considered two main forms of transport, coaches and private cars which are now being catered for; it is these arrangements that will be described first.

The main problem for those in private cars are parking and getting into the docks. The gate you need is number 20 and is signposted from the roundabout at the end of the M271, I am assured that there is plenty of space but advice that you arrive as early as you can. To get into the dock you will require a pass. This is simply a square piece of white paper or card on which you can draw a blue cross in the form of a plus sign (+). Unfortunately, our illustrator is away so we are unable to draw these ourselves, however this should not present too much of a problem to the more creative among you. It will be sensible also to take a letter with you (if you have been lucky enough to receive one) as further proof that you are meeting a particular member of the Task Force.

Those travelling on coaches have less of a problem but must first get to Seaton Barracks.

It is appreciated that for some this will be a problem on Sunday morning so coaches will be available at the following places.

0530 HORRABRIDGE –	at the junction of Town Farm Close and Chichester Road
0530 PLYMPTON –	Gateway Supermarket
0530 ST BUDEAUX –	Community Centre to call at junction of Budshed Road and Milford Lane
0530 TAVISTOCK FOLIOT –	NAAFI
0530 LOOSELEIGH –	Junction of Looseleigh Lane and Tamerton Foliot

All these will ferry passengers to Seaton Barracks, those with cars may park them at Seaton Barracks for the day.

Once on the coaches to Seaton you will be taken to Southampton, it will not be possible to stop other than for lavatorial facilities so you will need to take food and drink for the day, you will have to carry this with you as the coaches you return on will not be the one on which you travelled up.

At Southampton, whether in coaches or private cars, you will be directed to the area designated for 40 Commando relatives, from here you will be taken to the point of disembarkation as 40 Commando come ashore. Then you either accompany your relative to the coaches for the return journey together or return to your car. If you are intending to give your relative a lift back by car you must get him to Seaton Barracks by 0830 Monday 12 July 1982.

For those of you from Exmouth and Exeter we are providing a service from: -

0630 Exmouth –	FARMHOUSE, BRIXINGTON
0645 Exeter –	GRANADA SERVICES

For the return journey you will be able to get any coach for Exeter but only one will be returning to Exmouth, this will be clearly marked 40 Cdo RM EXMOUTH.

For all those travelling on coaches we will be providing guides from 40 Commando who will travel one between two coaches to help you with any problems you may have, they will then help to get you to the right area at the right time so please co-operate with them.

On return to Seaton Barracks we will marshal coaches to give as many as require it a lift home, this may be rather slow as we wait for people to get sorted out, however the wives' coffee shop and Naffi will be open for light refreshments. To catch a coach home simply move from the unloading area to the Education block and move to the classroom/ waiting room for your area. All the men will be required to parade in the barracks at 0830 on Monday 12 July 1982.

Anyone who can't make the trip to Southampton is very welcome to come and wait for the coaches at Seaton Barracks where the wife's coffee shop will be open from 1500 hours on the Sunday afternoon.

Finally, some information about the Wives' Club, below are listed the next meetings: -

Thursday 8th July 1982	Last informal morning coffee shop
Sunday 11th July 1982	Coffee shop open from 1500
Tuesday 13th July 1982	Last Tuesday meeting to formally close down the coffee shop all very welcome.

I have also been asked to tell you that the grand children's party planned for the 11th July 1982 has been cancelled for reasons unknown to me. And of course, don't forget there are still several places available for the trip to the Royal Tournament on 28th July, – Now the husbands are home you should have no problem arranging for the children to be looked after! £7 all-inclusive luxury coaches and ticket – too good to miss and too big for the screen! Absolutely the last word, whatever happens it probably wasn't what you expected, believe me, this way it's much more fun. Have a lovely day and please contact me on the above number if I can be of any help. Please pass on this information to any relative we may not have contacted.

Signed
S G T SCOTT
LT RM

Bibliography

Alden, John, The Falklands War from Defeat to Victory (Prominent Books, 2018)

Arthur, Max, *Above All Courage (Front Line First-Hand Accounts)* (Book Club Associates, 1985)

Badsey, Stephen, Rob Havers and Mark Grove, *The Falklands Conflict Twenty Years On: Lessons for the Future* (London: Frank Cass, 2005)

Bound, Graham, *Invasion 1982: The Falkland Islanders' Story* (Barnsley: Pen & Sword, 2002)

Bransby, Guy, *Her Majesty's Interrogator* (London: Leo Cooper, 1996)

Burnes, Jimmy, *The Land that Lost its Heroes: How Argentina Lost the Falklands War* (Bloomsbury, 2012)

Carrington, Lord, *Reflect on Things Past: The Memoirs of Lord Carrington* (London: Collins, 1988)

Clapp, Michael, and Ewen Southby-Tailyour, *Amphibious Assault Falklands: The Battle for San Carlos Water* (Annapolis: Naval Institute Press, 1996)

Dale, Iain, *Memories of the Falklands* (New York: Biteback Publishing, 2002)

Delves, Lt General Sir Frederick, *Across an Angry Sea: The SAS in the Falklands War* (London: C. Hurst & Co, 2018)

Ethell, Jeffery, and Alfred Price, *Air War South Atlantic* (London: Sidgwick & Jackson, 1983)

Fitzgerald, Warren, *All in the Same Boat: the Untold Story of the British Ferry crew who helped win the Falklands War* (John Blake, 2016)

Franks, The Right Honourable Lord, et al, *The Franks Report: The Falkland Islands Review* (Pimlico, 1992)

Freedman, Lawrence, *The Official History of the Falklands Campaign Part 1* (London: Routledge, Taylor & Francis Group, 2005)

Freedman, Lawrence, *The Official History of the Falklands Campaign Part 2* (London: Routledge, Taylor & Francis Group, 2005)

Freedman, Lawrence, Virginia Gamba-Stonehouse, *Signals of War: The Falklands Conflict 1982* (London: Faber and Faber, 1991)

Frost, Major General John, *2 Para in the Falklands* (Buchan & Enright, 1983)

Gardiner, Ian, *The Yompers: With 45 Commando in the Falklands War* (Barnsley: Pen & Sword, 2016)

House of Commons Defence Committee Report HC622, *Sunset for the Royal Marines? The Royal Marines and UK Amphibious* Capacity, Third Report of Season 2017-2019 (Published 4 February 2018) para 39-41.

Hunt, Sir Rex, *My Falklands Days* (David & Charles, 1992)

Hutchings, Richard, *Special Forces Pilot: A Flying Memoir of the Falklands War* (Barnsley: Pen & Sword, 2008)

Jolly, Dr Rick, *Doctor for Friend and Foe* (London: Conway 2012)

Jolly, Dr Rick, *The Red & Green Life Machine* (London: Harper Collins, 1999)

Ladd, James D, *By Sea, By Land: An Authorised History of the Royal Marines Commandos* (London: Harper Collins, 1999)

Lane, Andrew, *Royal Marines Commandos in the Falklands War* (Halsgrove, 2000)

Martin, Tom, *Falklands Gunner* (Barnsley: Frontline Books 2017)

McDonald, George, *Journey into the Unknown: 1982 HMS Hermes* (George McDonald, 2019)

McManners, Hugh, *Falklands Commando* (London: Harper Collins, 2002)

Middlebrook, Martin, *The Argentine Fight for the Falklands* (Barnsley: Pen & Sword, 2009)

Middlebrook, Martin, *The Battle for the Falklands* (London: Pan, 1983)

Middlebrook, Martin, *The Fight for the Malvinas: The Argentine Forces in the Falklands War* (London: Viking, 1989)

Middlebrook, Martin, *The Falklands War* (Barnsley: Pen & Sword, 2014)

Morgan, David, *Hostile Skies: My Falklands Air War* (London: Weidenfeld & Nicolson, 2006)

Muxworthy, Lt Cdr J. L, *Canberra: The Great White Whale Goes to War* (The Peninsular and Oriental Steam Navigation Company, 1982)

Norman, Mike and Michael Jones, *The Falklands War: There and Back Again: The Story of Naval Party 8901* (Barnsley: Pen & Sword, 2019)

Phillips, Ricky, *The First Casualty: The Untold Story of the Falklands War* (Edinburgh: BIEC Books, 2018)

Privratsky, Kenneth, *Logistics in the Falklands War: A Case Study of Expeditionary Warfare* (Barnsley: Pen & Sword 2014)

Southby-Tailyour, Ewen, *Exocet Falklands: The Untold Story of Special Forces Operations* (Barnsley: Pen & Sword 2016)

Thompson, Julian, *3 Commando Brigade in the Falklands: No Picnic* (Barnsley: Pen & Sword, 2016)

Van der Bijl, Nick and David Aldea, *5th Infantry Brigade in the Falklands* (Barnsley: Pen & Sword, 2014)

Vaux, Nick, *March to the South Atlantic: 42 Commando RM in the Falklands War* (Barnsley: Pen & Sword, 2007)

Vine, Andrew, *A Very Strange Way to go to War: The Canberra in the Falklands* (London: Aurum, 2012)

West, Nigel, *The Secret War for the Falklands* (Little Brown & Company, 1997)

Weston, Simon, *Walking Tall: An Autobiography* (London: Bloomsbury, 1989)

Woodward, Admiral Sandy, *One Hundred Days* (Annapolis: Naval Institute Press, 1992)

National Archive Files

ADM 202 828, 40 Commando Royal Marines Operation Corporate Occurrences

ADM 202 883, 40 Commando Royal Marines Operation Corporate Falklands Conflict

ADM 202 930-1, 40 Commando Royal Marines Commanders Diary Part 1

ADM 202 930-2, 40 Commando Royal Marines Commanders Diary Part 2

ADM 202 930-3, 40 Commando Royal Marines Commanders Diary Part 3

ADM-202-820, 40 Commando Royal Marines Casualties

ADM-53-189350, HMS *Hermes* (Falklands Conflict)

PREM19-0649, Handling the Falklands Crisis. Cabinet Documents

WO 305/5042, 1st Battalion Welsh Guards Operation Corporate (Falklands Conflict)

WO 305/5044, 1st Battalion Welsh Guards Operation Corporate (Falklands Conflict)

WO 305/5046, 1st Battalion Welsh Guards Operation Corporate (Falklands Conflict)

WO 305/5575, 1st Battalion Welsh Guards (5th Infantry Brigade) Operation Corporate (Falklands Conflict)

Unpublished Works

Cusack, Shane, OC A Company 40 Commando, *The Summer of 82*